Still Straight

Sexual Flexibility among White Men in Rural America

Tony Silva

D1713444

NEW YORK UNIVERSITY PRESS

New York

NEW YORK UNIVERSITY PRESS
New York
www.nyupress.org

References to Internet websites (URLs) were accurate at the time of writing. Neither the author nor New York University Press is responsible for URLs that may have expired or changed since the manuscript was prepared.

Library of Congress Cataloging-in-Publication Data
Names: Silva, Tony J., author.
Title: Still straight : sexual flexibility among white men in rural America / Tony Silva.
Description: New York : New York University Press, [2021] | Includes,bibliographical references and index.
Identifiers: LCCN 2020016691 (print) | LCCN 2020016692 (ebook) | ISBN 9781479801091 (cloth ; alk. paper) | ISBN 9781479801107 (paperback ; alk. paper) | ISBN 9781479801084 (ebook) | ISBN 9781479801121 (ebook)
Subjects: LCSH: Rural gay men—United States. | Heterosexual men—United States. | Rural men—Sexual behavior—United States. | Men, White—Sexual behavior—United States. | Gay men—Identity. | Men—Identity.
Classification: LCC HQ76.2.U5 S545 2021 (print) | LCC HQ76.2.U5 (ebook) | DDC 306.76/6208909—dc23
LC record available at https://lccn.loc.gov/2020016691
LC ebook record available at https://lccn.loc.gov/2020016692

New York University Press books are printed on acid-free paper, and their binding materials are chosen for strength and durability. We strive to use environmentally responsible suppliers and materials to the greatest extent possible in publishing our books.

Manufactured in the United States of America

10 9 8 7 6 5 4 3 2 1

Also available as an ebook

STILL STRAIGHT

CONTENTS

PREFACE

This project began in 2014. After reading some primarily theoretical work about straight men who have sex with men, I became fascinated by disconnects between how men behave and how they define themselves sexually. By this point I had also heard countless stories from gay men about hooking up with straight men, and I wanted to better understand what was happening. How could a man identify as straight yet have sex with other men?

Also on my mind at the time was the fact that most sociological research about sexuality and gender focuses on people who live in urban or suburban areas. How interesting it would be, I thought, to interview men from rural areas and small towns to find out how they approached this issue.

This focus builds on my personal background: I grew up in the 1990s and early 2000s on ten acres of woodland in Palo Cedro, California, a town of about twenty-five hundred people just outside of the city of Redding, which today has a population of around ninety-two thousand. This area is located in far Northern California, which is completely unlike the rest of the state culturally and geographically. The Redding area is over two hundred miles north of San Francisco and feels like a different world. Central California includes the San Francisco Bay area and Sacramento, the state capital, although most people—incorrectly, in my opinion—refer to it as Northern California. The far north is filled with farms, ranches, vast expanses of beautiful public lands, and communities that are mostly rural and small town in nature.

Redding is, technically, an urban area, and it is much larger than the towns from which I recruited men for this project. Still, having grown up where I did, I enjoyed many activities characteristic of rural areas and small towns, and I spent time in the surrounding rural areas. In part for these reasons I am familiar with many rural and small-town attitudes and norms, and I was able to bring that knowledge to this book.

Far Northern California faces issues similar to those faced by rural areas across the nation. These includes high rates of unemployment, substance abuse, and other social ills. Climate change is having an outsized impact on this area, too, as it is in many other rural areas and small towns. The 2018 Carr Fire destroyed over a thousand homes in the Redding area and almost completely charred the once green and beautiful hills surrounding Whiskeytown Lake, a popular recreation area. As bad as this was, however, the 2018 Camp Fire in the northern foothills of the Sierra Nevada Mountains has become the poster child for climate change, as it was the deadliest and most destructive wildfire in California history. Paradise, a city of about twenty-five thousand, was almost completely destroyed in less than a day. Ironically, many residents of rural areas and small towns either do not believe in climate change or typically vote for officials who block any attempts to address the problem. Sadly, this does not protect these people from the effects of climate change. These effects are becoming even more noticeable, too. In 2019, for instance, the electric company PG&E shut off power to millions of people in California to make sure no fires could accidentally start when record winds swept across the state. Climate change is affecting the day-to-day lives of people in California, and especially those in rural areas and small towns.

Many residents in far Northern California are also deeply conservative, so much so that some are trying to secede from California to create the State of Jefferson. Unsurprisingly, a majority of residents in the far north voted for Donald Trump in 2016 and typically vote for Republican congressional candidates. At the same time, far Northern California offers some of the most enjoyable outdoor activities of anywhere in the country. It contains incredible natural beauty, particularly in the wilderness areas known mostly by local outdoor enthusiasts.

While far Northern California is unique in many ways, it also shares similarities with other regions that are primarily rural, small-town, and home to a white majority. I point all this out to indicate that as a result of my background I am familiar with rural areas and small towns in the American West. I decided to focus on men living in these places in order to address the lack of research about gender and sexuality in these areas, taking advantage of my own familiarity with small towns and rural areas. It is useful to understand this context as you hear from the men who live in them.

This book contains information that will probably surprise you and challenge your beliefs. Sexuality and gender are complicated, and there is no right or wrong way to label people's attitudes or behaviors. While a reader might view these men's actions as contradictory, inauthentic, or disingenuous, they are not. In fact, many of the men I interviewed were fairly nonchalant about their activities. Perhaps most important, they did not think it was contradictory to have sex with men yet still describe themselves as straight and masculine. These men's stories are complicated and often filled with irony and paradox. The results are messy, as are most aspects of our social world.

I talked to sixty men between 2014 and 2017, and they lived in far Northern California, the Pacific Northwest, the Mountain West, and the Midwest. It was difficult to recruit men in such a secretive population, but I did so by posting ads on Craigslist. To protect their identities, I use pseudonyms instead of their real names, and do not report identifying information.

Several things are notable about the stories told by the men I interviewed. First, they identified as straight primarily because they are deeply embedded in institutions, communities, and networks that expect and reward male heterosexuality and masculinity. I refer to all of this as "straight culture." By "embedded," I mean they are a part of and feel connected to these institutions and communities. Most of the men I talked to did not identify as straight because they hated gay or bisexual men. Instead, they felt that most aspects of their lives were heterosexual. Those married to women wanted to stay that way and saw their role as a husband as key to their straightness. They considered their sex with men mostly irrelevant to their identity. All described themselves as masculine, too, and many felt that identifying as gay or bisexual would have threatened their masculinity. Wanting to avoid discrimination and enjoying being part of a socially dominant group played roles as well.

Second, most of these men were primarily or exclusively attracted to women. Many began having sex with men only later in life, and for a host of complex and sometimes murky reasons. Why they had sex with men is as interesting and complicated as why they identified as straight.

Third, the way these men saw themselves as men and perceived the world is shaped by their rural and small-town roots. For instance, marriage as an institution is generally considered more socially important in small towns and rural areas than in urban areas, which typically have more diverse populations and reflect a broader range of attitudes. Many of the men I interviewed were not particularly attracted to men, but reported that their wives had mostly lost interest in sex. The men I talked to wanted to continue having sex but without feeling as though they were cheating on their wives or harming their marriages. To them, sex with men was the perfect compromise. Many of the men I interviewed were not all that attracted to men, but liked being able to "get off" without feeling as though they were cheating on their woman partner.

Fourth, their stories show that even with remarkable increases in LGBTQ visibility, many men still identify as straight despite enjoying sex with other men. Today, nearly everyone in America knows that it is possible to identify as gay or bisexual, but that does not mean that all people with same-sex desires or practices identify themselves that way. Our world is more complicated than that. These men's narratives are filled with irony and paradox, as are those of most people, albeit for different reasons.

A key conclusion of this book is this: While attractions have biological roots and cannot be intentionally changed, identities are a social creation. How people label their sexuality and express masculinity or femininity will differ according to social context and time period. How these men understand themselves is unique, not wrong, even though their understanding contradicts the way most Americans currently understand sexuality. While men have been attracted to women throughout history, perceiving that being heterosexual is a key element of oneself is historically very recent. Classifying people on the basis of their sexuality only started in the mid-1800s. As this form of classification spread, laws and gender norms also changed. In other words, our social world today is regarded as primarily "straight," but it was not always this way.

Talking to men like the ones I interviewed, men whose actions appear to contradict their identities, helps uncover the social processes that socialize men to be straight and masculine, processes we take for granted. Identities like "straight" do not just indicate attractions or sexual practices. They also represent embeddedness in certain institutions and communities, and often adherence to certain attitudes and social practices. As the men I talked to explained: sure, they had sex with men, but that did not make them any less straight.

Introduction

Hundreds of thousands of straight American men have had sex with multiple men.[1] Not all are closeted gay or bisexual men. Nor are they all just experimenting. While most straight men do not have sex with men, those who do have thought a lot about their masculinity and why they identify as straight. It is rare to have an opportunity to study an identity that most people take for granted. What if heterosexuality, and particularly male heterosexuality, is not always what it seems? That is the issue this book explores.

Here are some of the questions driving my investigation: How do rural and small-town straight American men who have sex with men (a category sometimes labeled "MSM") understand their sexual identity and gender?[2] Why do they have sex with men? How do race and geographic location shape their experiences? My qualitative research helps us understand findings from national surveys.[3] While it is true that some men are closeted and come out only later in life,[4] although less commonly in an era of more tolerant attitudes toward sexuality in general, the men I interviewed were for the most part not like these men. The men I talked to actively identified as straight, and most were not looking for an opportunity to come out. Additionally, while some straight men have consensual sex with other men while in prison[5] or for money,[6] I only talked to men who reported sex outside of prison or sex work. Some men have consensual sex with other men out of desperation—or so they say—in all-male environments like prisons and the military. Many others do so, however, even when women are available as sexual partners. What could explain this?

The men I talked to provided answers that appear contradictory yet are also genuine. The findings in this book are complicated and messy. Even as their lives might to others seem contradictory or disingenuous, the men I interviewed did not see their lives that way. They identified as straight and saw themselves as masculine, and sex with men did not detract from either attitude. Most viewed sex with men nonchalantly. Several had sex with men for what they described as the "thrill" of it, and most did not develop emotional feelings for their male sexual partners.

One man in this group was Cain, a fifty-year-old man from Missouri who described himself as highly religious. This explains why he chose the pseudonym "Cain" for this study. Cain said he was simply looking for what he called a "regular bud," an ongoing nonromantic sexual relationship, to keep his "urges" in check. Until he found that regular bud, he was content with hookups (nonromantic sex). Cain admitted that he found risky, taboo sex exhilarating. "It's almost like the closer I am to being caught, the greater the thrill," he said. One of the hookups he found most thrilling involved topping[7] a man on a church pulpit when no one else was around. Cain also found it arousing to tell me about these situations, since he could not confide in anyone else. This is why he called me for several years after the initial interview to inform me about what he called "hot updates."

For Cain, sex with men was exciting in part because it was taboo. On at least two occasions, he had sex with another man while near his wife.

> I'll give you an example. My wife and I went shopping one time in the mall. She was picking out clothes for me, and there was this real cute college guy that was also trying on clothes. They had kind of like a bathroom setup in the stalls or whatever, and I kind of looked at him, and I could tell he was kind of interested. And so, I sat down and I just, kind of moved my foot just a bit, and fuck, he was all over me. And so, the thing is I was going back and forth getting clothes from my wife, who was right outside the dressing room. And here I was going back, and I worked the guy in my stall and he was nursing on my cock, sucking on my cock as I was going back and forth getting clothes. And fuck, she would have killed both of us, had she known, but it was just, fuck, it was so exciting, it was just, so thrilling. I don't know how to describe it.

In the other story, Cain described meeting a man at his home and having sex with him while his wife was upstairs, asleep. Cain enjoyed sex with men, but not emotional intimacy. Like several although not all of the men I interviewed, he was aroused by what he considered taboo sex.

While they shared a diversity of experiences, all sixty men I inter-viewed were embedded in straight culture, including the groups, institu-tions, and communities undergirding this culture. "Embedded" means they were a part of and felt connected to these groups, institutions, and communities. Most of these men felt more connected to other straight people than to gay or bisexual men. Those married to a woman wanted to stay that way rather than leave their wives and start a completely new life with a man. They had varying levels of attractions to women, differ-ent sexual histories, and distinct reasons for having sex with men, but all identified as straight. In order to maintain that identity, they prevented, cut off, or set boundaries on romantic attachments to men. Doing so allowed them to maintain their relationships with women partners and allowed them to remain a part of straight culture.

Additionally, identifying as straight ensured that these men could maintain their ties to others in their straight communities, which they did not think would have been possible had they identified as gay or bisexual. Identifying as straight, of course, also prevented them from experiencing homophobia or biphobia (an aversion to bisexuality). They enjoyed being part of a socially dominant group.

The men I talked to also felt that identifying as straight was a major part of how they understood themselves as men. The ways they had sex with other men—what I call "bud-sex"—both reinforced and reflected their straightness and masculinity. Embeddedness in (being a part of) straight culture, I argue, is a key reason the men I interviewed identified as straight. Those who still had sex with women saw this activity as tied to their straight identity, but it was only one of many reasons they iden-tified as straight. None of them considered sex with men an important aspect of their identity. As Mitch, a thirty-nine-year-old man living in Washington, said about having sex with men, "I wouldn't say it defines me or anything like that."

The experiences and behavior of Cain, Mitch, and the other men I interviewed make it clear that sexual identity does not necessary reflect sexual behavior. Identity also indicates feelings of belonging to certain communities and cultures and not belonging in others. Straight identifi-cation is also appealing to many because it brings social benefits unavail-able to LGBQ people, like never experiencing discrimination or facing rejection from loved ones on the basis of sexuality.

The men I interviewed were not closeted gay or bisexual men. They were straight men who sometimes liked to have sex with other men. This may sound contradictory, but one nationally representative survey I analyzed shows that a little over 1 percent of straight men aged fifteen to forty-four in the United States reported having had consensual sex with at least one other man. This equates to about 689,000 straight men.[8] About 221,000 of them identified as straight and had had two or more male sexual partners.[9] About a quarter of this group had had sex with at least one other man in the past year.[10] Understanding why these men identify as straight requires recognizing the difference between attractions, sexual behaviors, sexual identities, and sexual cultures. To explore and clarify these differences, I talked to sixty of these men, focusing on men from rural areas and small towns.

This geographic focus was intentional. Despite hundreds of news stories and academic articles exploring the politics and economies of rural and small-town America in the years after the 2016 election, which undeniably marked a watershed in American politics, few of these articles have examined the issues of sexuality and gender in these areas. We know that white residents of rural areas and small towns helped elect Donald Trump in 2016[11] and remain a key part of his base. We also know that over the past few decades such factors as outsourcing, deindustrialization, government deregulation, a greater concentration of economic activity in urban areas, and other economic and political changes have negatively affected many rural and small-town economies.

This shift has fueled both resentment and a desire for change.[12] Many small towns and rural areas are today facing major challenges: population loss, an aging workforce, a reliance on federal disability payments, low rates of educational attainment and labor force participation, opioid addiction, hospital closings, and an excessive number of deaths from heart disease and cancer.[13] While not all of America's rural areas and small towns face these issues, particularly in the western United States,[14] they are much more likely than urban areas, suburbs, and small- to mid-sized cities to be confronted with them.[15]

Many white rural and small-town Americans have responded to these economic issues by embracing the Republican Party, even though Republican office holders support many policies that harm them and oppose policies that could help them.[16] Rural and small-town America has increasingly turned toward the Republican Party within the past decade, even as large urban areas have moved further left.[17] These political divides will probably become more pronounced over time. Because of the way the Senate and the Electoral College work, rural and small-town America will continue to wield more conservative political power than generally liberal urban areas for decades to come.

These aspects of rural and small-town life are well documented. What we do not know much about is how men in these areas understand their sexuality and gender. This is a major oversight: about 20 percent of Americans, or sixty million people, live in rural areas,[18] and even more live in small towns that are not technically rural but could hardly be considered urban. Existing studies of sexuality and gender, and the theories they lead to, are limited by their focus on major urban areas. To help compensate for the urban focus in studies of sexuality and gender, I talked only to men in rural areas and small towns. I also did so because I thought the issues I examined might play out differently in rural areas and small towns compared to urban areas, where social norms are different.

Attractions, Behaviors, Identities, and Social Context

Sexual behavior, attraction, and identity are related but distinct.[19] Yet it is common for people to label others—incorrectly—as gay or bisexual because of even a single same-sex sexual encounter.[20] Nonetheless, same-sex sexual behavior does not require a gay/lesbian or bisexual identity, nor does the presence of same-sex attraction. People are metaphorically closeted only if they are hiding an *identity* that they see as a key part of themselves.[21] Many individuals secretly identify as LGBQ[22] (lesbian, gay, bisexual, or queer), but cannot be open about it because of the homophobic world in which they live. These people are in the closet. They differ from straight-identified MSM, who are secretive about having sex with men but still genuinely feel as though "straight" describes them better than any other identity. Straight MSM do not perceive sex with men as meaningful to their identity.

Simply put, not everyone who feels same-sex attractions engages in same-sex activity, and not everyone who enjoys same-sex activity feels same-sex attractions. Moreover, attractions differ in degree of strength: recent studies have found that 3.6 to 4.1 percent of men and 7.6 to 9.5

percent of women have limited same-sex physical or romantic attraction.[23] People who fall into these categories are somewhat attracted to members of the same sex, but not very. In this book, however, I do not explore in depth the complexities of same-sex attraction. My focus is on identity as opposed to sexual attraction or behavior, and how individuals derive meaning from their sexuality and their relation to social groups, like gay communities. Sexual identity often does not capture the complex ways in which people experience sexual attractions and practices. It often does, however, reflect the *sexual cultures* to which individuals feel they belong.[24]

Of course, identities are not entirely the result of individual choice. Prejudice and discrimination toward LGBQ people encourage straight identification, and homophobia is present in all areas of social life. By "homophobia" I mean a belief that LGBQ people are inferior to straight people or not deserving of equal rights, as well as individual actions that reinforce inequality. I also mean laws, institutions, and other macro social forces and processes that all together reinforce inequality between straight and LGBQ people.

For instance, it is legal to discriminate against LGBQ people in housing and public accommodations in over half of US states. Additionally, over half of US states allow parents to force their children into religious "conversion therapy" programs. Despite the fact that these programs are widely regarded by professional health organizations as harmful and ineffective, hundreds of thousands of young Americans have been forced into these programs.[25] Recently, Republican politicians, officials, and judges have worsened inequality by advancing so-called religious freedom and freedom of speech laws that legalize and protect discrimination.[26]

Many of these bills have been introduced in Republican-controlled states since the United States Supreme Court legalized same-sex marriage nationwide in 2015.[27] Cases such as 2018's *Masterpiece Cakeshop v. Colorado Civil Rights Commission* show that Republican justices often regard discrimination as a protected form of speech or religious exercise. Court decisions have major consequences because legal inequalities shape, and are shaped by, public perceptions of LGBQ people.[28] For instance, the legalization of same-sex marriage in the United States greatly reduced the proportion of Americans who support various homophobic attitudes.[29]

Legal equality declined in many ways during the Trump administration, so it is unsurprising that more LGBTQ people (the "T" here stands
for "transgender") reported discrimination in the years after President
Trump took office than before.[30] The Trump administration rewrote
federal rules to protect healthcare workers who discriminate against
LGBTQ people,[31] argued in court that civil rights laws do not apply to
LGBTQ people,[32] and made it easier for adoption and foster agencies
to discriminate against LGBTQ people.[33] Across the United States, over
half of LGBTQ people report having experienced discrimination.[34] Due
to concerns about discrimination, only 46 percent of LGBTQ Americans are "out" at work, a percentage that has barely changed in the last
decade.[35] This may be the case because LGBTQ employees are much
more likely to be bullied than their straight, nontransgender (cisgender)
counterparts.[36] In June 2020 the Supreme Court made employment discrimination against LGBTQ people illegal nationwide, but this ruling
only applies to organizations with fifteen or more employees.

Homophobia is still strong: despite advances, only about two thirds
of Americans support same-sex marriage.[37] Because of discrimination,
LGBQ people are much more likely to face economic hardship than
straight people.[38] They also experience higher stress due to homophobic social environments,[39] and this drastically affects their physical and
mental health.[40] LGBQ people living in areas without equal legal rights,
mostly in Republican states, have lower levels of mental and physical
well-being than straight people. This is due to prejudice, discrimination, and the stress of living in homophobic areas.[41] Unfortunately, few
federal laws protect LGBTQ people from discrimination. A bill in Congress that would do so, the Equality Act, has not advanced because most
Republican elected officials oppose it. Inequalities are present in all areas
of social life: as adults LGBQ people are much more likely to be denied
housing loans than straight people,[42] and as children they face harsher
punishment from school officials and higher rates of bullying by their
peers.[43] LGBQ people also experience higher rates of housing and food
insecurity than straight people,[44] and they feel less closely connected to
their neighbors than straight people.[45]

Overall, while discrimination today has lessened compared to what
it was prior to the 2000s, a great many institutions still operate in ways
that disadvantage LGBQ people compared to straight people.[46] Even

many straight people who support legal equality nonetheless believe that LGBQ people should not have the same "informal" rights as straight people, such as the right to hold hands in public.[47] Homophobia and biphobia come in many forms and sadly remain an integral part of the nation's social fabric. Prejudice and discrimination negatively affect LGBQ people and encourage straight identification. Feelings of belonging in straight culture are tied in part to the comfort of knowing that one will not experience either homophobia or biphobia. This is a major reason why the men I interviewed identified themselves as straight, although they did so for other reasons as well, as we shall see.

A Brief History of Sexual Identity

While attractions are shaped in part by biology,[48] sexual identities are not. Rather, they are shaped by history, culture, and social context. Economic and political changes helped form the framework for sexual identities in the late nineteenth and early twentieth centuries.[49] Some of these changes helped make gay/lesbian identities possible, whereas others helped spread the concept of heterosexuality. Interrelated historical developments from the mid- to late nineteenth century through the middle of the twentieth effectively created the identities of gay, lesbian, and bisexual that are now common in the West. Before then, individuals engaged in same-sex sexual practices, but these acts were not usually associated with a sexual identity.

Many people in the West regarded particular sexual acts between men, like anal sex, as something problematic that any man could feel temptation to experience.[50] As wage labor,[51] especially wage labor tied to corporations,[52] allowed for individual economic self-sufficiency, individuals were less reliant on the family unit to survive. This meant they could live on their own and have lives organized around work, friendships, and same-sex partners rather than biological families. This helped provide part of the framework for gay/lesbian identities. Additionally, urbanization allowed individuals with a common sense of sexual difference to form communities, facilitating the emergence of gay/lesbian identities.[53] All these developments were especially important for women, who historically had far fewer opportunities for economic self-sufficiency and consequently little opportunity to form a collective sense of sexual difference.[54] For both groups, the increase in personal privacy due to these historical changes also helped facilitate this shift.

While urbanization helped create gay and lesbian *identities*, sexual and gender nonconformity is not simply a product of urban culture. In the mostly rural American West, many people engaged in same-sex behaviors in the nineteenth and early twentieth centuries.[55] There were also many people who today would be considered transgender. Community and individual responses to these people varied greatly. Many were met with relative tolerance or even acceptance.

In the late nineteenth and early twentieth centuries, however, the American West was increasingly portrayed by the media and others as lacking sexual and gender diversity, effectively burying evidence that showed such diversity was commonplace.[56] The belief that rural areas were historically without sexual and gender diversity is one reason for today's widespread and incorrect assumption that LGBTQ people live only in urban areas. Understandings of purportedly healthy gender and sexuality changed in rural areas—and urban ones as well—as the national discourse about gender and sexuality spread across America by the mid-twentieth century.[57] Indeed, only during the 1960s, when the gay rights movement was linked to the civil rights struggle seeking racial equality, did Christian churches and conservative political movements in the American South cast it as a threat to social stability.[58]

Modern medical, governmental, and religious institutions played key roles in the creation and perpetuation of "heterosexuality" as both a concept and an identity. In the nineteenth century, emerging medical disciplines began to explain sexual practices as characteristics of particular types of people.[59] They helped create "heterosexuality" as a social category and constructed "homosexuality" as its undesirable opposite. Prior to the nineteenth century, most people did not perceive sex with men and/or women as proof of an internal disposition like "heterosexuality," "homosexuality," or "bisexuality." Twentieth-century bureaucratic practices in federal immigration, welfare, and military institutions helped legally define homosexuality and heterosexuality.[60] Government institutions also more often associated sexual "deviancy" with people of color and punished them accordingly.[61]

The US federal government helped spread a national discourse about what it termed "normal" gender and sexuality using idealized images of rural white people.[62] This was in opposition to what government workers and others perceived as immoral behaviors more common in cities. These ideas also penetrated rural areas through community organizations that reinforced the importance of heterosexuality, as well as the importance of men being masculine and women being feminine.[63] Today, government-funded efforts to encourage marriage similarly teach that marriages between men and women are key to social stability and in fact are the only truly legitimate unions.[64] The state thus helped to create the concept of sexual identities and continues to reward heterosexuality. Similarly, religious institutions traditionally placed considerable value on marriage and reproduction. This attitude became linked to the concept of "heterosexuality" once the phrase was more commonly used, particularly beginning in the 1960s.[65]

A variety of other historical changes in the late nineteenth and early twentieth centuries also helped to spread the concept of heterosexuality, especially those that threatened how middle-class white men perceived their masculinity.[66] Middle-class men lost some economic independence as they began to work for large businesses that were starting to dominate the American economy. This state of affairs challenged their previous understanding of business ownership and self-sufficiency as a basis for masculinity.[67] Men also became concerned that women were feminizing society.[68] Women increasingly entered the formal paid workforce and fought for political reforms, such as the right to vote. They also began teaching children and adolescents, which had previously been a male-dominated occupation. Additionally, many social settings became more integrated by gender and threatened men's sense of themselves as "opposites" of women.[69]

Already worried about these changes, middle-class men became concerned that working-class men and immigrants had stronger claims to masculinity due to their jobs, which often involved physical labor.[70] Middle-class men, in contrast, primarily held white-collar jobs that involved little if any physical labor. In response to all these threats to their masculinity, middle-class men began trying to underscore their masculinity through ties to fraternal organizations, interest in the outdoors, and competition through sports.[71] Yet middle-class men were also concerned about others interpreting their social interest in other men as having a sexual component.[72]

In part to prevent people from thinking this about them, middle-class men claimed "heterosexuality" as an identity. This identity showed others that they had "normal" sexual desire for women and were thus masculine, even when their masculinity was otherwise being challenged.[73] This identity also helped them distinguish themselves, at least in their minds, from working-class men and men of color.[74] The concept of heterosexual identification took longer to take root in working-class communities.[75] In short, the concept and identity of heterosexuality emerged in part to help relieve concerns about masculinity among middle-class white men, and this thinking eventually spread to most segments of society.[76]

Before this shift took place, social relations between men and between women were much different. Indeed, throughout history many societies defined "sex" as something that involved a penis, giving women the opportunity to engage in physically intimate encounters with other women without suspicion as long as they continued to be wives and mothers.[77] Furthermore, in the early nineteenth century, Victorians considered sexual passion and love to be mostly unrelated. This attitude facilitated socially accepted, romantic friendships between women[78] and between men.[79] These types of friends often sent passionate love letters to one another. Romantic friendships also contained various types and degrees of physical contact, like sleeping in the same bed or cuddling—and sometimes genital contact.[80] These friendships mostly disappeared as the modern system of sexual classification became widespread and pathologized them.

From the mid- to late nineteenth century to the middle of the twentieth, sexual identities as an organizing principle of social life slowly disseminated across the West. Today, mainstream understandings of sexual orientation link emotional and physical attractions, even though they are actually distinct.[81] For instance, it is possible for a man to fall in love with another man but not want to have sex with him or indeed with any other man. Yet current understandings of sexual orientation define all strong same-sex feelings, whether sexual or romantic, as gay or bisexual. This is why passionate emotional bonds are rare today between straight men.

In short, the current understanding of sexuality between men and women as "heterosexual" did not always exist. During the colonial era, sexuality was organized on a reproductive/nonreproductive basis; there was no social validation of sexual pleasure and most nonreproductive acts were viewed as offenses.[82] Much later, in the late 1800s, the emergence of heterosexual identification helped to normalize sexual pleasure between middle-class men and women.[83] Freud's insistence that humans were predisposed toward seeking sexual pleasure, especially different-sex (woman-man) genital pleasure, both reflected and helped solidify this shift.[84] Over time, most Americans came to understand themselves in terms of a sexual identity. Overall, historical research shows that sexual identities, including heterosexuality, are social creations rather than innate aspects of a person's identity.

Contemporary Heterosexuality

While most people consider heterosexuality to be only an identity or a sexual preference, in fact it is much more. Today, heterosexuality is both an identity and a set of social and sexual practices and experiences.[85] Heterosexuality is gendered, such that most people expect straight men to be masculine and straight women to be feminine. This attitude comes with assumptions about how men and women should interact with other people, both sexually and nonsexually. Gender norms built into heterosexuality help to create and reinforce social inequalities between men and women.[86] Heterosexuality today is also an institution and an organizing principle of social life.[87] Sexual identification as straight or otherwise is not a "natural" reflection of sexuality, because cultural norms affect the meanings and social practices that people attach to it. Most people take heterosexuality for granted and treat it as though it is disconnected from culture and society, when that is not true. While there are biological influences affecting sexual *attractions*,[88] sexual *identification* differs across cultural and historical contexts.

Because of this, sexual identification can differ within countries.[89] Within the United States, some people define themselves on the basis of their sexual attractions, whereas others identify in ways that reflect their current sexual or romantic partners.[90] Similarly, some people identify themselves on the basis of their romantic attractions but not their sexual attractions or behaviors.[91] Still others identify as straight because they believe stereotypes about LGBQ people, and do not think they fit those stereotypes.[92]

Additionally, legal rights or the lack thereof can shape identification. For instance, women who lived in states that recognized same-sex relationships before the US Supreme Court legalized that recognition nationwide were more likely to change their identity from straight to lesbian or bisexual than women who lived in more conservative states.[93] Coming from more educated and liberal family backgrounds may also make it more likely for people to identify as LGBQ.[94] Gendered social forces also affect sexual identification: men are much more likely than women to identify as exclusively straight.[95] One reason for this is that women are seen as less socially valuable than men, so they have more leeway to challenge gender and sexual norms.[96] For instance, most Americans do not see affection between women, like hugging or sharing a bed, as sexual, but they typically do with men. Hence, this behavior is perceived as gay for men but not usually for women.

Social patterns related to race also affect sexual identification. While men of all races and immigrant statuses are about equally likely to identify as straight, there are wide variations among women: Native American women have the lowest likelihood, and immigrant Asian women have the highest.[97] In short, a variety of social forces affect whether or not a person identifies as straight.

My study, which involved interviewing American men between the ages of nineteen and seventy-five who grew up in or currently lived in a rural area or small town, is part of a small base of qualitative interview research seeking to understand why some individuals with same-sex practices identify as LGBQ whereas others identify as straight. Other researchers have found that many working-class women identify as straight, despite enjoying sex with women, because they view their status as mothers or partners to men as incompatible with LGBQ identification.[98] Some middle-class women who have sex with women similarly feel that the identification of straight describes them best, in part because they do not want to end their partnerships with men.[99]

Interviews with straight men who have sex with men show that many of them bolster their straight identities by framing sex with men as emotionless and by emphasizing exclusive or primary attractions to women.[100] Some also feel that the word "gay" means feminine and that "bisexual" is too stigmatized or ambiguous to describe them.[101] Qualitative research such as this shows that many factors other than attractions and sexual practices influence straight identification, including the meanings individuals attribute to childrearing, different-sex partnerships, and gay or bisexual identities.

Moreover, while it is impossible to determine whether one can generalize from the results of qualitative studies, nationally representative surveys show that there are distinct types of straight-identified individuals with same-sex sexuality.[102] In one of my other studies, I found that about half of straight-identified men who have had two or more male sexual partners or who report substantial attraction to men are not overtly homophobic.[103] What links these men goes beyond overt homophobia: embeddedness in straight culture, enjoyment of being part of a socially dominant group that does not experience discrimination, and feeling that their straightness is a key part of their masculinity all likely play a role. Qualitative studies like the one in this book can explore these themes and mechanisms of identification in greater depth.

Straight Culture(s)

Identifying as straight may seem like a straightforward description of sexual attractions or practices, but it also indicates relationships to certain people, groups, communities, and institutions. Straight identification in part reflects embeddedness in a straight culture.[104] The existence of people, like straight MSM, who identify in ways that challenge the way most people understand sexual identity highlights how culture affects sexual identification. Straight identification, of course, is not purely conscious or voluntary: most societies confer unearned benefits on straight people relative to LGBQ people. Straight people do not experience discrimination, prejudice, or inequality on the basis of their sexuality; LGBQ people do. This fact encourages most people to identify as straight.

There are many straight cultures, although not much research has examined these cultures *as* cultures, since heterosexuality is considered "normal" in the United States, much like the racial category "white."[105] In contrast, there is a rich literature about minority sexual cultures, especially those involving LGBTQ people.[106]

Researchers, including Chrys Ingraham, a sociologist in the State University of New York system, and James Joseph Dean, a sociologist at Sonoma State University, do not analyze straight culture, but they do describe social practices associated with heterosexuality that altogether reveal that heterosexuality is more than a sexual preference or identity. Ingraham studied weddings, which she describes as "key organizing rituals" for heterosexuality.[107] Heterosexuality is not just an expression of sexuality, she argues, but also a set of social practices and rituals. Dean interviewed straight men and found that many express their straight identity through masculinity, relationships to women, and (often) varying degrees of distance from gay people.[108] The men he interviewed did not have sex with other men,[109] but their stories show that straight men today are more conscious of their straight identity than men were decades ago.[110]

One of the only researchers to examine straight culture as a culture is Jane Ward, a sociologist at the University of California–Riverside, who examined straight white MSM in urban or military contexts. Ward did not interview any men or analyze survey data. Instead, she did a content analysis of cultural materials such as Craigslist ads, popular films, and military rituals. From these analyses, she argues that same-sex sexual or erotic contact is a fundamental element of white heterosexual masculinity: "Homosexuality is an often invisible, but nonetheless vital ingredient—a constitutive element—of heterosexual masculinity."[111] I do not make this argument, since I have a different focus. Instead, I analyze how straight MSM construct their sense of themselves as masculine and straight, despite the fact that they have sex with men.

My argument following from this is that the men I interviewed help to show what straight culture is and how many men come to identify with it. Most straight men do not have sex with other men, but those who do help highlight how heterosexuality is more than a set of attractions or sexual practices.

Distinct straight cultures have many similarities and share considerable overlap. They vary from one another somewhat, but all are similar enough to be understood as part of the concept that falls under the umbrella of "straight culture." Most of these cultures encourage heterosexual identification, believe that men and women are "opposites" of one another, and normalize gender inequalities, in different ways and to varying extents. Similarities and differences can be recognized via cross-national research. For instance, the United States and the Netherlands, examined at the national level, have distinct straight cultures, as Amy Schalet, a sociologist at the University of Massachusetts–Amherst, has shown with her cross-cultural snapshot examining approaches to teenage sexuality in the two countries.[112] She finds that Americans tend to view teenage sexuality as dangerous and something that needs to be controlled, whereas many parents in the Netherlands support teenage sexual education and responsible sexual exploration.

A second example is the work of Gloria González-López, a sociologist at the University of Texas–Austin, who documented the sexual and romantic lives of straight Mexicans who immigrated to the United States.[113] Migration brought the people she interviewed to new social, economic, and political contexts, and interacting with new people exposed them to new attitudes toward sexuality and gender. International travel or migration can put individuals in contact with new straight cultures; this exposure can change how individuals experience their sexuality.

There are also distinct straight cultures within countries, including the United States. American evangelical Christians, for instance, have a distinct sexual culture that emphasizes heterosexuality, marriage, and sex for the purpose of procreating or maintaining fulfilling marriages.[114] This is in contrast to more liberal and secular straight cultures like those on many college campuses that normalize men and women hooking up.[115]

Regardless of the distinctions between straight cultures, however, a feature that ties most together is treating people as if they are either male or female, man or woman, when the world is much more complicated. Biologically, there are not just males and females; there are many individuals who are intersex and have characteristics of both males and females.[116] There are many different types of intersex conditions based on hormones, genitalia, and chromosomes.

Socially, there are a variety of ways that people express their gender that are neither hypermasculine nor hyperfeminine.[117] Most people express masculine and feminine characteristics, but to varying degrees. While some people are much more masculine or feminine than others, most people have a mix of traits. There are also many people who identify as genderqueer or nonbinary: neither man nor woman. While there is extensive gender diversity, treatment of people as either men or women persists.

For instance, institutions have responded to transgender people in ways that reinforce binary ideas about gender as well as sexuality. In gender-integrated settings, identity is often sufficient for the inclusion of transgender people, but in gender-segregated spaces, like bathrooms or sports competitions, biological markers are more important.[118] This is the case in part due to a cultural belief that men and women are biological opposites, as well as a belief that people with penises—however they identify—are basically heterosexual men who may prey on women and children.[119] One example of this is social panic over transgender women's use of public restrooms.[120] Increasing visibility of transgender and nonbinary people has modified how people understand gender, but not enough to fully change the fact that gender is usually understood as binary.

In short, while there is diversity when it comes to both biological sex and gender identity and expression (as masculine or feminine), in most straight cultures sex and gender are generally treated as binary. Beliefs about people belonging to one of only two "opposite" gender categories undergird how institutions and communities operate, as well as how individuals interact with one another.[121]

A colorful example of how this binarism is deeply ingrained in straight culture relates to so-called gender reveal parties for expectant mothers,[122] a recent but increasingly popular phenomenon, one fueled significantly by the explosion of social media. While these babies may be either male or female (or intersex), they have not yet begun to express gender, given that they are not yet even born. Yet gender reveal parties show that people assume a baby will behave in masculine or feminine ways simply on the basis of that baby's genitals. Many parents take these events very seriously. In 2017, one expectant father at a gender reveal party in Arizona shot a target designed to explode upon impact, and this accidentally caused a wildfire that scorched tens of thousands of acres of land.[123]

Parents celebrate what they believe their baby will be like on the basis of their sex, yet neuroscience research shows that gender socialization affects brain development in ways that create gender differences.[124] Toys marketed to boys and girls, for example, help create different kinds of skills. Many boys become somewhat more skilled at spatial tasks, for instance, because they are encouraged to play with toys and engage in activities that teach them these skills, whereas girls generally are not.

Gender imbalances in occupations like technology and teaching exist not because of innate sex/gender differences but because men and women are socialized to be more interested in certain skills and occupations than others (and also due to discrimination against women).

While there are some differences between males and females, most of these differences on their own do not greatly shape people's lives. When outcomes on any given criteria like test scores, mathematical ability,[125] and so on are charted, the distribution for males and females considerably overlap; there are generally not major differences between them. Further, society emphasizes gender differences (real or imagined, biological or social) rather than the many similarities between the sexes and genders. So, while there are some biological differences among the sexes, there are fairly few, and many of those related to brain structure are actually a product of whether a person is socialized as a man or a woman. Most gender differences are created by society.

Categorization of people as one of two "opposite" genders is important to straight culture because it is the foundation of "heterosexuality" as a concept: if there are more than two sexes or genders, then the assumption that heterosexuality is attraction to the "opposite" sex or gender is incorrect. Obviously, men and women have had sex with one another throughout history and will continue to do so. This is different from heterosexuality as a concept, however, because "heterosexuality" presumes that there are only two, completely different and complementary sexes and genders, which is not true.

In addition to categorizing people as one of two opposite genders, most straight cultures uphold inequalities between men and women in most areas of social life. For instance, women's sexual needs are often considered less important than men's, consciously or not. This is why men are more likely to orgasm during sexual encounters than their women sexual partners,[126] even though women are usually capable of more orgasms per encounter than men. The orgasm gap is due in part to how men are often not interested in better pleasing their woman partner,[127] and because women are taught to put men's needs before their own and to gain self-esteem through men's approval.[128] Relatedly, a sexual double standard stigmatizes women who hook up, but not men.[129] In the medical field, more attention is paid to men's sexual frustration than women's sexual pain: four times as many women than men experience pain during vaginal sex,[130] yet there are many more studies on how to address erectile dysfunction.[131]

Men are much more likely to sexually assault women than vice versa,[132] as well as to commit sexual harassment.[133] Men are also usually not punished for sexual harassment, legally or otherwise.[134] Indeed, Senate Republicans enthusiastically supported fellow Republican judge Clarence Thomas in 1991 and, more recently, Brett Kavanaugh in 2018 for lifetime appointments to the US Supreme Court, which routinely makes decisions about how much control women should be able to have over their own bodies. They did so even though multiple women credibly accused both of sexual harassment or attempted rape. One poll found that 55 percent of registered Republicans felt that Kavanaugh *should not* be disqualified even if allegations against him were true, whereas 71 percent of Democrats felt that he *should* be disqualified.[135] Similarly, despite President Trump boasting in 2005 that he sexually assaulted women ("grab 'em by the pussy"), not to mention the multiple women who publicly accused him of sexual harassment, groping, or rape,[136] most Republican voters chose him to shape laws and policies that will affect women for decades. Harassment and violence against a woman by a man is often normalized, especially when the man is wealthy, powerful, or well connected.

Even with consensual sex, however, most women are at a disadvantage relative to men, for many reasons. Inequalities between women and men are usually denied, ignored, blamed on women, or explained as biological. Yet research shows that even our understandings of biology are incorrect. For instance, most people are taught that active sperm race to inseminate a passive egg,[137] in line with understandings of men as masculine and women as feminine, even though the woman's body is just as active in insemination.[138] Other ideas about how women and men behave differently during courtship, sex, and reproduction are greatly affected by social context.[139] Gender inequality in straight cultures is present outside of the realm of sexuality, too, and structures most aspects of social life.[140]

In sum, straight cultures reinforce gender inequality between women and men in a variety of ways. Even though there is a huge literature on gender inequality, few researchers have analyzed how this issue is a key part of straight culture. This lack of data reflects how many people take heterosexuality for granted and do not consider how gender inequality or social practices of straight people are related to a straight culture. While I do not explore gender inequality at length in this book, it is important to keep in mind that it is a fundamental aspect of most straight cultures.

Another similarity between straight cultures is that they encourage straight identification. Part of this encouragement is achieved through homophobia and biphobia (as described earlier), and part of it is enacted through childhood socialization in both overt and subtle ways. For instance, most children's films portray heterosexuality as natural and desirable.[141] Parents also usually raise their children to be straight, in part by rarely discussing alternatives to heterosexuality.[142] In schools, most educational curricula and interactions between teachers, staff, and students socialize boys to be masculine, girls to be feminine, and all children to be heterosexual, with subtle socialization beginning even in preschool.[143] Similarly, peer interactions in elementary school[144] through high school[145] regulate how boys and girls express their sexuality and gender. In both obvious and subtle ways, most institutions and groups that are part of straight culture socialize children to become straight.

I introduce "straight culture" as a framework for analysis because it brings together different literatures in the sociological study of sexuality and gender. "Straight culture," I argue, is a concept that synthesizes different literatures and is an analytical framework that best captures my main findings. "Straight culture" is not simply a theoretical concept analyzing links between gender and sexuality. It is a framework for understanding social life that builds on past research and that I support with empirical data.

Obviously, not all straight people are homophobic, endorse gender inequality, or ignore the existence of more than two genders. Many straight people are genuinely committed to equal rights for people of all sexualities and genders. What I analyze when I use the term "straight culture" are social patterns that exist because of institutions, communities, and social norms that together perpetuate heteronormativity (the assumption that everyone is heterosexual) and gender inequality, even despite progressive individual straight people.

"Straight culture" is an umbrella concept that includes many different types of straight cultures, which overlap considerably but also have some unique differences based on how individuals in particular areas and with certain social identities perpetuate social norms about gender and sexuality. For instance, while most areas across America are home to a type of straight culture, specifics of this culture differ: marriage rates in urban areas are lower than in rural areas and small towns, for instance, showing that the institution of marriage is more central to rural and small-town straight culture.[146]

In this book, I analyze straight culture in parts of rural and small-town America in which the majority of the people are white. While I analyze this culture specifically, the findings also have implications for straight cultures in other areas and other populations, given that there is so much overlap between these cultures. "Straight culture" is an umbrella concept that encompasses specific straight cultures, and the rural and small-town, white-majority straight culture I describe is one of them. This culture shares extensive overlap with other straight cultures but is also recognizably distinct.

By analyzing straight culture *as* a culture, this book shines a spotlight on an underexamined organizing framework for social life. It synthesizes prior research about gender and sexuality, including gender inequality and homophobia, as well as the findings I documented, in a way that comprehensively describes them and explores their connections. This project is not a story of closeted gay or bisexual men, nor is it a look at a straight culture disconnected from broader American society. Its findings are not empirically representative, but they do have implications for better understanding straight culture(s) more broadly. Notably, they provide more detail for patterns researchers have found with nationally representative surveys. As we shall see, this research shows that some men have sex with other men yet still identify as straight. The stories they tell give us insight into how many men understand themselves as straight and masculine.

Queerness outside Urban America

Research about sexuality in America typically focuses on sexual and gender minorities who live in urban areas, especially near the eastern and western coasts of the United States.[147] This focus means that sociological research on LGBTQ life is quite lopsided. Although 2.9 to

3.8 million LGBTQ people live in rural areas in the United States,[148] only about 3.5 percent of the sociological research into LGBTQ people in the United States examines rural residents.[149] Most of the rest of the research focuses on major cities with large LGBTQ populations such as San Francisco, Los Angeles, New York, and Chicago. The focus on a handful of urban areas obscures the lives of rural and small-town LGBTQ residents. LGBTQ experiences differ in different communities due to different laws, customs, and levels of public support for equal rights.[150] Rural and small-town LGBTQ people are no less "authentically" gay or lesbian than their counterparts living in major urban areas.[151]

Because of the emphasis on urban areas when it comes to exploring LGBTQ life, there is less awareness of the complexity of rural LGBTQ life. One downside of rural LGBTQ life is that many rural LGBTQ people experience isolation and prejudice. For instance, LGBTQ youth in rural schools face more hostile climates than those in urban or suburban schools.[152] Rural LGBTQ people are also at greater risk of discrimination than their urban counterparts, for a variety of reasons. Rural areas are less likely than urban areas to have laws that protect equal rights, largely because cities tend to be more liberal than rural areas and straight rural residents are less supportive of equal rights than their urban counterparts.[153] Living in areas with lower concentrations of same-sex couples—the case in many rural areas and small towns—also reduces the chances of forming a same-sex relationship.[154] Not coincidentally, the risk of violence is high. For instance, the infamous 1998 murder of Matthew Shepard happened in Wyoming, the least populated state in America. At the same time, many rural LGBTQ people view rural locations as providing a number of advantages, among them privacy, easy access to the outdoors, and feelings of belonging in tight-knit communities.[155]

Rural LGBTQ residents often blend in with the local culture rather than being visibly queer, as is typically the case in cities.[156] Community interconnectedness and feelings of sameness are important for rural people, including rural LGBTQ people.[157] Indeed, research indicates that 42 percent of rural Americans feel very attached to their community and 39 percent feel somewhat attached, and 50 percent say their relationships with neighbors are very important to them.[158] Similarly, rural residents are more likely to know their neighbors than are suburban or urban residents.[159]

But community interconnectedness can be a double-edged sword. While some rural communities accept LGBTQ people who have long been part of that community, others reject them, thus subjecting them to painful social isolation that is even more pronounced in rural areas than urban because rural areas are typically sparsely populated. Many urban LGBTQ people involve themselves in communities of other LGBTQ people, whereas rural LGBTQ people often have communities of people different in gender or sexuality but similar in other ways.

Navigating the world differently than urban LGBQ people does not make rural residents miserable: LGBQ people report similar levels of well-being whether they live in urban or rural areas.[160] (Importantly, most research that distinguishes between urban and rural areas considers suburban areas to be urban, since they are part of a larger metropolitan area.) Rural life is not necessarily oppressive for those LGBTQ people who live in it,[161] despite disadvantages. Further, recent research shows that about 1 percent of rural residents identify as gay or lesbian, 3 percent identify as bisexual, and 1 percent, as transgender or genderqueer.[162] This combined 5 percent figure is about the same percentage as in the entire United States,[163] showing that not all LGBTQ people live in cities, as stereotypes suggest. Some certainly do, but even some members of this group think fondly of their rural background.[164]

In sum, LGBTQ people live in all areas of the United States,[165] and the rural/small-town/suburban/urban setting in which they live is not necessarily related to their level of well-being. It is undeniable that LGBTQ people typically face more discrimination in rural areas and small towns than in urban areas.[166] That said, LGBTQ people everywhere face problems, and while these problems differ somewhat on the basis of where they live, it is overly simplistic to conclude that one type of living area is better for members of this group than another.

Geographic location shapes social life in complex ways,[167] and research about gender and sexuality needs to take this into account. Addressing this issue will help us understand how physical location relates to how people understand their gender and sexuality. The fact that the men I interviewed identify as straight rather than bisexual or gay, as many would expect, highlights the unique ways in which rural areas and small towns affect how people perceive themselves. While some projects have researched rural masculinity or rural LGBTQ people, few have analyzed rural heterosexuality.

A Brief Overview of Masculinity

Masculinity is not a biological given. How American men understand and express masculinity has changed greatly over the last two centuries.[168] Masculinity is a set of behaviors, attitudes, and emotions that society shapes and gives meaning to.[169] Masculinity is something that is associated with men, but it is not necessarily tied to men, nor is masculinity simply a set of things that men do. Men can be feminine, for instance, and women can be masculine, and there are many people who identify as neither men nor women who also express masculinity in varied ways. At the same time, most people express their gender in ways that reflect what others expect them to do, given their gender identity, their biological sex, and the social situation.[170]

Masculinity is a continuing process: boys and men never "achieve" masculinity but rather must continually maintain it. Sometimes they do so through what are called "manhood acts," which take different forms but typically involve "claiming privilege, eliciting deference, and resisting exploitation."[171] Actions inconsistent with such behavior are policed by friends, family members, acquaintances, and others, and men often act particularly masculine in all-male spaces.[172] Masculinity is also relational; men's masculinity is shaped in part by how they interact with women,[173] as well as with other men.

There are numerous forms of masculinity.[174] They differ across social contexts and populations, and both shape, and are shaped by, other forms of masculinity as well as femininity. Additionally, different forms of masculinity exist in a hierarchy. Some forms have more power and influence than others, thus reinforcing social inequalities between men and women and among men.[175] Certain forms of masculinity seem progressive and do often represent an improvement in gender relations.[176] At the same time, many obscure and continue to reinforce various forms of inequality.[177]

Many men today seek to construct a masculinity in what Miriam Abelson, a sociologist at Portland State University, calls a "Goldilocks zone": not violent or emotionally stunted, but also not something that would be seen as obviously gay or feminine.[178] Rather, many want to be in control of their emotions with the ability to be flexible about how they express themselves.[179] These forms of masculinity seem progressive, but do little to challenge wider social inequalities.

What is common to most forms of masculinity is the importance of heterosexuality. More men than women perceive same-sex sexuality as a threat to how they perceive themselves in terms of gender. Nationally, men report greater homophobic attitudes on average than women.[180] Men are more likely to report homophobic attitudes when they feel their masculinity is threatened,[181] a dynamic that rarely occurs with women when they feel their femininity is threatened.[182] Put another way, heterosexuality is more strongly tied to masculinity than to femininity.[183] For many men, being masculine means being straight. Indeed, many of the men I talked to identified as straight in part to preserve their sense of themselves as masculine.

Additionally, masculinity differs depending on whether the context is rural or urban. "Rural masculinity" refers to masculinity as it is "constructed within what rural social scientists would recognize as rural spaces and sites,"[184] which are themselves difficult to define.[185] Rural and urban residents often understand and construct masculinity differently. In many rural areas, for instance, rural men construct masculinity in opposition to representations of urbanity,[186] emphasizing differences between themselves and urbanites. Forms of rural masculinity differ on the basis of local context and population, but they also share many common traits, such as an emphasis on physical labor and toughness.[187]

It is not socially acceptable for most rural men to express what might be considered "softer" forms of masculinity, as some urban men do. For instance, whereas many straight urban men pay close attention to grooming[188] or even dress fashionably in ways they consider somewhat "gay,"[189] most rural men do not. The masculinity they construct reflects fairly rigid expectations.[190] This is the case in part because rural areas and small towns tend to be socially homogenous and to reward conformity. Due to differing social contexts, forms of masculinity in rural areas are distinct from those in urban locations. People in rural areas, especially men, are much more likely to own guns than are suburban and urban residents,[191] and gun ownership is one way many rural men understand themselves as men.[192] Even as the issue of gun control becomes more popular in urban areas, it is unlikely to gain much traction in rural areas.[193]

Masculinity is critically important for rural gay men, as it provides them some social acceptance in their communities, which is otherwise lacking because of homophobia.[194] Similarly, in rural areas men and women of all sexual identities gain some community acceptance through masculinity.[195] Also, rural transgender men gain some community acceptance through heterosexuality and working-class masculinity, and by being white in settings in which whites are the majority.[196]

While rural and urban areas are tied together due to social and economic links, as well as easy travel between the two,[197] attitudes about gender and sexuality in these areas are often quite distinct. There are unique forms of masculinity in rural areas and small towns, and these are key to what it means to be a man in these settings. Consequently, central to the stories of the men I interviewed is a distinctly rural masculine outlook. This guides rural men's "thoughts, tastes, and practices." In addition, "It provides them with their fundamental sense of self; it structures how they understand the world around them; and it influences how they codify sameness and difference."[198] As we will see, heterosexuality is a crucial part of this rural and small-town masculinity. Being masculine, for many of the men I interviewed, meant being straight.

Where and How This Research Was Conducted

This book specifically examines residents of rural areas and small towns in the Midwest, the Pacific Northwest, the Mountain West, and far Northern California.[199] These areas are home to a white majority[200] and are socially conservative,[201] as indicated by voting patterns.[202] The areas I examine were historically part of the mythic American frontier.[203]

The rural focus is not meant to suggest that all rural areas and small towns are homogenous or the polar opposites of urban areas.[204] The boundaries between rural and urban areas are blurring due to their increasing economic, social, and political interdependence, and there are many types of rural areas and small towns that are not necessarily the binary opposites of urban areas.[205] However, research indicates that, broadly speaking, expressions of sexuality and gender do differ between rural and small-town America and its urban counterparts. Hence, building on operating definitions of the US Office of Management and Budget,[206] I concentrated my efforts to find people to interview on nonmetropolitan areas in my target regions: those with fewer than fifty thousand residents. I also interviewed men who lived in towns with a population of under fifty thousand that were located near similar towns.[207]

In total, forty of the men I interviewed were raised in rural areas or small towns with a population of under fifty thousand and not located near major cities, and forty-four currently live in these types of areas. Most either grew up or currently live in similar areas. Only five were raised and currently lived in large metropolitan areas with populations over five hundred thousand.

To find the men I interviewed, I posted advertisements in dozens of men-for-men casual-encounters sections of Craigslist, which is organized regionally.[208] Unlike most other apps/websites, Craigslist was, at the time of the research,[209] widely used, anonymous, free, and frequented by individuals with a variety of sexual identities. Of the 654 men who inquired about participation, sixty agreed to a semistructured interview. I did fifty-six of these interviews over the phone and four in person. During each interview I used an interview guide, but reordered and rephrased questions to make the interview less formal.[210] Interviews, which were conducted between 2014 and 2017, lasted between one and one and a half hours.[211]

The sample was racially homogenous but diverse in terms of who they were attracted to. One man identified himself as Latino and another as multiracial although he said that most people perceive him as white. About 65 percent of the men I interviewed were only or mostly attracted to women, and a majority were currently married to women. While all were secretive about their male sexual encounters, all also identified as straight—both to themselves and to others.

About two thirds were in their fifties or older. Although the men I talked to had a variety of educational and occupational backgrounds, most were middle class. Almost all had at least some college education, and a majority had at least a bachelor's degree. The sample was more highly educated than most Americans. Other studies have shown that straight working-class men also engage in secretive sex with men,[212] but the men who responded to my advertisement were overwhelmingly middle-class. (See tables A.1 and A.2 in the methodological appendix for more detail about the men I interviewed.)

The men I met in person were polite, expressed themselves in a way that most people would interpret as typically masculine (none were noticeably feminine), and dressed in conventionally masculine attire. Most wore jeans and a t-shirt, a polo shirt, or a button-down shirt that looked nice but was neither flashy nor expensive. All looked completely presentable, although not "fashionable" or "trendy." In other words: they were men most people would describe as resembling somebody's dad or grandfather. A "guy-next-door."

Rural and Small-Town Contexts

Straight men who have sex with men can of course be found all across America, including in large urban areas. They are all a part of some type of straight culture, and as a result there is quite a bit of overlap in terms of how they understand their sexuality and masculinity. Yet men who live in rural areas or small towns differ from their urban counterparts in several key ways, related to why they have sex with men, their specific sexual practices, and how they understand their masculinity.

Rural/urban differences shaped the reasons why the men I talked to had sex with men and how they began doing so.[213] A higher proportion of rural and small-town men are married (to a woman) than are their counterparts in large urban areas, a state of affairs reflecting the fact that marriage is more central to their identities. This attitude encouraged many of the men I interviewed to have sex with men rather than extramarital sex with women because they felt such behavior was not as threatening to their marriages. Counterintuitively, the enhanced importance of marriage to rural and small-town culture actually encourages sex between men in these areas. To many rural and small-town men, sex with other men is a loophole in their marriage contract: it does not really count, at least compared to sex with other women.

Additionally, unlike many urban and suburban men who first begin having sex with men in threesomes with their wives,[214] most of the men I talked to first had sex with men in one-on-one contexts. While some men I interviewed did have threesomes with their wives, this was fairly uncommon. Men in urban areas appear to be more likely to have three-somes than men in rural areas and small towns. The situations that led the men I interviewed to have sex with men, in other words, appear to be different from those that men in urban areas experience, despite some common aspects.

The sexual practices described by the men I talked to also differed from those of urban men. Some straight urban men post advertisements to find sex with men and write about women in these ads in sexualizing or demeaning ways, with the hopes of continuing this behavior during their hookups with men.[215] In contrast, the men I interviewed rarely talked about women to their male sexual partners and almost never watched heterosexual pornography (or any other type, for that matter) in their hookups. This behavior suggests that rural and small-town men do not feel the need to sexualize women in their male-male hookups in order to feel more straight. Thus, they were less overtly misogynist than many urban men, at least as urban men present themselves in online advertisements. This attitude may relate to masculinity: marriage, but not sex with women per se, is central to how many rural and small-town men understand themselves as men. In contrast, sex with women, but not necessarily marriage, appears to be key to how many urban men construct their masculinity.

Additionally, whereas a sizable proportion of white men in urban areas fetishize black and Latino men for being purportedly highly masculine,[216] the men I interviewed preferred white men. Being with men who looked and acted like them and other people in their rural and small-town contexts helped reassure the men I talked to that what they were doing was "normal" and thus compatible with heterosexual-ity and masculinity. Many of the men I interviewed also preferred men who looked and acted specifically like rural and small-town men: for example, men who hunted, fished, or wore jeans and a t-shirt. By con-trast, urban men often post ads seeking specific types of urban men—for instance, "skaters" or "bros."[217] In short, while urban men have a vari-ety of preferences because of the diversity of people to which they have been exposed in urban settings, the men I interviewed tended to prefer a more specific type of sexual partner that reflected the people who lived in their rural and small-town settings.

Also related to rural and small-town life, smaller social networks and greater community interconnectedness encouraged the men I interviewed to integrate their "friends with benefits" into the social fabric of their lives, allowing them to become sexually and emotionally closer to them. This behavior facilitated lasting bonds for the men who were open to such arrangements, even though other people had no idea about the sexual aspect of their friendships.

The way the men I talked to understood their masculinity also differed from that of men in urban areas. Most considered heterosexuality a key part of rural and small-town masculinity, so being masculine to them meant being straight. Many urban men also feel this way, of course, but they have greater options for expressing a "softer" masculinity than most rural and small-town men.[218] They also see a variety of sexual-identity options that are less overt in rural areas.[219] Similarly, a majority of the men I interviewed used elements of rural and small-town life to describe their masculinity: hunting, fishing, shooting, ranching, and so on. Thus, while most men across the United States construct masculinity in some way or another, the way they do so—and what their masculinity looks like—differs across rural/small-town and urban settings. Additionally, rural and small-town men tend to define themselves in opposition to what they believe men in urban areas are like.[220] So, even though there are many similarities between men in rural areas/small towns and urban areas, men in the former often strongly distinguish themselves from the latter.

Many of the men I talked to felt as if they could choose a gay or bisexual identity, on one hand, or a rural/small-town identity, on the other. They chose the latter. Many gay and bisexual men live in rural areas and small towns.[221] Yet they are usually less visible, since LGBTQ people in rural areas publicly look and act much like their straight counterparts, in part because there is less freedom of behavior outside cities.[222] There are also fewer LGBTQ institutions like bars and community organizations in rural areas and small towns than in urban areas. Thus, in rural areas and small towns, LGBTQ people are less visible, and there are fewer resources to support LGBTQ subcultures. To many men, including the ones I interviewed, it feels as if a gay or bisexual identity is simply not possible outside of a major city, even though—factually—it is. Urban men have more contact with visibly gay and bisexual men, so they know that being gay or bisexual is an option for them even if they distance themselves from the possibility.

Straight MSM and the Down-Low

While most of the men I interviewed identified as white, this does not mean that most straight MSM are white, nor does it mean that most straight MSM are black, as media portrayals suggest. My analysis of one nationally representative survey shows that there are no significant racial differences in sexual identification among MSM.[223] Thus, while popular culture treats the "down-low," or secretive sex between men, as a mostly black phenomenon,[224] in reality about the same proportion of men from different racial/ethnic groups identify as straight and have sex with other men.

The incorrect linking of blackness and secretive male-male sex reflects racist stereotypes about black sexuality and heightened scrutiny applied to black people.[225] Public health researchers have examined the down-low among black men to examine its relationship to HIV transmission.[226] HIV research is critically important to reduce rates of transmission. At the same time, public health research does not always take into account the fact that people of all racial groups engage in secretive sex.[227] Black and Latino men are at much higher risk for contracting HIV than white men,[228] but this reflects broader health inequities at the intersections of race, gender, economic status, and sexuality rather than the down-low itself.[229]

There is no single definition of what it means to be on the down-low. While some down-low men identify as straight, others identify as gay or bisexual. Many feel that "down-low" refers to men in relationships with women more than sexual identification.[230] Other black men describe themselves as down-low because they feel that "gay" means feminine and that "bisexuality" does not exist, is too ambiguous to make sense for them, or is too stigmatized and thus an unattractive identity to adopt.[231] Some men perceive the "down-low" as an identity, whereas others view it as a description that reflects their masculinity, level of secrecy, or romantic relationships with women. The construction of sexual identity for many black MSM is complicated because they navigate both racism and homophobia.[232] Because of the complex meanings of the term "down-low," I do not use it to describe the men I interviewed, and most of them did not use it to describe themselves either. It is, however, important to know that many men of all racial and ethnic identities are secretive about their sex with men, and that no one group is more likely to identify as straight than another. By analyzing white, straight MSM, this book helps correct what has so far been a focus on black and, to a lesser extent, Latino MSM.

Whiteness

In analyzing data, I draw on the rich theoretical framework of what is called "intersectionality."[233] Emerging out of black feminist scholarship, intersectional frameworks analyze how social inequalities shape lived experiences.[234] Everyone has multiple identities and statuses along the lines of race, gender, sexuality, economic status, and so on, and all of these elements shape people's lives. Larger social systems and social patterns affect all people, including parts of people's lives that seem very personal.[235] It is always important to consider how race, gender, sexuality, age, place, and other elements of social life interact to shape experiences and identities.

As part of an intersectional analysis, it is critical to consider how race, including for white people, shapes lived experiences. Racial preferences and partnering practices reflect how Americans are socialized in ways that differ on the basis of their race. People with shared backgrounds and social positions have similar dispositions, preferences, practices, and beliefs.[236] This helps to explain why white people have similar attitudes about race.[237]

White people also behave in similar ways. For instance, while most whites claim to support racial integration, most live in segregated residential areas and have all- or mostly white social networks.[238] Additionally, even though residential segregation has declined over the past several decades, most Americans still live in racially homogenous neighborhoods.[239] Their social networks are also homogenous: research shows that 91 percent of the most important people in white people's lives are also white, which is higher than the same-race share for black (83 percent) and Latinx (64 percent) Americans.[240] The segregated residential and social networks of whites create emotional bonds between whites and distance between whites and people of color. Segregated residential areas and social networks shape how white people act and perceive the world.[241]

It is also important to think about how race relates to rural America. Many rural areas across the United States are home to a white majority, and not by coincidence. For instance, Jason Pierce, a historian at Angelo State University, examines the historical construction of the mythic "white man's West."[242] Railroad companies helped reshape populations by encouraging Northern and Central Europeans to settle along their lines, for example by advertising in Northern and Central European nations, providing financial assistance to those Europeans who immigrated, and giving free land to those (Europeans) they sought to make customers on their lines. The US government subsidized these practices by providing land grants to railroad companies, helping to create an American West that was primarily white, rural, and small-town.

It is not surprising that the men I talked to have partnering practices reflecting racial preferences, since most whites across America do—and this differs by geographic location. Intermarriage rates are only about 11 percent in nonmetropolitan areas, as compared to 18 percent in metropolitan areas.[243] This reflects greater racial and ethnic diversity in metropolitan versus nonmetropolitan America, as well as a much lower proportion of rural and small-town individuals who feel that intermarriages are good for society: 24 percent, as compared to 38 percent and 45 percent of people in suburban and urban areas, respectively.[244] Similarly, when whites do marry a person of another race, they usually partner with either Latinx or Asian people,[245] reflecting continued anti-black racism. Overall, being white and living in a rural or small-town area shaped how the men I interviewed understood themselves and sexually partnered with other men.

Age and Aging

The men I talked to were skewed toward older ages, reflecting generational *and* life course dynamics. Many of the men I interviewed came of age between 1950 and 1980, a time that Steven Seidman, a sociologist at the State University of New York–Albany, describes as some of the most difficult years in which to express gender or sexual difference in America.[246] This state of affairs affected how they were socialized, what options they felt were available to them, and how they understood their gender and sexuality. About a third of the men I interviewed noted that the time period in which they grew up affected their identification as straight and masculine. Generational factors, of course, affect everyone. So, even though only a third of the men I interviewed specifically noted such influences, all were affected by generational factors to at least some extent. While American society today still expects men to be straight and masculine, today there is much greater social visibility and acceptance of LGBTQ people. Consequently, young men today have more options for identifying and expressing themselves as something other than straight and masculine. This is the case even as stigma and inequality remain.

We cannot dismiss older men's identification with straightness and masculinity simply as reflecting the era in which they grew up, however, for three main reasons. First, a third of the men I talked to were in their adult teens, twenties, thirties, or forties. This is unsurprising given that men across America are still expected to be straight. Relatedly, while women are increasingly identifying as bisexual, men are not.[247] Men are still constrained by expectations of masculinity to identify as straight, even if they are young. Second, some older men identify as gay or bisexual and have for decades—so clearly there are factors other than generational ones at play.

Generational influences affect people of all identities. If we reject older men's straight identification because of factors in their youth, then we have to dismiss all people's identities because of factors in their youth. Obviously, we should not do this. For the older men, generation was one factor of many that encouraged them to become, and remain, a part of straight culture. Some of the men I talked to did not have the language in their youth to describe what we now know as "gay" or "bisexual," whereas others did but did not see it as a realistic option for them. Again, though, many men in America identified as gay or bisexual in the 1960s and '70s, and many others did not but came out later in life. Gender expression and sexuality are both constrained *and* enabled in different ways across distinct time periods.

National data also show that some young and middle-aged men who report sex with or attractions to men identify as straight. My analyses of the 2011–2017 National Survey of Family Growth indicate that hundreds of thousands of American men aged fifteen to forty-four have had two or more male sexual partners yet identify as straight. The National Longitudinal Study of Adolescent to Adult Health also shows that it is common for young men to have disconnects between their behavior and how they identify themselves.[248] The practice of having sex with men yet identifying as straight is not limited to older men.

Third, one main reason the men I talked to had sex with other men has to do with the aging process. About a third of the men, mostly those who were older, began having sex with men or increased the frequency with which they had sex with other men because of the aging process. A handful experienced erectile dysfunction, while the rest reported that their wives experienced health issues or lost interest in sex as they aged. Thus, a major reason why more older men than younger men responded to my research advertisement is that the aging process itself encouraged straight men to have sex with other men. So it is not necessarily that participants identified as straight because they were older. Instead, many had sex with men because they were older. Thus, generational factors and the aging process were both reasons the men I talked to skewed older.[249] It is therefore likely that some men who are now young may also turn to men for sex as they grow older. Future research in aging and sexuality should investigate how the aging process itself can actually encourage same-sex intimacy.

Many individuals in their late fifties and older still have sex,[250] though the aging process often changes their sex lives.[251] A survey called the National Social Life, Health, and Aging Project indicates that men aged fifty-seven to eighty-five view sex as much more important and desirable than do women in the same group.[252] While researchers recognize the fact that straight men partnered to women may turn to extramarital sex because of this, few have considered that they may turn to men, as many of the men I talked to did. Other than research on older LGBTQ people, there is little investigation into the same-sex sexuality of older people who are not LGBTQ. Yet perhaps not surprisingly, my research shows that some straight men turn to sex with other men as they age.

Overview of the Book

The men I talked to identify as straight and masculine. What they told me shows that there is diversity within heterosexuality and that broad categories of sexual identity often do not represent the lived experiences of sexuality. Above all, my research shows that many people identify as straight because they are a part of a straight culture and want to stay that way. Part of the reason for this is that they can feel connected to a socially dominant group and not experience sexuality-based discrimination. Another part of it, for men, is that identifying as anything other than straight would threaten how they see themselves as men. As the men I talked to explained, it also made the most sense for them to identify as straight because all other aspects of their lives were straight. They had straight friends, most were partnered to a woman, and few felt that "gay" or "bisexual" described any social aspect of their life. Sex with men was mostly irrelevant to their identity.

Unsurprisingly, the stories these men tell are filled with irony and paradox, and seem embedded with contradictions, even though they are not. The findings that came from this project are messy, like most parts of social life, but I make sense of them through this book.

1

Why They Have Sex with Men

What I find attractive on men, and the only thing I find attractive on men, is a good-looking dick. I could care less about his shoulders or his muscles or his eyes or his hair, whether he's fat or skinny, it don't matter. Because I'm not interested in any of that. My only attraction to a man would be his dick, and I find that my attraction goes towards smaller ones rather than bigger ones. . . . I have no desire to do anal on a man, and I do not think that a man's ass looks good. I see comments on some of these places, "Oh, God, he's got such a good-looking ass on him." Not from my point of view he doesn't, I'm not interested. Like I said, the only thing I'm interested in is a hard dick and the only thing then is I want to make it come and then I'm through with it, I don't want nothing else to do with it. That's why I consider myself to be more straight than gay, I guess. (Richard, 75, Illinois)

Given that the men I interviewed identified as straight and that more than half were happily partnered with women, why did they have sex with men? What explained this apparent disconnect? It was not simply attraction: a majority of the men I talked to were predominantly attracted to *women*, not men. Even in terms of attraction, they were not simply closeted gay or bisexual men. What links these men as a group is their straight identity and their embeddedness in straight culture, not their level of attraction to men. Sexual identity and masculinity, not just attraction, are key factors that distinguish different groups of men." They are also linked by identity and culture rather than attraction, which is why men with identical attractions can identify differently.[1]

Hence, rather than describing their sex with men as a straightforward consequence of their attraction to men, the men I talked to described complicated situations, interpretations, and feelings that reworked sex with men as necessary and compatible with straight identification and masculinity. Even most of those attracted to men reported more complicated reasons for having sex with them. Several reported having sexual kinks for penises but not sexual attractions to men, just as some people have kinks for leather, knots, or floggers. Richard, the seventy-five-year-old man from Illinois who opened this chapter, offers one such example.

Some of the men I talked to desired sex with men to satisfy a kink rather than to act on an attraction. In other cases, they experienced changes to their bodies or sexual desires—or reported that their wives did—as they aged. About three quarters reported unintentional changes to their sexual attractions or desires as they grew older. This encouraged most to begin having sex with men or to do so more frequently. Additionally, over a third reported that their wives or women partners lost interest in sex, sometimes because it became painful or uncomfortable. This encouraged these men to have sex with other men, as they considered that less threatening to their marriages than extramarital sex with women.

Relatedly, most of the men I talked to preferred women for romantic partnerships, but were wary of casual hookups with women. The trait they felt made women better romantic partners—emotional compatibility—also made many uncomfortable with women as partners for hookups, as they felt that women would become too attached. Ironically, then, beliefs about men and women complementing one another emotionally actually encouraged these men to have sex with men. This was especially true for married men, most of whom did not want to threaten their marriage by having sex with another woman. Finally, several men reported that sex with men addressed needs related to masculinity.

Several had sex with men specifically to form nonromantic connections with other men: to relieve loneliness, experience connections with other men, or satisfy a need for touch. Others had sex with men to relieve the pressures of masculinity. Having another man penetrate them allowed some men to experience pleasure without having to be in control. Some of these themes have been documented in primarily urban samples of straight MSM as well.[2] This indicates that straight men throughout the United States experience a variety of reasons for having sex with men.

The stories I present are not the coming-out narratives of closeted men, nor are they stories of men "realizing" or "recognizing" their attractions to other men. Rather, they demonstrate that male sexual desires and attractions are flexible throughout life. Men often interpret this flexibility using identities they already hold. The men I interviewed already saw themselves as straight and masculine, and this perception did not change even as their attractions or practices did. Individual identities, and the interpretive frameworks that support them, are resistant to change even as sexual practices, attractions, and desires are flexible.

"I Like Dicks, I Don't Like Men": Sex with Men as a Kink

Several men reported cravings for sex with men, penises, or anal stimulation that conventional understandings of attraction do not capture. Those who described this theme either did not report sexual attractions to men or described sexual attractions to men mostly in terms of interest in a particular activity. For instance, Marcus, a thirty-eight-year-old man from Illinois, reported exclusive attractions to women, but occasional sexual cravings for oral sex with men, explaining, "It just seems like once in a while I'll just kind of get a craving, so to speak. It's like, hmm, I haven't done that in a long time, maybe I'll see if I can't do that. . . . I think it's just more something kinky, something taboo, something just a little bit different from the norm." Like Marcus, several other men I interviewed were primarily drawn to women yet reported openness to having sex with men in ways they found it difficult to explain. They found women's bodies sexually pleasing and did not generally feel attracted to men, but nonetheless felt occasional sexual interest in men if the possibility for sex arose.

Six other of the men I interviewed shared similar cravings, but their sexual interest was in penises rather than in the men attached to them. Richard noted that he is exclusively attracted to women, but felt that penises—though not the men attached to them—were a turn-on. As he explained, "It's not about the person, I'm only interested in the dick." Joe, a sixty-three-year-old from Idaho, similarly reported exclusive sexual attraction to women, along with a desire for penises:

It's strange, it's almost totally phallic. I don't know how to put it. Men don't attract me at all, whatsoever. The only attraction I have is women, but when men enjoy what I've got, I let them enjoy it. That's where I am. . . . I have no interest in hugging a man, in kissing a man, in suckling his nipples, or anything else. Everything about a man that would interest me is his cock and balls. And even then, it's not the guy, it's those parts. That's it. . . . I'm a straight guy. I do not lust after men whatsoever. I enjoy the company of a guy when it's correct, I do not like gay guys, I mean guys that are coming on to me, that want me as their partner, that doesn't interest me at all. A gay image, if I were to pull [one] up, I could get excited by a hard cock. But I'm not attracted to it, I don't seek it, I don't go out and go after it. A woman, a beautiful woman just lights my fire.

Joe, like Richard, enjoyed penises but did not find men attractive. He enjoyed giving and receiving oral sex with men, but no other physical activities.

The kink for penises likely comes in part from America's cultural fascination with penises. Penis references are almost everywhere. Boys and men tell "dick jokes," phallic imagery exists in art and architecture, and men are judged, insulted, or complimented on the basis of the actual or presumed size of their penis. Consequently, a kink for penises is a desire for masculinity and all things "man." Many straight men find penises fascinating. It is likely that a large number would act on this interest if society were not so homophobic. Several of the men I interviewed acted on it regardless.

A handful of men reported a kink for anal stimulation. Chad, a sixty-seven-year-old man from Northern California, reported that he was 95 percent attracted to women and 5 percent attracted to men; he began having sex with men so he could experience anal eroticism, which his woman partner was not interested in exploring. "I started becoming aware of those parts of my body that were sensitive in terms of not having used my anal region for pleasure in the past. . . . My partner, my girlfriend, does not want to engage in this fantasy part of my sexuality." While numerous men reported enjoying bottoming during anal sex, only a handful had sex with men specifically to give or receive anal stimulation in the absence of substantial sexual attraction to men.

The cravings for men, penises, or anal eroticism described by these men, many of whom emphasized their lack of conventional sexual attractions to men, may best be described as a kink. In the West, however, these interests are framed as indicative of sexual orientation. Yet dividing lines between sexual orientation and kink are social products. In the West, the biological sex of sexual partners is considered a marker of sexual orientation, whereas other sexual preferences are not. This emphasis on the sex of one's partners as the determining factor in one's sexual identity differs across cultures. For instance, in one Papua, New Guinea, tribe, members believe that it is critical for adolescent boys to ingest the semen of older boys to become healthy men.[3] As adults, men in this tribe are expected to have sex only with women. Hence, male-male sex is considered an important ritual without becoming a marker of identity or even of orientation, unlike in the West. Yet preference for partners that are several decades older, for instance, is not considered an important element of sexual identification. Even though age is a key component of attraction for many individuals, it is not considered an essential part of our identity.[4] Similarly, other traits that can also influence attraction, even to the point of being considered necessary—body build, amount and distribution of body hair, height, political beliefs, and so on—are not considered important for sexual identification in the West.

It may be fruitful to discard current Western understandings of sexual orientation in favor of a framework that incorporates multiple types of preferences.[5] Kinks for oral sex, penises, or anal eroticism can be simply three types of sexual preferences among many, existing distinct from or in conjunction with more conventional feelings of physical attraction. Men who are "mostly straight" in attraction—who find some men sexually attractive, under certain circumstances[6]—are distinct from men who sometimes enjoy a kink for penises but do not experience physical attractions to men. Both of these groups are distinct from men who identify as LGBQ. All three of these groups (and of course LGBQ itself is a group that encompasses many different identities and attractions) include men who have sex with other men. Yet there are important differences among them in terms of preferences, attractions, and identities.

Growing Older: Not Ready to Give Up Sex

About three quarters of the men I talked to reported unintentional changes to their sexual attractions or desires as they grew older, and more than a third reported that their wives or women partners lost interest in sex, sometimes because it had become painful or uncomfortable for them. These changes led some men to begin having sex with other men for the first time. "My wife and I stopped being sexually active," a thirty-seven-year-old man from South Dakota named George explained, but "I still had sexual desires to have sex or to do things sexually, but I'm also very committed to my wife about not doing things with other girls."

Others, who had had occasional sex with men before or earlier in marriage, said that the diminishing interest in sex of their women partners led them to have sex with men more frequently. A number of those men said they began to have sex with men because they considered doing so less threatening to their marriages than extramarital sex with women. Many also believed that sex with men was easier to find than sex with women. Additionally, most of the men I talked to preferred women for romantic partnerships but were wary of casual hookups with women. Many felt uncomfortable about casual hookups with women, fearing that women would become too attached to them.[7] Ironically, then, their belief that men and women complemented one another emotionally actually encouraged them to have sex with men.

Other key reasons many men reported having sex with other men involved changes to their bodies or their desires over the course of their lives. For instance, a handful of men described erectile dysfunction as encouraging them to have sex with men. Little research has examined masculinity and sexuality over the life course,[8] even though men may experience major changes to their sexuality and masculinity over the years. While researchers have focused on women's capacity to experience changes when it comes to their attractions, far fewer have examined men. The men I talked to show that men's sexual practices, desires, and attractions can be flexible over the course of their lives, even as they continue to identify as straight and masculine.

While only a few men noted disability or erectile dysfunction (ED) as a key reason for having sex with men, this condition was important in their narratives. Three reported having sex with men in part because of ED. Richard explained that a car accident left him unable to maintain an erection, even with medication. As a result, he began having sex with men:

I view myself as straight. And the reason for that is, the only reason that I will have anything to do with a dick is because I have no choice. If I'm going to have any sex at all, I'm going to have to have it with a man. My two choices of sex with a man is to either give him a blowjob or let him fuck me. That's the only two choices I got because I can't fuck him. If I could fuck anybody I'd find me a girl. If my dick could get hard, that would solve my [problem]. I'd get me a hooker on retainer.

While Richard preferred to have sex with women, he explained that it was too difficult to find women for sex, even without penetration, given his ED. His explanation provides another window on the way that conventional understandings of masculinity and man-woman sex can paradoxically lead men to sex with other men.

For Richard, sex with a woman without an erection was not an appealing option. Interestingly, even with ED he did have an ongoing sexual relationship with a woman for "damn near a year." He explained, "I'd suck on her titties and kiss her all over and kiss her on her neck and run my tongue down her belly button and eat her pussy until she couldn't stand it. She was quite happy; it worked out very well." She eventually lost interest in continuing the sexual relationship, however, and Richard guessed it was because she started hooking up with "a long dick guy" with whom they had a threesome.

Richard's description of her playing with his own "little bitty tiny flaccid dick" suggests that he found the experience in some ways emasculating. It appears that Richard came to see his inability to get an erection with a woman as more emasculating than having sex with another man. Social definitions of sex as necessarily involving an erect penis likely also affected Richard's motivations to have sex with a man who was able to penetrate him. A combination of these constructs led him to feel that sex with men was his only option.

Similarly, Tom, a fifty-nine-year-old man from Washington, described himself as "a straight guy that has ED and doesn't want to give up having sex," even though "I would rather be having sex with girls, if I could." He elaborated: "When I couldn't get hard anymore [I] kind of decided to switch teams. Probably the thought of touching another man's cock repulsed me three to four years ago, and now that I've done it a few times it doesn't bother me too much." In fact, for Tom, sex with men had become more than simply not bothersome. Unlike Richard, who maintained that he would prefer to be having sex with women if he could, Tom found that sex with men changed his attractions and desires:

It's more like, it's like a forbidden thing, kind of makes it exciting. . . . Just strictly because I've got ED and I don't get hard anymore. So, I can take the submissive role with a guy and it's kind of nice that I don't have to perform. It's like I'm in control, like women are with guys. I still got to perform, but it's kind of a power thing over the guys. . . . They want to have sex, and I can provide that for them, and if I say no then I can't. When having sex with girls you're always afraid you're going to come too fast, or you won't be hard or you won't stay hard. Being a submissive, sex with guys, you're kind of in control, it's up to them to perform.

While Tom began having sex with men because of ED, he came to enjoy it: "If I could get hard good and stuff like that, if I could get hard all the time I never would have started with guys. And now, if I get my ED under control, I still might stay with guys too, just because I like making them happy. I like the attention they give me."

As Tom gained more experience with male-male sex, he began enjoying it more. Indeed, he turned his erectile dysfunction into a kink, such that he could experience sexual pleasure through bottoming and performing submissiveness. Tom, like Marcus, enjoyed the "forbidden" or "taboo" aspect of having sex with another man. Moreover, interpreting bottoming as a way to maintain control helped Tom continue to see himself as masculine. This interpretation required rejecting mainstream associations between being penetrated and being vulnerable. He concluded his explanation by noting that "I've always been a little bit kinky. . . . But for me it's only recreational, it's not a physical attraction at all." He understood that his sexual activity with men required an alternative attitude distinct from conventional understandings of men's sexuality and masculinity.

Again, these decisions to have sex with men rather than nonpenetrative sex or physical intimacy with women reveal the degree to which many straight men see penetration as a key aspect of man-woman sex. Mutual masturbation and oral sex with women (giving or receiving) were inadequate for Richard and Tom. As Tom said of his reason for having sex with men, "The most deciding one is that I can't get hard for girls. I had some girls suck me off, but I [was] not hard. It was okay, but I didn't feel too good about it." Similarly, Richard's statement that he had "no choice" but to have sex with men is an oversimplification that helped him justify sex with men while retaining his sense of himself as straight and masculine.

Men who are exclusively attracted to women yet want to be anally penetrated can ask women to top them with a dildo, something known as "pegging."[9] However, since many men fear that their women partners will see them as gay or feminine if they ask for pegging, some instead turn to other men for anal stimulation.[10] Hence, cultural beliefs about the importance of penetration for heterosexual sex, and the association between receptive anal sex and gayness or femininity, counterintuitively encourage some men to have sex with other men.

The way many rural and small-town men construct masculinity perhaps makes the seemingly paradoxical choice to bottom because of ED even more understandable. Their masculine ideal involves a relationship to women that is protective, nurturing, and sometimes in charge—presumably making it particularly difficult for these men to challenge conventional ideas of man-woman sex. While difficult even for urban and suburban men,[11] this may be particularly so for men from rural areas and small towns.

The desire to bottom for another man because of ED may be related to the kink for penises. Penises, and particularly erect penises, are associated with manhood. Wanting to bottom for another man suggests a desire to reclaim masculinity through the association with a penis, even if it is someone else's. Additionally, bottoming feels good. Prostate stimulation is intensely pleasurable, sometimes even more so than penile stimulation.[12] It is no wonder that several of the men I talked to turned to bottoming.

Over a third of the men I talked to noted that sex had become painful, uncomfortable, or less desirable for their wives due to disability or age-related bodily changes, or simply because their wives lost interest in sex as they grew older. Because these men wanted to continue having sex, they turned to other men. They felt that sex with men was more enjoyable, easier to find, or less threatening to their marriages than extramarital sex with women, and that having sex with men benefited everyone: they continued having sex while their wives stopped having sex or had sex less frequently.

It should go without saying that these women did not "cause" their husbands to have sex with men or that it was their "fault" the men I talked to did so, since people have every right to stop having sex for any reason. Rather than trying to pressure their wives into unwanted sex, the men I talked to turned to other men because doing so allowed them to continue having sex without feeling as though they were cheating on their wives. Some had sex with men for the first time as a result of not having sex with their wives, whereas others increased the frequency of sex with men that they were already having.

A sixty-three-year-old man from Montana named Chris, for instance, divulged that his wife "has a horrible lack of interest anymore. And I've just gotten to accept it, don't argue [or] try to get it anymore." As he explained, "Even though we're sixty years old we still have desires. And if you can't get it at home, well, you get tired of yourself." Chris began having sex with men in the late 1990s, after his wife lost interest in sex. At the same time, he gained access to the Internet, which allowed him to explore sexual possibilities he had previously never considered, including sex with men. This increased his desire to try it. Aaron, a man in his midsixties (he was not more precise) living in North Dakota, also started having sex with men after his wife lost interest in sex:

> As it [our marriage] went on and we had children, frequency decreased. And I can remember a situation after we were either close to empty nest-ers or just before we were empty nesters I decided just to see what would happen if I never initiated the sex with my wife, and this was probably late forties or early fifties. And that time that I never initiated sex with my wife we had it like twice in a year. And that may have been the tipping point for seeking sex outside the marriage.

Prior to this, Aaron had begun to develop an interest in sex with men "once there was accessibility to Internet porn. Then my curiosity and sexual nature just led me to widen my range as to what I watched." Like Chris, Aaron explained that Internet porn shaped his desires for men. (Internet porn can also, similarly, shape men's attitudes about women and sex in general.)[13] This coupled with lack of sex at home encouraged him to turn to extramarital sex with men. Similarly, a sixty-three-year-old man from Iowa, Jared, noted that his least favorite part of his sex life was the infrequency of sex with his wife: "My first priority would be to always have it with my wife, but when it's not very frequent that's when I tend to look for others. . . . She used to have a higher sex drive so I would say it's less than when we got married, and it continues to decline." Jared had previously had sex with men, so his wife's lack of interest in sex encouraged him to have more frequent male-male sex.

Other men experienced no desire for men and no sex with them prior to their wives losing interest in sex. Brian, a fifty-five-year-old man from Colorado, was one such man:

Just to give you an example, the last time was just before Thanksgiving. I romanced the wife all day Friday, romanced her all day Saturday, thought I was going to get lucky on Sunday, nothing happened. And literally by Monday, before Thanksgiving, I genuinely had a bad case of blue balls. I thought I was going to explode. I was in pain, wife went to work, called my buddy, he came over, and he goes, "Oh crap your scrotum is really swollen," and I says, "Well I tried romancing my wife Friday Saturday Sunday, blah blah blah, and she's just not interested." It's like eh, even when we have sex, okay, I'll get around to it. It's like eh, I'm sorry. He and I put on some porn, watched some porn, two or three movies, these are like fifteen-minute clips, they're not like full-length clips or anything, jerk each other off and we're good to go for another month or so.

Brian hoped that his wife would regain interest in sex, but in the meantime, he hooked up with friends, which he found easier than trying to have sex with his wife. Pat, a seventy-three-year-old man from Illinois, similarly explained that no longer having sex with his wife was the sole reason he decided to have sex with men:

Wife gave up sex after [our last] child. I think she finally figured out what caused it. After all [of our] children left the house, and got their education started, I thought maybe sex would start up again, but it didn't. Well, that was our first bout with breast cancer. And part of the chemo removed any estrogen she had. And then she informed me she wasn't sleeping in the master bedroom anymore. I said that's fine. We had three other bedrooms. And I said I'm not leaving the master bedroom. So, I guess about five years ago I finally decided well, I can't live this way anymore, I've got to have some blowjobs. Or the little woman has to start spreading her legs.

Pat's crude statement about his wife needing to "start spreading her legs" indicates that he felt entitled to sex. It took Pat "like fifteen, twenty years" during which "I didn't have any sexual activity at all" to come to the decision to have sex with men. Eventually, he said, "I decided this is for the birds. And I decided I'll find some guy that likes to suck cock and get my cock sucked, and that's what I've been doing." Dissatisfied with his lack of sex at home but unwilling to leave his wife or feel that he was being unfaithful, Pat turned to men. For many of the men I talked to, changes in their wives' sexual desires were the catalyst for changes in their own sexual activities, but not a change in their sexual identification. Some seemed genuinely understanding, empathetic, and respectful of their wives' changing needs; others, like Pat, expressed annoyance, frustration, and even misogyny. Several of the men I interviewed made statements that were sexist and demeaning toward women.

Of course, it is common for people in relationships to have different levels of sexual desire, and people respond to this problem in different ways. Secretive extramarital sex is, arguably, more ethical than pressuring or manipulating partners into sex. And while the possibility of STI transmission means that it is potentially unsafe for men to have secret extramarital sex while continuing to have sex with their wives, this issue is nonexistent when they no longer have sex with their wives. Not all the men I spoke to had stopped having sex with their wives altogether, but many of them had.

Only two of the men I interviewed communicated with their women partners about currently having sex with men; both were in open relationships. The rest were not open about their sex with men.[14] Open or polyamorous relationships[15] are a solution to differing sex drives within relationships for some people. Since these solutions necessitate consent and awareness of all partners, they do not constitute infidelity. Although there is little research on consensual nonmonogamy (which itself reflects stigma regarding this topic), open relationships or polyamory do work well for many people.[16]

Nonetheless, these relationship models are stigmatized because monogamy is culturally constructed as normal and virtuous, making it difficult for people to conceive of, much less talk to their partners about, opening up or expanding an established romantic partnership. Moreover, the cultural emphasis on monogamy means that many nonmonogamous couples may be discreet about their open or polyamorous relationships, and these relationships are seldom represented in the media. As a result, many people are not aware that consensual nonmonogamy is an option. Few Americans are in consensually nonmonogamous relationships: only 4 percent of American couples are open or polyamorous, with greater frequency among gay male couples than other groups.[17] Most of the men I interviewed said that extramarital sex with men was less threatening to their relationship than extramarital sex with women would be.

The men I talked to lived in rural areas and small towns where the cultural emphasis on monogamous heterosexual marriage was especially strong. Because male-male sex and nonmonogamy are stigmatized, particularly in conservative rural areas and small towns, most men were afraid to discuss their sex with their wives and did not think their wives would accept it even in the context of an open relationship. Similarly, most did not think their women partners would be willing to have an open or polyamorous relationship and did not discuss the possibility with them. Hence, given the cultural importance of heterosexual marriage and the stigmas surrounding open/poly relationships and male-male sex, the men I interviewed did not discuss their extramarital sex with their women partners. They were able to meet their sexual and romantic desires by having sex with men while remaining married, and without feeling as though they were threatening their marriages or their identities.

Because I only talked to the men, I cannot know how their wives would describe these same situations. Perhaps many stopped having sex with their husbands because it was unsatisfying. Men are much more likely to orgasm than women in sex,[18] in large part because many men focus more on themselves or do not do what is necessary to best please women, such as clitoral stimulation.[19] That could have been the case with several of the men I talked to, and they may not have even been aware of this. The perspectives of the wives are just as important as those of their husbands. Unfortunately, I do not know what they think, because I could not interview them. It is, however, important to keep them in mind when thinking about why they and the men I talked to no longer had sex, or had sex less frequently than in the past.

Changing Sexual Attractions

While a number of men attributed having sex with other men to their wives' changing sexual desires, a majority—forty-five out of sixty—reported changes to their own sexual attractions or desires too. These changes were unintentional, unexpected, and long lasting. Some men reported that they occurred in response to their wife no longer having sex with them or having sex less frequently. Others described the change as unrelated to their sex life with women. While some men had experienced changes in their teens or twenties, for most these changes were in their thirties, forties, fifties, or even sixties, well after youth.

This remarkable finding shows that men's sexual attractions can be flexible throughout adulthood. Most of the men who reported such changes did not indicate that the changes were radical, however. Instead, most said that their sexual attractions or desires shifted from "exclusively" to "mostly" being focused on women or reported that preexisting attractions to men grew stronger. Nonetheless, these subtle shifts were profound. They encouraged many men to begin having sex with men for the first time as well as leading others to seek out sexual encounters with men more than they had in the past. In either case, aging affected how the men I interviewed experienced their sexuality. Sexuality is not necessarily fixed from a young age. The men I talked to identified a variety of circumstances, situations, and events that they felt were related to their attractions changing, encouraging them to seek sex with men.

Some men noted that their attractions changed after they began having sex with men, whereas others said their attractions or desires for men preceded their having sex with men. Some felt that changes to their desires and attractions were "caused" by having sex with men. Of course, causality is a complex topic when it comes to sexual attraction and activity. Indeed, several of the men I interviewed had sex with numerous men but remained exclusively attracted to women. Some psychologists have concluded that shifting attractions are caused by a complex interplay of environment and biology.[20] My own interest, as a sociologist, is less in what causes these attractions to change than in how men report experiencing them. Again, the stories here are not about men "recognizing" latent desires; rather, they demonstrate sexual flexibility over men's lifetimes.

Many men pointed to a key event as the beginning of changes to their attractions, reporting that their sexual interest in men increased after having sex with a man. Ernie, a twenty-one-year-old man from Kansas, said that his attractions to men "probably first shifted after my first experience with a man. Because I used to not have any attraction to men and then after it happened it became more." He said that he experienced a "pretty sudden" shift in his attractions, from being exclusively directed towards women to an 80–20 women–men split.[21] David, a seventy-four-year-old man from Oregon, had previously had group sex with his wife participating, and also found his sexual interest change from being focused on women to 80–20 women–men after a particular experience:

> Well, up until about ten years ago I didn't have any sexual, physical attraction to men, in any way. That all came on fairly recently. Up until then it was all women. Even when we had three-ways, two guys and my wife, I didn't feel any sexual attraction to them. They were just part of the mix, they were just doing their thing and I was doing my thing. And then I was in my late fifties, I met a couple in a motel room that I talked to online. . . . [F]irst thing I noticed about him was that he was shaved. I had never seen a man shaved before. And so was she, she was sitting on the bed and he was just standing there.

David continued, explaining how this sexual experience profoundly affected his sex life.

> Anyway, something, I don't know what it was, I just reached out and held him. For some strange reason, it just dawned on me, and he didn't mind at all, and I said, "I've never seen them shaved like this." Anyway we went through the process and I was screwing her, and they had both told me to be sure to tell them when I was ready to come. And so I was about ready, so I said, "Okay, I'm ready to come," and he reached out and held my balls while I came in her. And that was probably one of the best feeling things in my life. I could not believe it, and after it was all done and I had left and I was thinking back on that, it was like wow, that was mind blowing. I thought hmm, there might be something worth pursuing there, with a guy. And that's kind of how it started. It took a long, long time, it was

probably four to five years before I actively started targeting guys online, but that's really what started it.

While David had had group sexual encounters that included men previously, he felt that it was this experience that began a process whereby his sexual attractions changed. He began meeting up with men one on one "because I knew that sex with men could be fun, and I hadn't realized it up until then."

Kevin, a sixty-nine-year-old man from Missouri, in contrast, had long experienced minor attractions to men, but after he unexpectedly hooked up with a man in his midthirties, his sexual interest in men increased. He estimated that his attractions to women and men changed to 75–25 after his first sexual experience with a man:

> I grew up in an area where that wasn't an option, in a time and area both. And I never really thought about it. I had attractions a time or two, a few times, but never was with a guy, never touched a guy, never anything. Until I was in my midthirties, and that kind of happened by accident, and I liked it, and been kind of doing it ever since. . . . After that, I was attracted more, I wouldn't say more to men than women, but my attraction, my thoughts about men, shall we say, escalated. It did change, it changed a lot. And I seen it was an option, and it was good.

Kevin also saw for the first time that it was possible to have sex with men even as he continued identifying as straight. Many other men similarly reported suddenly realizing that sex with men could be enjoyable, putting them on a new sexual trajectory. These situations were diverse, ranging from prearranged threesomes to spontaneous hookups with random men. Ernie, David, and Kevin were three of several men whose attractions to other men shifted after an unexpected sexual encounter that helped them realize that sex with men was a possibility for them, and an enjoyable one.

Many other men described their attractions shifting as a process and noted general life changes rather than a specific event as the beginning of the shifts. Harrison, a fifty-five-year-old man living in Oregon, explained that his attractions increased "dramatically, much more towards men" after divorcing his wife. It was at that point that he also began seeking sex with men, which he did not do during marriage. Relatedly, Will, a fifty-two-year-old man from Missouri, explained that his wife divorced him in middle age for reasons unrelated to his male-male attractions, and said that the divorce allowed him to sexually explore after their separation.

Will's sexual attractions shifted from mostly women to about equal women and men, leaning toward men. "I would positively say it has changed, when checking out people, I probably check out more guys than I do females." This changed from before, when "it would have been female, and then an occasional checking out a dude, he looks good, he's fit, he's clean. You know, just wondering."

Seamus, a forty-seven-year-old man from Indiana, described sexual attractions shifting from 95–5 women–men to 80–20 women–men after joining the military. He explained that this major institutional change led him to notice men more: "Probably just noticing guys, when I was in the military. Just proximity, because I grew up in a small town. And when I joined the military I was around a lot more men than women. . . . It was a process." Importantly, although he eventually left the military, his sexual interest in men did not revert to what it had been prior to joining it. While many straight men in mostly male contexts like boarding school or the military, which is still a mostly male world, attribute their sex with other men to desperation, many do so because of genuine interest or bonding rituals.[22] As Seamus discovered, new social and institutional contexts may actually shape attractions and desires.

A number of men attributed changes to their attractions specifically to gaining Internet access in the 1990s or early 2000s. Prior to the Internet, it was much more difficult for men in rural areas and small towns to meet other men for casual sexual encounters. While all of the men I interviewed felt that the Internet made hooking up easier, several identified the opportunities it provided to meet other men for sex, talk in chat rooms, and view gay pornography as catalyzing shifting sexual desires. Chris, for instance, described his attractions shifting from exclusively to women to about 75 percent women and 25 percent men: "Probably with the advent of the Internet I've acquired a little bit more interest in guys. . . . I didn't really know that much about anything with men prior to that because it's just been a straight life my whole life. . . . It would have been all women, 100% women. . . . My interests extended when I was online, just checking out different areas." Internet access allowed Chris to explore his sexuality and begin having sex with men as he felt increasing sexual attraction to them. Several other men similarly explained that being able to access new information online opened their eyes to new sexual possibilities. Thus, historical and technological changes may help shape sexual attractions and desires, as well as make it easier to find sexual partners.

In sum, many men experienced a wide variety of situations, events, and circumstances that they felt contributed to unexpected and unintentional changes in their sexual attractions or desires. Some experienced this as a single event, though most described it as a process. The most common themes that contributed to this change included declining sex with their wives, growing older, or having sex with a man.

Regardless of what caused the change, these stories show that men's sexual desires and attractions can be flexible over the course of one's life in conjunction with and distinct from sexual practices. Even fairly small changes to attractions or desires can facilitate major changes to sexual practices. Significantly, the changes the men I talked to experienced were primarily sexual, and most either did not have emotional attractions to men or actively avoided situations where they might emerge. They pointed to both generational and aging-related factors. Lessening social stigmas attached to male-male sex made them more open to trying it, while at the same time other changes specifically related to aging encouraged them to have sex with other men.

Sex with Men: Easier or Better

About half of the men I talked to felt that casual sex with men was better or easier than with women. They attributed this to various factors, including the belief that women are less capable of, or uninterested in, casual, nonromantic sex. Some also believed that because men are naturally more sexual than women, sex with men is consequently more straightforward, exciting, or pleasurable.[23] The belief that men are naturally more sexual than women is common in American society and relates to how men and women are socialized differently. Hence, while most of the men I talked to preferred women for romantic relationships, many felt that other men were a better choice for casual sexual encounters.

Again, we see the effects of straight culture on their perceptions: men and women often learn that they are "opposites" sexually and emotionally. Men are sexual and emotionally not very complicated, whereas women are less focused on sex and are very emotional. Men and women are taught that while they are different emotionally, this difference also makes them compatible; they are complementary. These beliefs encouraged romantic relationships with women and shaped their desires for romantic partnerships with women. These same beliefs about women being emotionally suited for men, however, made them wary of casual sex with women. Many felt that women were naturally emotional and nurturing and that men and women were naturally attracted to each other, emotionally speaking. Emotional women were matches for emotionally uncomplicated men. Consequently, seeking out women for casual sex was too difficult—because women were less inclined to casual sex—or too risky, since there was such a great potential for emotional attachment.

Thus, beliefs about men and women matching one another emotionally actually encouraged sex between men. These men's stories reveal a broader contradiction within the institution of heterosexuality, which is dependent on understandings of men and women as sexual and emotional opposites. According to this logic, the qualities that make men and women emotionally match one another also make them unfit to fully satisfy one another sexually. Men will continue wanting an active sex life, whereas women will lose interest. Certainly, most straight men who are frustrated with their sex life, whether they are single or in a relationship, will either accept that they are going to have less sex than they want or will try to have more sex with women. Yet the stories of the men I talked to show that many instead take conservative beliefs about men and women to their logical conclusion: men can have fulfilling, long-term romantic, but not sexual, relationships with women.

Conservative gender beliefs also suggest that men cannot trust women: even if women say they desire casual sex, they are likely mistaken, and perhaps cannot be trusted to keep a secret or be empathetic about issues related to ED. Men, in contrast, can be trusted to be direct about what they want, to not change their minds, and to keep secrets.

Men can also perhaps be trusted to not emasculate other men in specific circumstances with clear boundaries, as Tom and Richard explained about other men penetrating them. Thus, conservative (and sexist) beliefs about men and women matching one another emotionally, as well as about masculinity and femininity more broadly, all encouraged sex between men.

Compatible Desires

Just as most of the men I talked to considered women complementary *romantic* partners, several considered men to be better *sexual* partners. Ten said directly that sex with men was better than sex with women, either because men engaged in sexual practices women did not enjoy[24] (e.g., oral-anal stimulation: "rimming") or because they found that sex with men was more pleasurable in other ways. David, like several others, related this to the aging process: "Sex with men right now for me is very gratifying. Older men particularly are a lot more receptive to sex. They're more enthusiastic. They seem to get more pleasure out of it. Senior women have kind of lost their desire to do much of anything. Generally my wife is the one who is real passive, she's nice enough and willing in that, but not a lot of fun." It is not necessarily true that older women have lost sexual desire. Those who have, however, may have lost it because of unsatisfying sex they do not want to repeat. Regardless, David explained that sex with men had helped him rethink the relationship between sex, pleasure, and masculinity: "I think the way we're raised has a lot to do with it. There's so much social pressure to be a straight, he-man-type thing, they completely forget the pleasurable side of sex, and we're taught not to do that. Now when you find out your wife no longer wants to do it, you get retaught." As David grew older, his sexuality changed. As a younger man, he had pursued sex with women in part because doing so bolstered his masculinity, regardless of the amount of pleasure he experienced. Later in life, however, he began focusing on pleasure—with men.

David's wife still consented to sex but was not "enthusiastic" about it, as men were, leading David to feel that sex with men allowed him to pursue pleasure more thoroughly than sex with women did. His experience and explanation again demonstrate that men's sexual practices and understandings of their masculinity can change over time, even as they continue to identify as straight and masculine. They also illustrate the ways that strict constructions of heterosexual masculinity and messages that men and women are "opposites" of one another can paradoxically decrease intimacy and pleasure between men and women.

Jordan, a sixty-four-year-old man living in Colorado, also found sex with men more pleasurable than sex with his wife and, by extension, with women in general.

> I think that for us men it's hugely physical. But in a monogamous relationship with a woman, it becomes more than that, it becomes very mental, very emotional. And then all of a sudden no matter what you do, they can't orgasm, and pretty soon it becomes a very one-sided thing. Pretty soon for us we couldn't even have intercourse, and it just became a very one-sided thing. I was always getting off and shooting my load, and that was it. And that became very frustrating.

Sex with men, according to Jordan, is more arousing than sex with women.

> A man, I can watch him shoot his load and know he's having as much fun as I am. And I'm more turned on by that than a one-sided deal with my wife. . . . I love oral, my wife has given me oral, but not like a man. I want her to just get so aggressive and suck my dick to the point where I'm saying I'm going to shoot and then jacks me off. But that's never happened. And I loved giving her oral, but she didn't like it so much.

Jordan was very interested in oral sex, and said that men were more interested in that than his wife was.

> So we just never went there hardly at all. And I always wondered, how can you not like that, oh, my gosh, I like it. And maybe it's a man thing, I don't know. . . . You always hear that a man gives a better blowjob than a woman ever could. And I love my dick sucked, I love to come, and yet women do not so much want to do that, and especially to climax. [To] have an orgasm and [for a partner to] swallow, I've never had that happen with a woman, ever.

Because his wife did not experience as much pleasure from their sex as he did, Jordan's own pleasure was curtailed. He sensed his wife's lack of interest in sex and turned to men. Jordan, along with others I interviewed, felt that oral sex in particular was better with men than it was with women, in part because their male partners seemed more enthusiastic. Jeremy, for instance, cited oral sex as "the reason for my initial sexual experience with a male, and that continues to be probably the major attraction, a major goal that I'm looking for." In fact, he found it "very difficult to reach an orgasm when a woman is performing oral sex on me," so that, he explained,

> There are very specific reasons or specific instances when I would be more attracted to seeking of a sexual experience with a man. . . . I don't have any problems at all reaching an orgasm when a man is performing oral sex on me. . . . I think part of it is because it is another man, there's something about, it might be a power thing seeing another man subjugate himself to me whether it's on his knees or in between my legs. Somehow it's a very powerful feeling to look down and see another man's mouth filled with your penis and wanting you to have an orgasm in his mouth. There's something about that, and I find that men, in my experience anyway, are much more likely to want you to ejaculate in their mouth. Whereas in my experience very few women want it, some will allow it, some won't allow it at all.

Jeremy felt it was more sexually exciting to penetrate another man than a woman, but he also felt that women were less enthusiastic than men. For both reasons, Jeremy's sex with men—receiving oral sex— bolstered his masculinity. While many men find sexual dominance over women arousing,[25] Jeremy found that consensual power dynamics with men were more pleasurable. Although Jeremy was one of the few who fetishized penetration with men in this way, a sizable portion of the men I talked to felt that sex with men was simply better than sex with women, even as they preferred women for romantic relationships. Interestingly, forty-nine-year-old Jeremy was one of the few men I talked to who lived in an urban area (in Florida).[26] His perception of oral sex as a form of sexual dominance was one of a few topics where his attitudes differed

from those of the other men I interviewed, and it may relate to him living in an urban area rather than a rural area or small town.

Like David and Jordan, other men also explained that they were not
only interested in their own sexual pleasure. They wanted their partners
to experience it as well. Hence, men who did not believe their wives
genuinely enjoyed sex might seek it with others, though this phenomenon was not limited to married men. Seventy-year-old Zach, who was
single and living in Oregon, shared similar sentiments:

> I think men understand men sexually better than women do. And
> therefore I felt that a man can please a man better than a woman can
> at times. . . . [T]he experiences that you have with women are the same
> all the time, but men are a little bit different, men do things differently.
> Women [are] kind of just the same. . . . The reason I meet up with men
> is, I feel like strangely if my need is being met then I'm able to meet their
> needs. Once again I can tell the difference. When you're with a woman,
> they don't really express themselves like a man does, and they don't react
> like a man does. A lot of times they're just passive and they expect you
> to do everything, so to speak, and I guess that's the way it's always been.

Of course it is not true that all women are passive, nor is it true that this
is "the way it's always been." But Zach believed this to be true, and consequently enjoyed having sex with men more than with women.

> But when you're with another man they're not always passive, they may
> be aggressive, and so I find that exciting and a little bit challenging to see
> what role is going to come out or what's going to happen. . . . So you just
> never knew what was going to happen, and I think that's what's so dif-
> ferent, and that's what maybe makes it more exciting, I guess. You don't
> know what's going to happen, whereas when you're with a woman the
> same thing always happens, it doesn't change any.

Zach explained that "I would prefer to be with a woman, but they're
dull. . . . [I]f there's going to be a romance I'd rather it be with a woman,
but I'm not really sure if she could meet all of my needs or not, and that
would bother me. That's kind of why I just stay the way I am right now

[single]." Zach's blanket statements about women are untrue and sexist. Still, what matters for his identity and his decision to focus on men for sex is that he believed these statements to be true. While Zach preferred to romantically partner with a woman, he was not willing to sacrifice what he thought of as a natural sexual pairing between two men. It is remarkable that Zach so strongly believed that women and men were natural emotional partners, but that men were natural sexual partners.

To sum it up, many men reported that other men were better sexual partners than women because men are naturally more interested in sex and, thus, are more enjoyable and exciting sexual partners. Conventional ideas about men's and women's sexual natures—that men are constantly desiring and pursuing sex whereas women are not or should not—encouraged the men I interviewed to seek men for sex. Conservative beliefs about natural differences between men and women actually facilitated sex between men.

Compatible Goals

While some men reported that male sex partners expressed and elicited more pleasure than women, many others believed that women were less capable than men of separating sex from emotion. Women partners for casual sex were more difficult to find, and riskier to deal with, than were men. It is sexist to say that most women are emotionally clingy and untrustworthy; these are stereotypes. Nonetheless, this belief encouraged many of the men I interviewed to have sex with men. Thus, while almost all the men I interviewed preferred women as romantic partners, and many felt that women and men were emotional (if not sexual) matches, it was this very belief about being emotionally suited for one another that raised red flags for them. Casual sex with men was just easier, they said, because they felt that it mostly avoided the possibility for romantic attachment. As Ian, a forty-two-year-old man from Idaho, said, "Whereas men are able to more easily separate a sexual encounter from feelings or emotions, they can categorize that, yeah, this is just to get together for sexual release because, they're needing [it]. [Guys] can be more readily available. If you're looking for a hookup off Craigslist for example, you're much more likely to be able to do that with another man. . . . so part of it is effort and availability." Ian believed that men were more sex oriented than women. Men could "get off" and leave, with no added complications, making it much easier to find men who were as interested in casual sex as he was. As fifty-seven-year-old Adam from Wisconsin said simply, "I think men are a lot less complicated and that it's just easier. It's sex, but there's no attachment. I don't think women can do that." Connor, a forty-three-year-old man living in Oregon, also felt that no-strings-attached (NSA) sex was easier to find and, importantly, safer with men:

> I prefer women and I date women, but I sleep with, or have sex with guys just because it's a lot easier and more convenient. Casual sex with men is a lot simpler than it is with women. So I guess, I really never have casual sex with women. . . . I'm actually a little bit wary, more wary about female casual sex, like if I looked on a Craigslist ad or something like that, and it had a woman wanting to hook up, it would be more off-putting. Like it would be a little bit scary, like what's wrong with her, [laughs] or what's going on, that she's looking for casual sex.

Connor distrusted women who sought casual sex and felt that women who were looking for casual sex had something wrong with them. His belief that women tied emotion to sex meant that women who seemed not to do so were flawed and thus potentially dangerous. This belief demonstrates the sexual double standard: it is okay for men to seek casual sex, but not women. Many Americans hold this sexist belief. Pat, who also said that women were unsuitable for casual sex, explained his preference in more pragmatic terms:

> Now your next question is why didn't I choose women. I could have, and would have, but you've got to think the whole thing through. You've got to be logical. Were I to have an affair with a woman on the side, women are going to talk. They're emotional. They're going to talk. They're going to let the secret out. As opposed to meeting up with a straight man, they're not going to talk. They're not going to let the secret out. So I guess that's when I decided.

Pat continued talking about why women are untrustworthy: "Men are more discreet. Men won't talk, women will talk among themselves, and it's been my observation that sooner or later if you hook up with a woman then word gets out and we have a terrible knock-down, drag-out situation. I thought about that before I decided to hook up with men, and then I thought no, men are in the same boat I am. And will not talk." Given that Pat was married, he felt that sex with men was the easiest and most secure way to get off without threatening his marriage. He felt that women were too emotional and prone to talking among themselves, and therefore too risky. These beliefs are based on sexist stereotypes, but very much influenced him. Similarly, Richard, who was single and divorced, explained that women were not interested in sex but demanded considerable investments of time and money. As he argued,

> Women my age, the only thing they're interested in is they want you to take them to church, buy them things, and take care of them, basically. I'm not into taking care of a woman. They're not interested in sex, that's for sure, no way in hell. . . . Now I'm quite sure if I coughed up enough money, and I got my hair cut, and I went out and bought me a real nice suit, and I cleaned my car out really, really good, and detailed it a lot, and contacted one of these women and played the courtship game for two or three weeks, I could probably get a date with her, and take her out to dinner, and buy her whatever the hell she wanted for dinner, and spend a pleasant evening talking.

His disdain for women already apparent, Richard continued.

> And then I could take her home and let her go home, and that would be the end of it, and after ten to fifteen dates like that she might possibly consent to maybe doing a little necking. But that's it, I'm out three to four thousand dollars. I'm sorry, I'm not interested, I just don't want to deal with the drama, and I've dealt with drama and women all my life. And my buddy and I, there's no drama. He gets horny, he wants a blowjob, I go give him one, he's happy, I'm happy, we discuss politics.

For sex without romance, Richard felt that the answer was obvious: have sex with men. He felt that sex with his "buddy" demanded little to no emotional, financial, or time investment, or, at least, that the emotional and time investments were less onerous since they shared similar interests. Hence, after his divorce, Richard preferred sex with men over romance with women. Richard shared Pat's disdain for women.

Significantly, these men felt that sex with men was almost guaranteed, unlike sex with women. As Otto, a fifty-two-year-old man from Oregon, joked, "I would rather be with a woman, but given my circumstances, it's easier to be with men. . . . [Sex with women is] too hard. . . . [W]ith a man, it can happen almost immediately if you're attractive or you have a big dick or, I don't know, not a leper." The belief that men are naturally more sexual than women reflects ideals of conventional masculinity. In youth through adulthood, most men learn that they are more sexual than women and that this is part of what it means to be masculine. Thus men learn that it is acceptable, and even expected, for men to be sexually active, express sexual interest, and always be ready for sex. Many women, on the other hand, are victims of a double standard in which peers treat them as defective for being as sexually active as men.[27] This may mean that fewer women than men are interested in casual sex, but of course there are still many women who enjoy nonromantic sex. Just as important are perceptions of gender differences, which lead some men to be more comfortable with and interested in nonromantic sex with men than with women.

Paradoxically, beliefs about men and women being natural emotional matches actually encouraged the men I interviewed to have sex with other men. This paradox partly reflects their views on the essential nature of gender differences, which they felt made romantic ties between men and women natural but casual sex much riskier. Men could be counted on for sexual interest, and for emotional detachment when needed. The very traits that made women preferable as emotional and marital partners made them problematic casual sex partners. Conventional understandings of masculinity and femininity sexually connected men but stifled mutually pleasurable intimacy with women.

Many of the men I talked to made comments about women that are sexist. Richard, and several of the other men I interviewed, characterized women as untrustworthy, sexually unpleasurable, selfish, and even a waste of time. Many blamed women for issues with their sex life. Women in their lives would probably describe these situations very differently. Saying that most women are clingy, sexually boring, or untrustworthy reduces them to stereotypes. There were likely other factors the men did not report that contributed to issues with their sex life. These could include not focusing enough on their women partner's pleasure, having poor hygiene, being physically unattractive, not doing an equal share of housework, being poor communicators, having an irritating personality, or being rude, demanding, or entitled. I cannot know for sure which of these possibilities, if any, were contributing factors. But regardless of the exact issue, men are not entitled to sex with women and should not blame all women for issues with their sex life.

There are two additional factors that are important when considering women having casual sex. First, many women desire, and have, casual sex. It is not true that women are inherently untrustworthy in casual sexual encounters. Second, there are likely more men than women seeking casual sex, overall, but this is due to gender inequality. Stigma about women having casual sex, and fear of sexual assault, likely discourage some women from having more casual sex.

Most of the men I interviewed did not consider these factors. It is important to remember that many of their statements are sexist, and that we are only hearing the stories of men, not women. The beliefs many men shared, while sexist and untrue, nonetheless greatly shaped their decision to turn to men.

Compatible Feelings

Many of the men I talked to described sex with men as a way to connect or bond with other men or to relieve the pressures of masculinity. For those looking for connection, sex was not necessarily their main goal in meeting up with a man. Sex, however, helped them reliably connect with another man in a way they considered masculine. Sex with men also allowed them to enjoy nonsexual physical affection, such as cuddling, which they were not sure how to do platonically. Because these men saw sex as necessary for connecting with other men, particularly in a masculine way, they saw sex with men as compatible with straight identification.

Sharing feelings of loneliness or expressing a desire for male cuddling or physical affection might be taboo, stigmatized as feminine or gay. Having sex, counterintuitively, was not. Platonic touch, which many men avoid because they associate it with femininity, weakness, or gayness, increases individual well-being on a variety of measures.[28] To address their need for touch and connection with other men, some men I talked to turned to other men for sex. Pursuing sex was masculine, and therefore acceptable in ways that simply seeking nonsexual physical intimacy was not.

Sex with men provided several of the men I talked to a reason to meet up with, and thus connect to, other men. Meeting up for sex made the encounter feel masculine. It also helped prevent them from feeling vulnerable in seeking to connect with other men. As sixty-six-year-old Trevor from Oklahoma explained, "I don't think I meet up [with] them so much for sex as I meet up with them for companionship, and sex is the vehicle for meeting up." After his wife's death, intimacy with women remained painful for Trevor; being with other men helped him find companionship without bringing up painful memories. Seeking men for nonsexual types of companionship was not possible, he said, because "Craigslist just doesn't have a category for fishing buddies or hunting buddies." This is not actually true: Craigslist at the time of the interview did have a section for people to platonically meet. Sex was a way for Trevor to reliably connect with another man, though, even if he would have typically preferred a nonsexual encounter. A fifty-two-year-old man from Oregon, Jack, shared similar sentiments:

> And the only reason that I would do it would be just for the physical need of wanting to hold a man, I guess. . . . It wasn't for, it wasn't to get my rocks off per se, because I just wasn't that horny. It was just because I like that physical connection with a man. . . . [M]y wife and I were having some hard times, we're divorced now, but we were going through some pretty hard times, and I just could connect with a man. But it wasn't, no emotions were ever involved. It just felt good to be in the company of a man for sex.

Despite Jack saying that "no emotions were ever involved," he did experience emotions when hooking up and cuddling with other men, just not romantic emotions. Like Jack, a number of men said they desired nonromantic companionship or touch. Sex with men was the way they were able to fulfill this need, since they did not know of another way to intimately connect with men.

Harrison also shared the fact that he has sex with men because "I think it's loneliness. . . . [that makes me want] just holding, healthy holding. Being single it's a deprivation, people are meant to not be alone. So it's something I like." Building on this, seventy-two-year-old Val, who split his time between two states in the Pacific Northwest, explained that he enjoys cuddling because it is "just, somewhat [of] a bonding experience I guess, and you just enjoy each other's body without being overtly sexually active, although it usually eventually leads that way." In contrast to those men for whom sex was the primary goal, and men were the means to get it without emotional entanglement, these men sought out nonromantic intimacy with men. Sex helped them achieve this intimacy, even if they were not looking for sex per se. Without knowing how to intimately connect with men in ways other than sex, or because they were uncomfortable with the emotional vulnerability displayed by seeking intimacy with other men, these men sought sex as a way to connect emotionally.

Joey, a sixty-six-year-old in Minnesota, had a particularly thoughtful explanation for why he specifically sought out sexual intimacy with other men:

> Maybe a reason that an aging male would reach out to other men is that as one's testosterone declines and your sexual prowess declines, you maybe want to be seeing that close up in other men, sort of reclaiming it, in a way. I think that's no small matter. All things start to slow down a little bit, the time it takes to get an erection, the volume of semen and so on, and to be close to men who are maybe more potent than I am, that's a good thing to see. It's stimulating to see that, and it reminds me of powers that I had and still have but maybe in a somewhat diminished capacity.

Sex with men allowed Joey to rekindle his feelings of masculine virility. Seeing younger men get off reminded him of his own youth and helped him accept age-related changes to his body.

Another reason many of the men I talked to sought sex with other men was to help relieve the pressures of masculinity. Sex with men was an opportunity to *not* have to be in control. Relieving the pressures of maintaining their masculinity allowed them to experience sexual pleasure without additional pressures and expectations. Other men's masculinity could allow the men I interviewed to play a less dominant or controlling role, freeing them to enjoy being pleasured. Hooking up with men who topped them was a gift: sexual enjoyment outside the gendered constraints of conventional heterosexual sex. Men partnered with women could theoretically have played nondominant roles to experience sexual pleasure while relieving masculine pressures to maintain control. But rather than express this vulnerability, they turned to sex with men. Bottoming for another masculine man allowed them to satisfy a desire for masculinity without feeling as though they were losing control to a woman or a feminine man.

Other men found that being penetrated allowed them to experience pleasure outside of the strict confines of typical heterosexual sex, in which men pursue and penetrate women, reflecting themes found in online interview studies.[29] In fact, more of the men I talked to described enjoying sexual submissiveness to relieve the pressures of masculinity than meeting masculine expectations through sexual dominance over other men. Connor, for instance, explained that "I guess if I had to admit it, it's a small ego boost to have somebody attracted to you, so you get a little bit of that encouragement. And a physical release, it was kind of refreshing to actually go to a bar and be the person somebody chased, rather than the guy who is constantly chasing women around."

Similarly, Chris said that "my job demands that I'm in control of things quite a bit, and I like to have that control taken away from me," while Neil, a thirty-four-year-old from South Dakota, divulged that "in my everyday life I'm a straight, macho, masculine guy, an alpha male type of a guy. So sometimes when I'm spending time with guys, I want to be the opposite of that, be the submissive." For these and other men, being pursued or submissive represented a welcome break from feeling constant pressure to be in control. Rand, a fifty-two-year-old living in Oregon, explained that "part of it for me has been about trying to tap into feminine sexuality and what women feel. And so topping has never even come close to being interesting for me. Bottoming is about being the receiver and surrender," while fifty-seven-year-old Sam from Colorado shared that "it kind of makes me feel like a sexy object, and not having to be in control all the time is nice." For these men, bottoming was a temporary relief from the daily enactment of their own masculinity.

2

Friendship, Intimacy, and Love between Men

One man I interviewed, thirty-seven-year-old Larry, fell in love with Nolan, whom he met on Craigslist while both were in relationships with women. Larry and Nolan lived in rural Wyoming. They introduced one another as friends, and even spent time together as couples with their women partners, to whom they explained that they had met through their jobs. Nonetheless, the sexual and romantic aspect of their relationship was "very secretive." As Larry explained,

> Our connections weren't real frequent. [There was] anticipation of the next time we get to see each other. We did go for a couple weekends away. We could do that because of what we did and it was off the radar and it was something that we both could say, "Hey, I'm headed up with Nolan to, whatever, we're going to go do this." So that was very, very normal, so you didn't have to hide in that respect, where you were going to be. You could answer the phone if you were in the truck with him or whatever. And same on his side, so it was very easy for that.

Larry enjoyed spending time with Nolan and even fell in love with him. He found some men attractive and enjoyed spending time with them, both sexual and nonsexual. He was like many others in that regard, several of whom developed sexual friendships with men. Unlike most other interviewees, however, Larry fell in love with another man. Larry and Nolan had sex with no other men while they were together. Yet even as they enjoyed sexually and romantically intimate weekend camping trips, they also saw themselves as unquestionably straight. Larry described their dynamic as similar to that of the two main characters in *Brokeback Mountain*, a 2005 film directed by Ang Lee that was based on a short story written by Annie Proulx. This film follows two publicly straight men who fall in love while sheepherding in Wyoming, and who secretly maintain a relationship after they meet.

He's actually one of our prominent community members, and he is married, has family, great guy, still friends today. We consequently do not hook up anymore. It's weird to say this, but I feel like we kind of started falling in love with each other a little bit. You have to understand Wyoming. Did you ever see *Brokeback Mountain*? That is very, very in line with how things are. . . . [T]hat would be very true to how things would happen in Wyoming.

Larry described a deep sense of connection, and even love, for Nolan. The fact that their women partners knew about the friendship between the two men (although not including their sex) meant it was easier for them to spend time together. This, in turn, gave them the opportunity to form a deep emotional attachment. Eventually, however, they felt as if they were becoming too close and decided to end the sexual and romantic aspect of their relationship. "I think we both reached a place where we kind of, gosh, weird to say, but I felt like we were starting to fall in love with each other, and we both decided, look, this is only going to be a nightmare, we have to stop. I got to quit you [laughs]." ("I wish I knew how to quit you" is a defining quotation from the film *Brokeback Mountain*.) In spite of his laughter, Larry found the end of their romantic and sexual connection very painful. "Oh, Tony, it was horrible. Really, I felt like I was going through a breakup. And he did too. It's difficult because you can't talk about that with anybody, you can't say, 'Oh, kind of splitting up right now, so I don't feel like being social.' You have to be on top of your game like nothing ever happened, and on the inside you're shattered."

Being open about the nonsexual aspects of their relationship gave Larry and Nolan the opportunity to become emotionally close. But being only partially open meant that they could not reach out for support when they separated. Larry's feelings about his breakup with Nolan were especially difficult because they had to hide their relationship from other straight people and were not socially involved with networks of gay or bisexual men. They were on their own, without support from either the dominant (straight) culture or a gay subculture. Interestingly, they remained close friends despite breaking up:

We are still friends so that aspect is still happening. I went up to his ranch last night and had dinner with his family. And it lasted for probably a year. I worked with him, so we did lots of things together. I would say a good year of us being in a relationship. Back to the question of could you ever see yourself in a relationship with a man, I could. With this guy, different place, he's wonderful, we connected on that level. And that's the closest that I felt to feeling romantic or having a relationship with a man.

Notwithstanding his feelings for Nolan, Larry was not a closeted gay or bisexual man. He identified as straight, and even reported that his sexual attractions were predominantly to women. Yet he experienced sexual and romantic passion with Nolan. In that respect Larry differed from most of the men I talked to, most of whom did not report feelings of love. Larry was also one of only a handful of men I interviewed to experience a "breakup" with another man. Like the rest of the men I talked to, however, and unlike the men in *Brokeback Mountain*, Larry and Nolan worked to ensure any feelings they had for men did not affect other parts of their lives.

What kinds of relationships did the men I talked to have with their sexual partners? They described four main types. First were casual, sex-only relationships that provided comfort, convenience, and security, but no deep or lasting emotional ties. Second were genuine friendships. They involved activities other than sex, including talking about politics over coffee, hunting, camping, and even going on dinner dates together with their wives. Many men I interviewed formed these friendships because they genuinely enjoyed the time they spent with the other person, even aside from sex. These friendships were like those between many gay men,[1] who consider sex to be one activity of many that friends can enjoy together.

The third form was deeply intimate but nonromantic friendships, which were more intimate than most friendships but less involved than romantic connections. In the context of these friendships, I define "deeply intimate" as involving extensive time commitments, unprotected sex, or sexual exclusivity as far as sex with men was concerned. The men I interviewed did not necessarily state directly that they were deeply intimate, reflecting how straight men often avoid thinking about relationships with other men in these ways. Yet their practices and their descriptions of these relationships show just how intimate they actually were. The final category was explicitly romantic relationships, which I define as involving love. Men like Larry, who fell in love with Nolan, perfectly illustrated this. Unlike deeply intimate friendships, the men in them described these relationships as involving love or something close to it.

Most of the men I talked to formed continuing sexual relationships with at least some of their male sexual partners.[2] The ways they navigated these different types of relationships reveal how they needed to control their emotions for men in order to maintain both their straight identity and their masculinity. The way men express and act on feelings toward other men reflects social context, as well as the constraints associated with masculinity and straight culture.

Regardless of relationship type, all of the men I talked to engaged in emotion work to prevent attachments that would have affected other parts of their lives, especially their romantic relationships with women. The few who did experience feelings of love toward men set tight boundaries for those relationships or eventually cut them off. None sought to leave their women partners to romantically partner with a man.

This is not to say that they cut off all emotional feelings for men. Some experienced temporary romance. Others formed friendships with male sexual partners, some of them quite intimate. Although many described their sex with men as emotionless, this is not entirely true. It may have been true for their one-time hookups, but not for their longer-lasting sexual relationships. Most were nonromantic, but the men I talked to often felt comfort, safety, or friendship within the sexual relationships they formed. These feelings were compatible with straightness and masculinity. It was lasting romantic attachments that were incompatible, and that they consequently sought to avoid.

Masculinity and heterosexuality take a lot of emotion work to uphold. By regulating the emotions they felt toward men and channeling romantic sentiments towards women, the men I talked to formed relationships compatible with rural and small-town straight culture. Male peers often discourage intimate emotions, such as expressing nonsexual love and affection toward other men.[3] This affects how boys show emotion and form friendships as men.

Today, men's same-sex affection is often viewed as a sign of gayness, bisexuality, or femininity, and thus is incompatible with masculinity and heterosexuality. As a result, many straight men are wary of showing much affection toward other men, even if platonic. Historically, however, deep emotional ties between men were compatible with masculinity. They were also not necessarily tied to sexuality. For instance, Victorians considered sexual passion and love to be mostly unrelated. Many men of that era formed deeply intimate—and sometimes romantic—friendships with other men.[4] At the time, these relationships were seen as completely normal. They involved various types and degrees of physical contact, ranging from sleeping in the same bed to cuddling. Thus, this type of emotion work is not inherent to either masculinity or heterosexuality. It reflects changing understandings of both masculinity and heterosexuality over historical periods.

Most of the men in relationships with women explained that they loved their wife or woman partner, and none had plans to leave them. They were not miserable, closeted gay or bisexual men, even as they prevented most deeply emotional relationships with men. They navigated a host of complex emotions and regulated their feelings for people in ways that they felt conformed to rural and small-town straight culture.

Emotions towards men were usually handled in one of a handful of ways. They could be prevented altogether, as in one-time hookups; kept fairly basic, as with feelings of comfort in purely sexual relationships; regulated and contained, as with short-term romantic relationships; or channeled into friendships compatible with masculinity and heterosexuality. These friendships—except for the sex involved—were similar to friendships many men have. Their romantic sentiments were usually directed at women, except for a handful of men who were divorced or had been single for a long time. In those cases, they generally did not seek any romantic bond. They were not waiting for their male soul mate so they could come out. Instead, they regulated their relationships with other men to preserve their life as it was.

Sex-Only Relationships

In total, fifty-five of the men I interviewed had past or current male sexual partners with whom they had sex more than once, two did not but were looking for or open to this arrangement, and just three were not interested in recurring sexual relationships with men and had never had them. In practice or preference, the men I talked to leaned toward forming sexual relationships in the past or the present.[5] Most were open to one-time hookups, and many enjoyed them as much as, or more than, sexual relationships. Nonetheless, many also enjoyed longer-lasting but tightly bounded sexual relationships. These ranged from casual, sex-only relationships to genuine friendships.

I call the latter "friends with benefits" (FWBs), mirroring slang that many people today use.[6] Some lasted for only a handful of meet-ups, whereas others lasted for dozens. In total, forty-five reported sex-only relationships, and twenty-seven reported FWBs (not including highly intimate friendships, which I will discuss in the next section).[7] Many formed both sex-only relationships and friendships, with different men. These relationships lacked romance, but the men I talked to said they enjoyed them for other reasons: convenience, safety, and comfort with their sex-only relationships, and enjoyment of time spent with their FWBs. Thus, when they described their hookups as emotionless, what they meant was that they usually avoided deep romantic attachments.

Their lived experiences with male-male relationships contrast with Craigslist ads posted by straight men, many of which state they are looking for emotionless encounters.[8] How they present themselves in online settings is often different from their actual relationship practices. Non-romantic relationships did not affect their familial relationships or other aspects of their lives. Sex-only relationships and FWBs were entirely compatible with the rest of their lives, as long as the sex was kept secret. Most of the men I talked to channeled their feelings toward other men into these types of relationships.

Many men formed sexual relationships with other men for simple reasons like safety, comfort, and convenience. They wanted to know that the other person was not going to harm them or reveal their identity and was available for the kind of sex they wanted. As thirty-eight-year-old Marcus from Illinois said, "For convenience I think it would be better . . . somebody that you kind of knew, and you wouldn't be wondering about, is this person a weirdo, or whatever else, kind of a comfort thing more than anything." He described one sexual relationship that fit this pattern: "There was a guy that, I guess we went on for about a year. He was married, [had] kids, and every once in a while we would hook up. It was kind of an understood thing that he knew the days that I worked, I knew the days that he worked, and if you're in the mood for something, we could always give each other a call and it would be there." This type of relationship was potentially ongoing, but not intimate. Because of the casual nature of their connection, it was also likely to end suddenly. Marcus, for instance, expressed regret that his sexual relationship ended abruptly after the man stopped contacting him. Aaron reinforced the utility of sexual relationships when he said, "In general I would prefer a regular partner. I would like the safety part of it, the ease when you walk in the door of somebody you've met before. That would be my preference, but it is hard to make reality."

Forming these sexual relationships was especially difficult given that rural areas and small towns have fewer potential sexual partners, and there are fewer ways to safely meet them (like bars or through community organizations). Thus, it was convenient and practical to form a sexual relationship when the opportunity arose. Fifty-year-old Mike from Illinois noted that "once I find a person I like, then I stick with that. . . . [R]epeat people, once I've built people like that, then I don't need anybody else. And so I just kept those ones over and over and over."

Mike and his hookup partners did not discuss sexual exclusivity, nor did they spend time together outside of sex because "I have other interests and too much going on. . . . [O]nce we're done it's over until the next time they call." Mike sought sexual relationships that provided convenience, safety, and a guaranteed opportunity to bottom, not a chance to just hang out with another guy. Relatedly, Brian indicated that "you just get to a point where, oh, my God, I feel like I'm going to burst, and it's nice having, I would love to have a steady guy."

While his regulars were not necessarily friends, Brian did screen them before they had sex: "In all three cases we met at a coffee shop, a Starbucks nearby, met for coffee, talked. Don't hook up the first time, want to meet, get a judgment of their personality, second time judgment of their personality, third time okay, let's go jerk off together." Convenience, safety, and comfort were hallmarks of nonfriend sexual relationships. Many of the men who described these types of relationships made sure they did not have any more emotional involvement. Some of the men I talked to were not comfortable forming friendships with their male sexual partners and limited their relationships with men to ongoing sexual meet-ups.

Friends with Benefits

Other sexual relationships were genuine friendships. They involved sharing hobbies or mundane activities that are hallmarks of many friendships between men. The men I talked to did not feel as though sex substantially transformed the friendship. Sex was simply one of many activities they enjoyed. Sex was great, but it was not the only tie holding the men together. It also did not indicate undying love or romance. They were friends who also happened to occasionally have sex. As Vince, a sixty-seven-year-old man from Michigan, explained,

> [He] was a friend that I had known since childhood, and we reconnected at a time when we were both out of college and were going through a period of unemployment and had some time. We went on a long camping trip. So, à la *Brokeback Mountain* [laughs]. . . . I know that I was eager to get together with him and do things, and sex was not as important as getting together and doing things. [Sex] wasn't the main focal point. . . . I wouldn't call it boyfriends. We were just men, were friends, and occasionally we had sex.

Vince and his friend enjoyed spending time with each other, both sexually and nonsexually. This did not mean that they were in love, however. Similarly, Joe shared the fact that he and one of his FWBs "get together at either his house or mine, we'll cook, and we'll eat, and then we'll play. It's only two to three times a year, so it's not that often. . . . [W]e know when we get together what's going to happen, and it happens." While sex was part of their friendship, it was only one aspect of many Joe enjoyed. Similarly, fifty-nine-year-old Billy from Oregon engaged in a variety of activities with his five regulars: "road trips, drink beer, go down to the city, look at chicks, go out and eat, shoot pool, I got one friend I hike with. It normally leads to sex, but we go out and do activities other than meet and suck." Richard also described a friendship that involved regular sex, as well as discussions of politics over coffee:

> I'm not just going to take Joe Blow off the street, [he would] have to be somebody I know or can get to know. . . . Over the last couple of years, we have settled into a routine. He's not into men and dicks at all, he simply

wants to get off. And since mine won't get hard, that's no big problem for me, so I meet with him periodically, not as often as he would like [laughs], but I meet with him periodically. And I get him off. And I get an emotional satisfaction out of it. Probably once every one month to three months depending on a whole bunch of factors, I'll get a little bit horny. . . . He and I share the same political views. We're both staunch, dyed-in-the-wool Republicans. We both think Obama is a bumbling idiot, we both feel the same way about it. I'm totally 100 percent pro-gun; so is he.

Despite their connection, Richard made clear that they were not emotionally attached.

So, whatever, we share a lot in common, we get along, we're friends, but as far as an emotional attachment, no, not any more so than you would have for any friend. Is it, a friendly thing, I don't feel any love or anything like that for him. No. . . . I don't have to worry about making a mistake and mentioning him, I mention him all the time, talking to him, talk about him all the time, and we talk about a lot of other things other than sex. Sex is a very small part of our relationship. It's more friends, we discuss politics, and we discuss all sorts of shit.

Richard liked sex with his friend but enjoyed the companionship of a like-minded conservative just as much. He expressed frustration at how difficult it was to find sexual friends, and appreciation of those men he did find. Friendships for Richard and other men fulfilled multiple social and sexual needs. Introducing FWBs to loved ones (as purportedly platonic friends) meant that the two were more fully integrated into each other's lives, even as these relationships remained nonromantic. Similarly, Chris enjoyed his past FWB in part because of the opportunity it provided for male bonding:

We'd go have coffee, just visit in restaurants and go for walks. . . . [It is nice to] just [have] somebody to be able to talk to once in a while. I don't know if you're married or not, but sometimes you can't discuss some things with your spouse, and it's nice having another guy to talk to and knowing it's going to stay right there. . . . We were discussing politics, things we like to travel to and what we've done in the past, general discussion.

Sexual friendships were ideal for Chris in two main ways: they provided sexual satisfaction and a chance for masculine, male-male bonding. While he loved his wife, he also wanted to have "guy time." Many others described similar feelings: they loved their wives and needed friendships outside of their marriages as well. If those friendships involved sex, even better. Relatedly, Trevor explained a friendship with one of his past FWBs: "When he and I get together, we might spend two or three hours together and talk politics, religion, news, and just, maybe spend more time together just as associates than as sex partners." Trevor, like a few others, used sex with men primarily as a way to build connections and spend time with other men. Sexual friendships usually involved in-depth conversation or activities outside of sex, and genuine enjoyment of time spent with that person. It was not necessarily more intimate than other types of friendships.

Being in a rural area also shaped the friendships that the men I talked to formed with other men. Pat, the seventy-three-year-old from Illinois I introduced in the last chapter, for instance, owned a hunting cabin and met his friend there for sex and coffee: "We met out here in the country at my hunting cabin and proceeded to get naked. And we talked maybe for an hour before then, had a very wonderful conversation about nothing in particular but the world in general. He was a little bit older than I was, and he gave me a wonderful blowjob. And became a regular." Both Pat and his friend enjoyed this friendship.

> He would want to get away and talk to another human, as he called it, somebody that was knowledgeable and sane. And he would drive thirty miles to get here, and we would have coffee and talk about politics and the world events. And before the meeting would be over we would be naked and I would get a blowjob. And he would leave and we'd wait a day or two and one of us would get ahold of the other one. And we would meet up again out here at the cabin, where I'm at now, and I'd have the coffee pot on and we'd talk for an hour.

Pat enjoyed having conversations with his FWB. The sex was pleasurable, but so too was the company. He appreciated this arrangement because, as he put it, he liked "somebody you can say, 'Hey, what are you doing today, want to come over for coffee? You want to get together and see what happens?' The conversation, the good fellowship, being able to depend on somebody." This extended to times where they met and no sex was involved: "If they need help, I'll go over and help them. They don't live around, well, this is not in a town, this is in the country, rural setting in the country, but if they need help, yes, I will go to their house and help them. Sometimes I take them with me when I go shopping. Yes, we have meetings where sex is not even mentioned."

Although Pat formed relationships with these men for sex, they transitioned into friendships involving other activities. Remote hunting cabins, like Pat's, were ideal for meeting friends for sex (and coffee). Most of the men I talked to did not have a cabin, but many did enjoy hunting, hiking, and other rural activities. For instance, thirty-nine-year-old Jon from Oregon had had two FWBs in the past and explained that "we drink beer, hang out, go do stuff that isn't sex. . . . We go hunting and hiking." Bob, a forty-six-year-old living in Missouri, also enjoyed rural hobbies with his sexual friends, which sometimes directly led to sex:

> [The last time] we took a walk out in the country and we went to this private place that he knows and we walked around, looked at the birds, different places, go fishing, we talked about getting together and going doing some fishing and so forth. "Hey, well, let me show you this little cabin over here, blah blah blah, I've never been there before," and the next thing you know, clothes come off and the game's on.

Bob enjoyed having spontaneous sex with his friends in the outdoors. He met most of these friends through networks, especially through military contacts, rather than online. He was able to do this by being highly perceptive about other men's intentions. One situation where that played out involved a buddy who came to live in his in-law cottage:

> The guy that used to be really good friends with me, he actually lived with us for a short time, before I lived where I live now. We had a separate building from our home and actually him and his wife got displaced through a big family knockdown, and they had to have a place to go. . . . [H]e and I wound up being pretty much a daily thing. Every day, whenever it got time for him to get up and go to work or the evening, he got woke up in a special way because she was at work, my wife's busy with

kids, so nobody knows anything. But that was pretty much an everyday thing with me and him.

Thanks to having an in-law cottage, Bob was able to hook up with this friend. This, in turn, was possible thanks to inexpensive land and housing costs in the rural Midwest. Thus, while being in a rural area constrains opportunities for male-male sex in some ways, it also enables them in others. That Bob was able to have sex with many men indicates just how perceptive he was in gauging people and social situations. His ability to hook up with men was also due in part to a gendered division of labor: his wife's care of their children meant that he was able to find time to have sex with friends. Few men described convenient situations like Bob's, but they nonetheless found time for sex. Adam, for example, described having friends with whom he enjoyed rural hobbies as well as mundane activities:

> Some of them I actually become friends with. Do things like go fishing, see a movie, go out to dinner with their spouses and my spouse, those types of things. . . . bike riding, going to coffee, just sometimes talking, getting together to talk. Physical activities sometimes, assisting with personal projects like helping install a patio door or paint a room, the things that any normal people would participate in. Just day-to-day things. Sometimes riding shotgun when one has to go out of town for a few hours or something like that, just generally enjoy each other's company. The last time we met up we didn't have any sexual interaction with each other.

Men like Adam enjoyed friendships that sometimes involved sex but were otherwise just like other friendships. Friendship activities ranged from rural hobbies like fishing to more intimate activities, like spending time with each other's spouses for dinner. This is particularly striking: many men did not hide their FWBs from their wives. They just did not tell them about the sex they occasionally enjoyed. Several integrated their FWBs into the social fabric of their lives. FWBs met their social and sexual needs. Because no romance was involved, they did not threaten the men's marriages, relationships with their children, or their embeddedness in straight culture.

Deeply Intimate Friendships

Despite some men's efforts to keep emotion separate from their sexual relationships or friendships with other men, others formed relationships that were intimate in ways that the word "friend" cannot fully capture. They clarified that these friendships did not involve love, but instead involved activities or emotions unlike the friendships described in the last section. Many involved sexual exclusivity (as far as sex with other men is concerned), sex without condoms,[9] deep emotional ties, or extensive time commitment. None of the eleven who described this type of friendship secretly hoped it would blossom into a long-term romance. Instead, they regulated their relationships to ensure they did not transition into anything that may have affected their marriages. They enjoyed their friendships in their current forms, and most did not hope they would change into anything else. While most did not overtly state that these relationships were intimate, their practices indicated a deep degree of intimacy. The exceptional trust or deep emotional ties of these friendships distinguished them from other FWB friendships. Given that both were nonromantic, however, they did not threaten other aspects of their lives.

Hallmarks of intimate friendships were extensive time commitments, sexual exclusivity, or unprotected sex. Together, they show that the men I talked to enjoyed spending time with these friends and often felt extensive trust towards them. Sometimes these types of friendships started as casual hookups. For instance, the friendship of Sean, a fifty-eight-year-old from Oregon, transitioned into something involving sexual exclusivity:

> This guy started out as just a sexual, meeting-behind-the-tree thing, and then I think we've kind of become friends. We stay in touch with each other and we talk, [but] I haven't seen him or been with him for some time. Since I've been with this guy I haven't been with any other men. . . . [W]e didn't make an agreement or anything, he's free to do what he wants [and] I'm free to do what I want. But I have spoken with him that I haven't been with anybody since we were together last, we text a lot, and he's texted back the same thing that he hasn't been with anybody else since our last encounter.

Although Sean and his friend were not bound by monogamy, they were each other's only male sexual partner. Underlining their rural location, Sean shared that the first time they met in person, "We met at a predetermined spot and went another place out in the country that he knew about that's pretty secluded in some woods, and that's where we had sex the first time." While Sean and his friend did not see each other very often, their sexual monogamy suggests the nonromantic intimacy they shared. Kevin, a sixty-nine-year-old man living in Missouri, in contrast, had semi-regular weekend retreats with his FWB, Warren, and enjoyed topping him without a condom: "It's just been about three weeks ago. I've got a guy I see every once in a while, maybe [a] couple, three times a year. He lives quite a ways away from me. And he was here, everybody was gone for the weekend except for me, and he stayed all night, on Saturday night, and we had some sex that Saturday night. That Sunday morning again before he left, we did some more." Kevin's friendship with Warren involved weekend getaways with one another. Given that Kevin was married and Warren lived three hours away, it took extensive logistical coordination to find time they could spend together. They trusted each other so much, Kevin reported, that they did not use condoms.

David, too, spent weekends with his FWB, Marley, which involved time engaging in mundane activities other than sex. He described this friendship fairly nonchalantly. The sexual activities he and Marley enjoyed, however, reveal just how trusting and intimate they were with one another:

> Right now, there's only one guy that I see. We get together maybe twice a month. [There is] nobody else, and the reason for that is we're both safe, and want to stay that way. So by not doing anything with anybody else, we can guarantee that. Because neither one of us are pursuing people for conquests or anything, we have sex with each other because we enjoy it, we like it, and we do things we both like to do. And by keeping it between the two of us, we keep it safe. Because neither one of us like condoms.

David explained what their meet-ups usually looked like:

> We always take our clothes off, then we'll hug each other, kiss a little bit, fondle each other, a lot of handling, massaging, that kind of thing, then

we shower together, wash each other, spend a lot of time washing our cock, balls, asses, stuff like that. Then if I haven't given myself an enema before I get there, then he gives me one and cleans me out. Then we'll generally go lay on the bed and just hold each other, play with each other, go back and forth because laying on your back, one or the other can do something but it's hard to, neither one of us is left-handed so it doesn't work very well. And then usually either he sucks me or I suck him, not necessarily to completion, but just for pleasure for a while. And then before long he'll say, "Are you ready for me to fuck you?" and I usually say, "Yes. I am," then we'll talk about which position to use. He likes me to get on the edge of the bed on my side with my butt hanging out on the edge of the bed so he can stand on the floor. That's the way we do it most of the time. We vary, we do other things too. Then after he's come in me, he likes to watch it run back out. Then he'll go get some wet wash rag or something and clean me up with that, and at that point he usually sucks me off until I come, to completion.

Rather than leaving at that point, David and Marley continued to spend time together, both sexual and nonsexual.

Then by that time it's usually time for dinner or maybe we're going out to the theater, to the adult theater, or something else, and we'll do that. And we'll come back from that and then we'll have more sex, sometimes he'll screw me again, sometimes not, sometimes we'll suck some more, but all the time it's naked and hands on. That's the big thing, the tactile thought of just touching each other, playing with each other, feeling each other. We sleep together, and he loves to wake up in the middle of the night and start playing with me, and that's usually how I wake up, either his hands on me or his mouth. . . . I've been with him probably, jeez, eight to ten times, maybe more, but since I met him too I haven't really been looking for anybody else.

David's friendship did not contain romance or strong emotional ties. It was deeply intimate, however, as indicated by cuddling, sleeping together, sexual exclusivity, unprotected sex, and even assistance with enemas—activities most often associated with couples. Not even most gay men give one another enemas, so David's story reveals the deep intimacy he shared with Marley. As with others, David described this friendship with nonchalance. He did not consider it meaningful for his identity, but rather enjoyed the relationship in the form it took: compatible with all other aspects of his life. It is interesting that Marley was gay *and* a top, yet David did not find that threatening to his own straight identity or masculinity. The secrecy of their meet-ups, as well as Marley's masculinity, helped David feel more comfortable having this type of sexual friendship.

Jeremy also shared a deeply intimate friendship with a sexual partner, Cody, with whom he tried new sexual activities. He had sex with Cody after developing a friendship with him. Jeremy described his first orgasm with Cody as so good it was "almost frightening":

> He started to perform oral sex on me, at which point it was the first time I found that I was more interested in watching what he was doing to me than watching the porn on the screen. Up to that point in my life I probably had the most shattering orgasm I've ever had. It was almost frightening how powerful it was, and it really was a head-to-toe experience. When it was over with I was shaking and I just felt like that was the first time I had a real orgasm. I think it was exciting because I had known him for a while and there had been this playfulness back and forth between us.

Jeremy and this friend were not extremely close, but were familiar with one another. This familiarity made sex even more arousing for Jeremy.

> Although up until the very last moment, until I said yes, I had never really entertained that it was ever truly going to happen. And we weren't best buddies, but we were well acquainted enough that I did see him on a regular basis, more than a couple of times a week because of work. So I think it was the familiarity, looking down and seeing somebody that I knew, somebody that I respected, somebody that I found attractive. And somebody who, I think this might be the most important part for me at that time, somebody who seemed to be really enjoying what they were doing. He came at the same time that I did, which I found terribly exciting.

Of all the men with whom Jeremy had sex, he only kissed and had anal sex with Cody:

I found the kissing very erotic. In fact it was when I started to kiss him and we were naked, I was on top of him, and when I felt both of our erections pressing against one another, I found that feeling very erotic. And the more we kissed, the more I wanted to be inside of him. And so the first time I kissed him also coincided with the first time I ever performed anal on a guy.

Jeremy felt so comfortable with Cody that he tried new physical and sexual activities. At the time of the interview, he had neither topped nor kissed any other man. He felt a strong connection to Cody, albeit not a romantic one. The sexual friendship he developed with Cody was so rewarding that it encouraged Jeremy to begin exploring sex with other men. While intimate friendships involved no love or romance, they were intimate in ways that the word "friend" cannot capture.

Several men described friendships that *almost* turned romantic. Because they were not looking for romance with a man, they reworked the relationship to ensure that it did not interfere with other aspects of their life. The difference between these situations and the ones described in the next section is that these men were much warier about the potential for romantic involvement, and proactively prevented romance from forming. Jack, for instance, "became good friends" with one hookup partner, Nick, and Nick's wife. Seeing Nick was difficult, as they lived two and a half hours away from each other, but they nonetheless arranged trips to see one another. Jack eventually cut off sex with Nick because he felt as if their relationship threatened other aspects of their lives:

It was really getting to the point where I was afraid his wife was going to start suspicioning things, and I really, really like his wife and I did not want to destroy his family. I needed to put my physical attraction aside and he needed to do the same, and we made a mutual agreement that it would be best that we stop. That was one of the exceptions to all those, he was one of them that, we did fuck, and it was very enjoyable for both of us. And we did kiss, I spent the night at his house when his wife was gone. That was a little more intense, but there was no love, per se. I would not allow myself to go there. I didn't have an interest in falling in love for one, and number two, he was married, it's complicating. We had a great time. And we still do, we still talk. But we just know we can't go there.

Jack felt a connection to Nick that lasted for years. Afraid their relationship might affect Nick's marriage and even cause Jack to fall in love, Jack
asked that their sex stop. In so doing he protected his heterosexuality
and masculinity. Both would have been threatened had he fallen in love.
While Jack experienced some feelings for men, he made sure that he
would never form a romantic bond. Indeed, Jack explained that his ideal
romantic partner would be a woman. He did not seek to develop this
type of relationship with a man:

> I've thought a lot about that. Thought that what if I decided, because I've
> been single for a while now, what if I just let, I don't know if you'd call it
> nature, but let myself have feelings for a man. And then I just, no, I don't
> have any desire, don't want to go there, because I like the physical attrac-
> tion and emotion involved with a female I've had since I was divorced.
> I've had [several] live-in women, long-term relationships; of course none
> of them worked out, but I just prefer that with a woman.

While Jack considered partnering with a man, he instead partnered
with a woman. Given that he was embedded in rural straight culture,
he found fulfillment in relationships with women, not men. He did not
seek to change any aspect of his life, which would have been necessary
had he partnered with a man. This is why he tightly regulated his friendship with Nick.

Like Jack, Larry had no plans to openly form a relationship with a
man. Even so, Larry formed emotional friendships with several sexual
partners, even other than the one with Nolan that turned romantic.
Larry integrated his FWBs into his everyday life, even going so far as
to arrange activities with their women partners. A similar emotional
connection developed with Larry's college roommate. While they both
identified as straight and had girlfriends, they began watching pornography together. This later transitioned into other sexual activity, as well
as feelings of emotional attachment:

> I wouldn't say romantic. I would say emotional, though. I don't know
> [how] I would make the distinction between the two, but it wasn't roman-
> tic in the way that we were romantically involved, but it became emotional
> and if I had a girlfriend or he had a girlfriend, there were some difficult

emotions there. But it was just awkward. I don't think we ever talked about it or thought about it or anything. It wasn't like you're my lover and you're bringing a girl over! [laughs] Or something like that. So I don't think either of us even knew how to identify those things, it was just awkward, where you'd find yourself a little bit pissy or something like that.

Despite not being romantically involved, they did care for each other.

[After moving out] I missed him, and I think he missed me too. I think we both made phone calls hoping the other would take the hook, and it never happened. I would say on both of our ends. Text messages like, late at night, "What's up, how have you been," all of those little indicators that would lead us to something before didn't transpire with anything on both of our ends. It was kind of difficult for a while. Yeah. I enjoyed it, but it kind of opened the door to kind of more of a conflict, an internal conflict with me.

This roommate-turned-sexual-friend situation was not romantic, but it was emotional. Larry even reported feeling jealousy when his friend's girlfriend visited. Preventing romance with men had costs, such as the "internal conflict" Larry experienced after this relationship ended. Nonetheless, he continued to enjoy forming emotional attachments to other men, so long as they did not affect relationships to his women partners.

Overall, numerous men reported deeply intimate but nonromantic friendships. They often involved time spent together outside of sex, including with one another's women partners; sexual exclusivity; unprotected sex; or feelings of emotional connection. These friendships were compatible with rural and small-town straight culture because they did not affect any other aspect of their lives, including their relationships with women.

By preventing romantic attachments to men, the men I talked to sacrificed the potential for loving partnerships with other men. This also, however, allowed them to continue enjoying fulfilling and loving relationships with women. It also allowed them to remain embedded in straight culture, and to continue reaping the benefits of it. While they did not necessarily identify these friendships as deeply intimate, their descriptions and practices reveal how intimate they actually were. More broadly, these friendships show that straight men are capable of deeply emotional relationships with other men, and that expectations of heterosexuality and masculinity shape the forms they take. Unlike the relationships that will be described in the next section, though, intimate friendships did not involve love or romance.

Love towards Men

Only eleven men I interviewed reported love or past romantic relationships with other men, but these relationships had a great impact on them.[10] Cutting off or preventing this love shows the costs of identifying as straight. These costs are considerable even as men reap other benefits, such as pleasure from marriages to women (as well as the gender inequality usually present within marriages), good relationships with their children, and comfort knowing they will not experience stigma because of their sexuality. Psychological research indicates that sexual attraction and romantic attraction are distinct,[11] and the men I talked to differed from one another in their level of sexual and romantic attractions.

Regardless of what romantic capacity they experienced, however, what linked them was their investment in regulating their emotions towards men. Previous research has shown that a key difference between straight and gay/bisexual MSM is their willingness to experience romantic attachments to other men.[12] My research shows some straight men can and do enter into romantic arrangements with other men, but eventually cut them off. This reflects and reinforces their embeddedness in straight culture. It also reflects how their particular way of engaging with other men necessitated restrictions on romance. Their stories show the romantic possibilities men can experience, but that they usually prevent or cut off to preserve their masculinity and heterosexuality.

The minority of men who formed romantic relationships with other men always ensured that those relationships did not affect their marriages or relationships with their children. They were fulfilled in their roles as husband and father and were not willing to threaten those relationships. Val provided one example of this. He and one man, Dominic, had been close friends for several decades, and were roommates in graduate school. In the past they enjoyed several hobbies together: "hunting, fishing, we'd go to movies together, we travel a lot, camped a lot, we're both married and the four of us are all very good friends. [We did] just about everything." In addition to being sexual partners, they were socially involved as well. Val expressed that he was in love with Dominic but took steps to ensure that never affected their lives:

> The closest to being in love was the one roommate that is still a very close friend of mine. I was pretty much in love with him and still am, but we have a very workable agreement. In that we spend a lot of time together and so forth and don't allow it to get in the way of each other's marriages and so forth. We like each other's marital partners as well. We're all very good friends. . . . [He lives] quite a ways away, and he's had some health issues and wives are close friends and so forth, so [we] just agreed to not do that. Although there have been times when it was extremely tempting. We do talk about things that we did together, sex that we had together. We talk about our sex lives now with women, and even when we were hooking up we talked about sex with women that we both had, and we actually had a threesome with a woman while we were in grad school.

Although Val was "pretty much in love" with Dominic, they agreed to stop having sex and set emotional boundaries so their marital relationships were not affected. Like Larry, Val and his wife enjoyed the company of Dominic and his wife. No one but Val and Dominic knew the relationship they used to share. Although Val and Dominic still desired sex with one another, they did not act on that desire because "we don't live close together anymore and usually when we're together our wives are with us too, and so forth. And he's had some physical problems lately but definitely would love to spend a weekend in bed together. Definitely would be a turn on for me."

Their growing feelings of love for one another also influenced their decision to stop having sex, lest their relationship grow into something that would have affected their marriages. Over time, due to health issues, the physical distance separating them, and their efforts to stifle feelings of love, their relationship grew more platonic. Nonetheless, Val noted that "we talk about sex quite a lot, even still," when they were together. Numerous men felt romantic or loving feelings for another man, but they made sure that these romantic relationships would not develop into anything that could threaten their marital or familial relationships.

This was the case even for men who described themselves as currently being in love. Like Larry, Bob described a deep feeling of love for one of his sexual partners, Ken, but had no plans to divorce his wife. Bob envisioned himself partnering with Ken only if his wife died or divorced him, neither of which possibilities looked likely in the foreseeable future. He noted that with Ken there was "more than a physical attraction, with him it was a little bit more than just the sex and the physical contact, it was a little more emotional. Not crybaby shit. It was more of an emotional attraction there as well, not just the physical side of it. . . . I know I sound sissy-fied as hell. This is where it goes against my grain as far as being masculine." Bob was uncomfortable expressing feelings of love toward another man, since he feared that doing so was too feminine. He nonetheless felt love for Ken. At one point, when Bob and his wife were experiencing major marital problems, he came close to divorcing her, but he did not do so because of his children:

> Had it not been for my kids at that time in my life, yeah, I would have been gone in a heartbeat because I felt so strongly about being with Ken. He never asked me to do that and wouldn't ask me to do that, I know he wouldn't, but with the circumstances I was dealing with at the time it was very, very imminent that it could have happened. Had it not been for my children, it most definitely would have happened.

Bob's decision to avoid divorce because of concern for his children is not surprising. Fatherhood is a key element of rural and small-town straight culture, and Bob was not willing to threaten his relationships with his children to partner with a man. Fatherhood is entirely compatible with being gay; many same-sex male couples raise children together, although this has only become more common in the past few decades. Yet Bob still perceived a relationship with a man as a threat, since it would change many parts of his life. Still, even years after this incident, Bob felt love for Ken:

> To be honest with you, I'm in love with him. There's no other way for me to describe it, I love everything about him, his personality, his looks, the

way he cares for me. I'm in love with him, have been since the day I laid eyes on him. . . . Of all the guys that I've been with he's probably, if I had the opportunity to be lifelong partners with him, he would be the one. There wouldn't be no other.

Bob remained married to his wife at the time of the interview, even as he continued to fantasize about partnering with Ken. His arrangement was acceptable to him: he was able to see Ken every once in a while, during which times they enjoyed both sex and emotional intimacy. Bob was also, at the same time, able to maintain his current relationships with his wife, children, other relatives, and members of his rural community. The arrangement was not perfect, but it worked. The ways in which men navigated romantic relationships with other men show the costs of being secretive about their relationships, but also the benefits the men were able to reap, including avoiding stigma from loved ones.

Other men also experienced romantic feelings for men, but in the context of a more established relationship with that man. Harrison, for instance, entered into a romantic arrangement with a man named Robert for five years. He described the two of them as being "deeply connected friends," but friends who were sexually exclusive. They met several months after Harrison and his wife divorced, and he felt very connected to Robert: "Just deeply connected friends, saw each other exclusively. Never lived together or anything, but that's the only person I saw. Do things together, listen to their life story, inner circle, the type of friend that you can only afford to have one because it's so time consuming; you make such a great investment." Even though Harrison referred to Robert as a friend, he also noted that they "saw each other exclusively" and described them as being in a relationship. Harrison actually identified as gay during the time they were partners: "When I was with him I identified as gay. [That changed] when we broke up. When you're exclusive with somebody, that is my definition of being in a relationship, a partnership, a union. When you aren't exclusive, uh-uh [no]."

Their relationship was secretive, both because Harrison kept it hidden from his loved ones and because Robert was already in a partnership with a man (Robert was cheating on this partner with Harrison and except for his male partner was exclusive with Harrison). After Harrison and Robert separated, however, Harrison again began identifying as straight. This was the case even as he told his children about his relationship and referred to Robert "as the guy I've been seeing."

Harrison defines himself in part on the basis of the people with whom he is in a relationship. While he and Robert separated, they established a friendship after several years of not talking. As a result, Robert remains an important part of Harrison's life. As Harrison explained, when they became friends several years after separating, "that's when the healing began. When we weren't talking, it was toxic. But when we started speaking, that's when I at least was able to start mending." As Harrison is single now, he identifies as straight, reflecting how he is embedded in straight culture.

Few other men described a similar situation of shifting sexual identities several times. Research has long established, however, that many individuals define themselves in part on the basis of the people with whom they are sexually or romantically involved.[13] It is also not uncommon for people to shift to straight identities from nonstraight identities. For example, in the National Longitudinal Study of Adolescent to Adult Health, a nationally representative sample of adults who are currently in their thirties and forties, a substantial percentage of women and men shifted to a straight identity in the years between survey waves.[14] One reason may be that individuals form same-sex relationships and later end them, thus no longer feeling as though an LGBQ identity makes sense for them without that partnership. Even if some individuals, like Harrison, identify as LGBQ for a time, many eventually reclaim a straight identity. By doing so, they re-embed themselves in straight culture. In any case, even the men I talked to who enjoyed romantic connections with a man eventually ended the relationship or tightly bounded it.

Some men who had never experienced love for another man acknowledged that they might have partnered with a man had their life turned out differently. All, however, made clear that they loved their women partners and had no plans to leave them. This attitude reinforces the fact that marriage and family formation is a key aspect of rural and small-town straight culture. Having made the choice to form those relationships, these men planned to stick with them. Considering a hypothetical romantic partnership with a man was one thing, but actually taking steps to undertake it was another. As Mike said,

If I hadn't gotten married, I would probably let the other side have more "me time." But because I got married, I kept that in, kept it hidden, and still do, to some degree. But if I had not gotten married, I can't promise I would be with a woman today. . . . I think that if I had to do it all over again, I would not have gotten married for one thing. Even if I had liked girls, I probably wouldn't have gotten married. I mean, I don't have any problems with my wife; don't get me wrong, I have [several children] and they're wonderful. So, I don't have any problems with that, I just think that if I would have had more options at first I probably wouldn't have made the decision I made.

Mike expressed considerable nuance in his attitudes. He loved his wife, did not want to leave her, and enjoyed being a father. Yet he might not have chosen this path had it been more socially acceptable to be gay or bisexual when and where he was raised. Other men similarly noted that they might be open to romantically partnering with a man if their wives died or divorced them, but none wanted this to happen.

In sum, eleven of the men I interviewed experienced love or a past romantic relationship with a man. A handful stated that they might have partnered with a man, but their life trajectory or unwillingness to be gay or bisexual prevented that from happening. In all cases, they made sure to control their emotions for men. Those who did experience love for men ensured that it did not affect their relationships with their women partners or children. Those who were open to the possibility of romantic feelings for men, or who were currently in love with another man, kept those relationships tightly bounded. They did this so that these relationships would not affect other parts of their lives.

Most simply avoided deep romantic attachments with other men, by, for example, sticking to ongoing sexual relationships or FWBs. For those relationships that transcended those boundaries, however, we see the emotional work it took to maintain the men's masculinity and heterosexuality. The associated costs were particularly difficult for the men who reported love for another man. For them, romance was gendered: even as they felt feelings of love for men and women, they cut off the former to preserve the latter.

3

Straight Culture

> Maybe only a few times I've ever mentioned this; I can't exactly in a po-
> litically correct world. I think there's a definite disconnect between gay
> and homosexual. There's the homosexual community, which isn't a com-
> munity, there's the homosexual proclivity, and then the gay community.
> It's like you can be an athlete without being a jock. And you can be ho-
> mosexual without being gay, or into all of it. It just becomes so politically
> charged now. (Connor, 43, Oregon)

Some men can be, and are, straight even as they enjoy sex with men. As
Connor put it, men who enjoy sex with other men have "homosexual
proclivities" but do not have to be gay. He later elaborated, "I consider
gay a little different than homosexual." Another man, Val, shared similar sentiments in explaining why he identifies as straight: "For me it's a
matter of the all-around time that I spend with individuals that I like. [It
is] more than just the sexual aspects of a person. And I like being with
women, particularly my wife."

The men I talked to considered straightness as an identity, a way of
life, or a community. Identifying as straight meant they could continue
relationships with their women partners, children, extended family,
friends, and other people in their straight communities, relationships
they did not think possible with a gay or bisexual identity. It also meant
they could avoid stigma and could feel connected to a socially dominant
group. In terms of identity, having sex with men was largely irrelevant.
They were not "closeted" gay or bisexual men. They identified as straight.

In short, the men I talked to were secretive about their *sex with men*,
not their *identities*.[1] People interpret similar sexual acts differently depending on how they identify. Specifically, straight-identified MSM
interpret their sexual practices in different ways than gay- or bisexual-
identified men. For the former, embeddedness in heterosexual culture re-

inforces their straight identity, regardless of the fact that they might have sex with men. Most institutions and social interactions assume that men are straight and masculine. This is a central aspect of straight culture.

Key straight institutions the men I talked to described included their childhood families of origin; religion; school or youth sports; and the adult families they formed by partnering with women and, often, having children. Because of the importance of these institutions, sex with or attractions to women were not the only reasons these men identified as straight. While many did interpret sex with or attractions to women as related to their straight identity, those were only two of many reasons they identified as straight. Multiple institutions, groups, and communities—collectively comprising straight culture—socialized them as straight and masculine. Their stories help show us what straight culture is and how it affects the identities and perceptions of many men.

The specific straight culture to which the men I talked to felt attached was shaped by race and geographic location. Most grew up in or currently lived in white-majority rural areas and small towns. The straight culture to which they felt connected was a *white* rural and small-town straight culture. Though generally they themselves did not identify whiteness as a crucial component, it nonetheless affected their identities and desires. The institutions that affected their lives were rural and small town, as were the communities they felt reflected their values.

Most of these men felt that part of a straight man's life in a rural area or small town was being a husband or father and found great meaning in this. Not coincidentally, many also perceived partnerships with women or childrearing as central to their straight and masculine identities. Because rural heterosexual culture is tightly connected to masculinity,[2] their masculinity went hand in hand with their straight identity: their identification as straight was deeply tied to their sense of themselves as masculine. Many felt that identifying as gay or bisexual would threaten their sense of themselves as men, and thus avoided this. Most saw themselves as straight, masculine, rural or small-town men, reflecting their embeddedness in the institutions and communities that comprise rural and small-town straight culture.

Of course, most straight men do not have sex with men. Those who do, however, have thoughtfully considered why they identify as straight.

Little research has explored how men become straight and masculine and maintain these identities. The men I talked to provide insight into these social processes. Talking to them highlights how straightness is cultivated in a variety of institutions and contexts and is maintained through various social practices. Embeddedness in straight culture explains why men who have sex with men identify as straight. Straightness is not just an identity: it is an entire social world. For the men I talked to, their straight identity encompassed their embeddedness in mainstream heterosexual institutions, like marriage, and in the straight communities to which they and most people they knew belonged. Collectively, these institutions and communities comprise straight culture.

The reason I use the term "straight culture" as a framework for analysis is that it refers to both past research and my research findings. It is not simply theoretical; it is backed up by data. It incorporates research on how anti-LGBTQ discrimination, expectations of heterosexuality, and gender inequality structure most institutions and aspects of social life. It also captures the various communities, institutions, and relationships that the men I talked to described. Finally, it reflects how individual practices, attitudes, identities, feelings, and beliefs are shaped by these various social forces. The term "straight culture" is a shorthand for all of these things at once. The men I talked to identified as straight not because they hated gay or bisexual men but because they were embedded in straight culture and wanted to stay that way. This helped them feel more masculine, avoid stigma, and enjoy the benefits of being a part of a socially dominant group.

Heterosexuality in Rural and Small-Town America

For most of these men, growing up in or currently living in a rural area or small town encouraged both heterosexuality and masculinity. This was manifested in subtle and overt ways, and through multiple institutions and individuals. Heterosexuality and male masculinity were central to their rural and small-town cultures. Many of them expressed varying degrees of dislike toward male femininity, which they associated with gayness even as they also recognized that not all gay men are feminine. With few visible alternatives to straight masculinity, male femininity or open gayness/bisexuality seemed difficult or even impossible. Notwithstanding some of the challenges of rural living, such as the difficulty of finding sexual partners and fear of discovery in small communities, rural life also provided many benefits. This included easy access to activities like hunting, fishing, camping, and hiking; a slower pace of life; proximity of family members; close-knit communities; and privacy. The positive attributes compensated for the difficulty of finding male sexual partners and the need for extreme secrecy.

These men's stories also show how central heterosexuality is to rural culture, and how rural areas and small towns encourage masculinity and heterosexuality simultaneously. As thirty-five-year-old Jose from Colorado explained, "You don't really see any gay couples or men and women that live together that people know around here, as compared to the city where you would see more of that. Here where I'm at there's not much of a, I guess you could say gay scene around here. It's mainly straight." Donald, a seventy-four-year-old man from Montana, also noted a lack of gay couples where he grew up: "There wasn't anybody in observation to show me that there was any alternative. Sort of an innocence."

Echoing this, forty-year-old Joshua from Colorado noted that "I don't know, when I was growing up there wasn't really a lot of gay or bisexual people that at least identified that way. But mostly I mean just in general it seemed like more masculine people than feminine as far as men." Because men were expected to be heterosexual and visibly gay and bisexual men were absent, many of the men I talked to were not even aware of alternatives to straightness for many years. As Richard said when referring to the initial thought of sex with men, "I was a farm boy straight off the farm." Similarly, Kevin noted, "I grew up in an area where that wasn't an option, in a time and area both." While LGBTQ people do live in rural areas,[3] a fact backed up by large-scale survey research,[4] it is true that they are often less visible than rural residents who are straight and follow norms related to masculinity or femininity.

The men I talked to described their rural environments as expecting heterosexuality and masculinity, with heterosexuality "distilled in a lot of the kids here," as Chris put it. Their rural surroundings encouraged masculinity and heterosexuality in many ways, including through the implicit or explicit threat of violence were they not to conform to prevailing attitudes. As Mike explained,

This is what's called the Bible Belt. So you have, back then, a lot of people that was very stern religiously, politically, socially . . . very stern against this kind of stuff. You didn't want to get that name out because you would be ridiculed or whatever it might be, shunned . . . because it was not a popular way to be. Or beat up, even, for that matter, because there was a lot of people that would just knock the tar out of you if they thought that you was gay, or doing anything like that. Not even gay, just doing anything like that.

This was one of only a few explicit statements about the role of violence in enforcing expectations of heterosexuality or masculinity. However, implicit references to violence are evident in some of the other men's descriptions of their rural surroundings. For instance, David remarked that "there's no leniency" in what he described as "really a straight life, rurally, it just is." Neil described his "straight world" as including the threat of social isolation for outliers: "Definitely a straight world, definitely, everybody just expects that you're going to get a girlfriend, drink beer, get married, and have kids. And if you don't then you're that crazy weird guy who lives at the corner of town or something." So too does Jordan's explanation that being openly gay or bisexual "would be horrible because everybody knows everything in those communities. . . . [Y]ou would be scrutinized pretty rigidly." Whether through the threat of violence, social isolation, or rejection from loved ones and community contacts, the men I talked to knew that visible gayness or bisexuality could carry severe consequences in their communities.

Heterosexuality was part of the foundation of their rural communities and small towns. As sixty-four-year-old Brett from South Dakota explained, "I think ruralness in South Dakota probably means conservative. I think people in this area are maybe a little more close-minded, not so accepting of being bisexual even, not to mention gay, so you tend to hide, you suppress your feelings more so than a city." George, too, explained that "a lot of peer pressure growing up was to date other girls, and I think that's kind of the route I went." Heterosexuality and masculinity were the fabric of their rural areas and small towns, in part because tight community ties encouraged conformity. Several men acknowledged expectations of heterosexuality in positive terms. As Bob explained,

As a kid growing up, I really liked it. I think the whole experience growing up in a rural community made me a lot better person than I probably
could have been had I been say growing up in metropolitan St. Louis or
Kansas City. [In those cities] there was more exposure and the larger the
population is, the more exposure. Had I grown up in the city, I probably
would have been the biggest flaming homo you ever seen. But growing up
in a rural community, it was help your buddy out kind of thing, nobody's
looking, and it was all kept under wraps, and nobody knew anything. But
I thoroughly enjoyed growing up in a rural environment.

Basically, Bob enjoyed growing up in a rural area because it helped
ensure he would be straight. The main drawback to living in a rural
area, he said, were "the fucking mosquitoes." Similarly, Larry explained
that he identified as straight because of where he lived: "Primarily just
the culture that I live in. I am in rural Wyoming. . . . [I]t's kind of a small
town . . . and it's just not a community or a state that's very diverse as far
as different sexualities, different ways of life. I would say straight because
that best suits our cultural norms around here." In fact, Larry had grown
up in a city and moved to a rural area intentionally: "I kind of weighed
all my options and this is conducive to what I wanted as far as what I
valued in my life, so I moved to a smaller place, rural, like a hometown
type of place. . . . I like so many things. I like the simplicity, the pace of
life is slower. I like that it's very high on the value on relationship, friendship, family." Like Bob and Larry, many of the men I talked to saw the
rural and small-town straight culture in which they were embedded as a
good thing. It supported heterosexual family life and men's masculinity,
both of which they valued. Thus, while all recognized the constraints of
the social norms where they lived or grew up, many believed that these
affected them positively, even if they negatively affected LGBQ people.

Learning Masculinity and Heterosexuality in Rural and Small-Town Straight Culture

Most of the men I talked to did not use the term "straight culture,"
though they did discuss feeling more connected to straight institutions,
people, and communities. As thirty-two-year-old Peter from Montana
explained, sexual identity is a "way for groups of people to kind of come

together or separate, and so I feel like as a community, straight sexual identity is where I feel aligned." He went on, "Personally, I don't really believe that anyone is just like completely heterosexual or completely homosexual, I think everybody's got some place on the spectrum of that. . . . I very comfortably wear that label of being a straight white man, because culturally and socially that's what makes the most sense for me. I'm not interested in trying to get my environment to acknowledge me as some different new fluid sex thing." Like Connor, Peter felt connected to a straight community. His attractions to and sex with men did not detract from his feelings of belonging within straight culture.

Within rural areas and small towns, four key institutions—pillars of rural and small-town straight culture—teach men how to be straight and masculine. Childhood family of origin, religion, childhood youth activities and schooling, and marriage and adult families strongly shaped how the men I talked to understood their heterosexuality and masculinity. Put another way, they *learned* how to be straight and masculine through these institutions. Importantly, these institutions are often racially segregated in rural America.

Because of this segregation, race was not mentioned by most of the men I talked to. Nonetheless, the ways in which whiteness affects their identities and practices can be discerned throughout their stories. In short, the men I interviewed did not identify as straight simply because they did not want to identify as gay or bisexual. Instead, they found great value in what they considered a rural or small-town straight man's life, especially marriage or childrearing.

By and large, the men I talked to expressed satisfaction and comfort with their straight lives. Their rural and small-town institutions reinforced their identification as straight and masculine. Certainly, identifying as gay or bisexual, or being less masculine, would have been difficult because of prejudice and discrimination. Most institutions, social contexts, and interactions reflect social norms and standards that assume heterosexuality.[5]

Most of the men I interviewed felt that heterosexuality and masculinity were normal and expected of them. As sixty-year-old Matt from Oregon put it when explaining his masculinity, "I appear normal. Straight, I guess, whatever you want to call it." Expectations to be "normal" encouraged the men's identification with heterosexuality and masculinity.

As fifty-seven-year-old Todd living in Ohio explained, he married his former wife in part "because it was just what was supposed to be done at that point, I guess." Importantly, however, they did not identify as straight simply because of prejudice or social coercion. Indeed, only a minority of men voiced overtly prejudicial thoughts of their own, and few wanted the opportunity to "come out" as gay or bisexual.

Instead, we see the numerous ties these men had to straight culture. As with most facets of social life, we see the effects of both personal choice and structure.[6] Structurally, the institutions and contexts of their child- and adulthoods shaped their preferences and the options available to them. On a personal level, they chose not to distance themselves from straight culture or identification. Given that they were embedded in straight culture from birth, it is not surprising that they felt connected to it. Personal choice and social structure interacted, and both shaped their identification with straightness and masculinity.

Childhood Families of Origin

Most parenting practices implicitly or explicitly encourage straight identification. This is true of both mothers[7] and fathers.[8] Even parents who support LGBTQ civil rights often unintentionally—or knowingly—raise their children to be straight and follow conventions of masculine and feminine behavior.[9]

Several men explained how their families encouraged their identification with straightness and masculinity in both overt and subtle ways. They learned that being straight and masculine was just what men did. It was normal and expected. As fifty-two-year-old Will from Missouri explained, "The straight life is according to everything you learned when you're growing up. [A] man and a woman get married, have children, you have a house, and it doesn't always work out that way, but that for me is what a straight life [is]." Similarly, Chad recalled, "I think I followed the role model of all the people around me, and just did what I was supposed to do." These men internalized subtle messages from their family, such that identifying as straight and masculine felt "natural."

However, several men did remember overt familial encouragement of heterosexuality and masculinity, sometimes due to conservative religious teachings. Mike, for instance, stated that "we were taught that no matter what, that you're a straight male, and you're supposed to get married, you're supposed to do all these things, so I've always identified with that because that's how I was raised." Jordan, similarly, said, "For lack of a better way to put it, that's the way I was raised. It was taboo to even talk about anything else, you're going to hell, certainly, if you're gay, so it had a lot to do with upbringing." Mark, a sixty-one-year-old living in Oregon, experienced a similar dynamic when he told his uncle about his desires for other men: "Like my uncle said when I was about eighteen, he said you get married, you have a family, and all those desires will leave you, and so I got married and had a family. . . . [N]othing was accepted except being straight." Families expected heterosexuality regardless of the attractions or desires of the men I talked to. Some even feared violence from family members. As Ryan, a sixty-year-old from Illinois, explained,

> Back in those times you were a fag or were a queer. And there's no way I was going to pigeonhole myself as that, I wasn't that way. If I was my big brother would beat me up. I had three other brothers and a very masculine dad, and no way I was one of those, okay? I think you have to have a certain amount of confidence and maturity to start accepting things about yourself. And, for a long time there was no way, I wasn't one of those people.

Ryan's narrative is a powerful reminder that there can be severe consequences for deviation from heterosexuality and masculinity. Fear of violence is a major reason many men identify as straight and masculine. Though few men echoed Ryan's fear of violence, most families nonetheless influenced how they understood their sexuality as straight and gender as masculine.

Similarly, for many men, positive relationships with their fathers reinforced heterosexual and masculine norms. Zach described the influence of his father in positive terms: "Growing up at home, our dad was always, he was the leader of the house and he kept things going and he kept everyone in line. But yet, he spent time taking us to activities that a man would want to go to, and he spent a lot of time with us. We were around our mother a lot, but we did things with him and I think that helped contribute to the masculinity." Zach experienced his father's role as so positive that he felt that men were feminine if they did not have a strong father figure: "I think a lot of people today, the reason why they're feminine or they lean that way is maybe because they're from a broken home unfortunately or they never had a father as a role model. They only had the mother and that's what they saw. And that's how they relate." This is factually untrue and stigmatizing toward single mothers and same-sex couples, but Zach believed it. Todd also described his father positively:

> Probably just seeing my dad I guess, being the way that he is, my dad's been dead for years but knowing what he did. He was very construction oriented, worked a lot, did what he had to do, just a symbol of masculinity right there. Plus uncles and cousins and stuff like that who were more manly, they were in the service and stuff like that, I think it was a little more of an idol role like that.

For men like Zach and Todd, fathers were key figures in shaping their masculine identity as adults, and they appreciated what their fathers did. Others, however, described the influence of their fathers or other male family members less positively. For instance, a fifty-five-year-old man from Iowa, Paul, explained, "I had a very dominant father, and he was older when I was born so he was actually more the age I am with my grandkids, so he's more like my grandfather, so he was very much this is women's work, this is men's work. It was the traditional male-female roles of a hundred years ago, and that's the way he raised me." As a child, Paul saw gendered household divisions of labor as natural, in part due to his father. However, as an adult, he found that this upbringing did not serve him well, requiring him to change his perspective. "It took me some getting used to, to realize that in modern society, especially if you're not going to live in a rural area, those things don't hold true anymore. It took me a while to figure out that just because you cook the meal and do the dishes, doesn't mean you're not masculine."

For Paul, and several others, fathers served as an example of what not to do as men. Relatedly, Richard reported that his father had substance abuse issues, which affected Richard's family: "He was a drunk, and when he was [in his twenties] he owned a five-hundred-acre farm and was leasing a thousand acres and farming it. And he drank it all up." Richard saw his father as a lesson in the importance of avoiding substance abuse.

Yet despite criticizing his heavy drinking, Richard admired his father's work ethic, a conventional measure of masculinity, and understood his father's drinking as in part an adaptation strategy that allowed him to work hard:

> Dad got a job as a night watchman, a guard. . . . He worked graveyard shift. He'd go to work at 11:30 at night and get off at 7:30 in the morning. He would come home, mother would have breakfast for him. He'd come home, he'd eat breakfast, he'd go out and get on that tractor and plow all day. He'd come in, she'd have dinner ready for him. He'd eat dinner, he'd go to bed, she'd wake him up at eleven o'clock and he'd go to work.

Richard's father drank heavily to help him keep working.

> He got to drinking in order to stay awake. I remember he used to keep a case of whiskey underneath the bed and he'd wake up at eleven o'clock at night, pull that case out, open up a brand new bottle, break the seal on it, and direct from the bottle he'd drink about a third of that bottle, glug glug glug glug. Put it back down, go back, mother would fix him some breakfast, a little bit of dinner or whatever, and he'd take off and go to work. When he came home from work the next morning, he'd find that bottle, and drink about half of what was left, and he'd go get on that tractor and plow all day. And he'd come in from after that and he'd kill that bottle and go to bed. Next morning he'd open another bottle.

While Richard learned from his father to avoid substance abuse, he also saw the importance of working hard and taking care of one's family.

Family members were key agents encouraging, in various ways and to different extents, straightness and masculinity. While the men I talked to shared different familial experiences, all of their stories indicate that they nonetheless came to understand masculinity and heterosexuality as important. Some, like Zach and Todd, explained that their fathers were positive figures who showed them how to be properly masculine. Others, like Paul and Richard, described how their fathers affected how they saw themselves as men, although they eventually recognized their fathers' faults and sought to avoid them. Thus, while some found family members as role models for healthy masculinity, others perceived them as examples of what they should not become in order to enact masculinity they found less problematic.

School and Sports

The importance of schooling and sporting institutions to how men perceive their masculinity is well established. How boys and girls are treated differently in preschools,[10] peer interactions in elementary school[11] through high school,[12] and formal and informal curricula in educational institutions[13] all shape boys' expressions of masculinity and heterosexuality. One man, Paul, explained that school-age bullying continued to impact his ability to form relationships with men:

> Well, in school I was always, I guess, the bullied child. So I didn't ever have a lot of friends, I guess, and I think that's affected me as an adult because I still don't have a lot of friends. But I think I've just kind of, because of all of the bullying I went through in school, I think I just kind of decided it wasn't worth it having friends if you had to deal with that kind of stuff.

His childhood bullying was so traumatic that Paul mostly stopped trying to make friends and relied on his wife and family for companionship. In his case, aligning himself more closely to heterosexuality helped him compensate for threats to his masculinity, especially bullying from other men.

Sports, in particular, are a central way for men to construct masculinity and heterosexuality.[14] Most of the men I talked to did not discuss schooling or sporting activities,[15] but many of those who did indicated its importance to how they perceived themselves as men. Positive experiences in childhood sports, particularly football, helped several men bolster their masculinity. Eli, a fifty-two-year-old from Idaho, for instance, when detailing childhood influences on his masculinity, explained that "I played football in school, all the way through my high school years." Joey, who described himself as a "typical jock in high school, athlete and so on," explained the importance of sports for how he saw himself as a man: "That was very traditional, very structured role. Guys in schools were athletes and girls were cheerleaders or in the band and so on. . . . I was captain of my basketball team, good baseball player and so on, so athletics was important to my gender identification as well, to be an athlete." Participating in organized sports was key to how Joey, and several others, saw themselves as men, since "athletes" were "guys." Positive experiences with sports helped these men construct their masculinity in a fairly straightforward way.

In contrast, lack of interest in sports or lack of athletic skill during their school years negatively affected how several understood themselves as men. Harrison, for instance, noted that he "was always the last one picked for the team. . . . [and] I was a Scout dropout, [was] forced to play Little League." In part because he was different from other boys in this way, Harrison felt that "it was tough" to grow up in his community. Similarly, growing up in a conservative community and not enjoying sports challenged how Mitch saw himself as a man: "A lot of people always identified me as different because I wasn't into sports and stuff like that. I was never really accepted on those levels. [I was] a little different. I was always just more sensitive, and I cared about different things. I cared about art, and music, and movies, and stuff like that. Versus sports." While community members identified Mitch "as different," Jordan explicitly identified his lack of interest in sports as impacting his sense of his masculinity: "I was raised on a farm, I was raised in a small community. So, in a small community, a small school, you were masculine if you were good at sports. And there were times I did not feel masculine because I wasn't that interested in sports."

Even men who had played sports as children felt the experience impacted their emerging masculinity if they were not particularly talented. Vince was explicitly pressured by his family to play baseball and football:

Well, back in the day I had a brother who was on the football and the basketball team. I played in the band. I would get shit from my football star uncles that I was big and I should play football, I could plug holes, and I was just not the slightest bit interested in that. So I equated that with being less masculine than they are. My brother coerced me into going out for Little League. I hated it, I absolutely hated it. He talked me into going out for football, I hated that more. And lasted a couple of weeks. Is a guy that plays football more masculine than a guy that plays in the band? I think the general population would say yeah. But I quickly learned to not give a shit.

In Vince's case, family pressure to play sports appears to have been more formative than peer influences. Vince explicitly challenged the equation of sports with masculinity, having later rejected sports entirely and constructed masculinity in other ways. In contrast, Adam discovered as an adult that he had had a congenital heart issue that affected his athletic ability. This greatly shaped his childhood:

> I didn't have a really good childhood. I had some physical issues, which I was often teased for. Sometimes it seemed like I did better having female friends than some male friends. And believe it or not, six weeks ago I found out what my issue was. It was actually something I was born with, a [congenital heart issue]. And so I didn't excel at sports or anything like that. I did swim on swim team and I did play football in high school, but physically there were a lot of things I couldn't do. . . . So it always left me somewhat weak and unable to do some of the things that the other guys did. It kind of dominated who I became. So I didn't always, I couldn't always keep up with the pack, let's put it that way.

Despite being on the swim team and playing football, Adam's physical limitations made him feel weak and inadequate. This negatively affected how he saw himself as a man.

Because male peer interactions in school and participating in sports affect how men construct masculinity,[16] for many men I interviewed who experienced school- or sports-related issues, heterosexual identification helped them feel like men. The men I talked to perceived masculinity and heterosexuality as tightly linked. Thus, heterosexuality helped them bolster their sense of masculinity when it was threatened in other ways. Difficulties with peers and sports meant that straight identification helped some men relieve consequent threats to their masculinity. Given the links they drew between masculinity and heterosexuality, threats to the former seem to have encouraged these men to double down on their straightness.

It is interesting that sports are a main way many men express masculinity, since sporting environments are typically single-sex and often homoerotic. In locker rooms men undress and shower together, often secretly admiring their teammates' bodies. It is also common for men to slap each other's butts in highly masculinized sports like football, yet this is not perceived as gay in that context. Sports are a socially acceptable site for men to express same-sex desire, but in limited ways. Men in many sporting environments valorize masculinity, build intimate bonds with other men, and admire other men's bodies or sporting capabilities. This is often homoerotic. Yet none of this is perceived as gay or even bisexual. It is perhaps counterintuitive that sports are a way to build masculinity and reinforce straightness, given how homoerotic they are.

Partnerships with Women

For most of the men I talked to, having children or forming partnerships with women was central to their straight and masculine identities.[17] People in rural areas and small towns are more likely to marry than those in large urban areas,[18] suggesting that the institution of marriage is particularly important in rural areas and small towns. This helps to explain why so many men raised this topic when describing their straight identification and masculinity. They placed great meaning on being husbands, providers, or fathers. The men I talked to identified as straight in large part because of what they valued—family—rather than what they did not value, such as gay culture.

As Ryan said, "I desired having a wife and a family and I sought that lifestyle." He reflected on his wife, children, and grandchildren, explaining that "I would think that I'm most comfortable as straight or I probably would have changed to a gay lifestyle several years ago. So to me a straight lifestyle is being a family man and acting that way." Of course, "lifestyle" is a problematic term, since it suggests that sexual orientation is a choice, which it is not. Still, his explanation shows that he valued what he associated with heterosexuality, like marriage and childrearing.

Many men equated marriage to a woman—and often childrearing—with straightness. Asked to define what it meant to be straight, Adam replied simply, "basically [being in] a heterosexual relationship." In discussions of their sexual identity, this came up repeatedly. Brian declared definitively, "I consider myself straight. Married over thirty years and like women." Chris "guessed" that he was straight, "because I'm married and I've got children. And I do love my wife." Peter decided, "I would say that I don't really identify as bisexual because I am in a heterosexual relationship." Jared similarly concluded, "I think that [straight] describes me best because I am married, have children, adult, grown children—but I also have urges to be with men." In short, being straight was a way of life, indicated most clearly by being in relationships with women and perhaps raising children. Being in a relationship with a woman meant being not gay, nor even bisexual, despite sex with men.

Even those men who had not yet married described wanting to partner with women as a marker of straightness. James, a twenty-eight-year-old who lived in Tennessee,[19] explained that straight described him better than other identities because it reflected "the degree to which I want to get married and have a wife. That's kind of how I see myself in the future." Similarly, Jose noted, "I definitely would love to have a wife and kids one day, but I guess I'm just one of those late bloomers and it's just taking me now into my thirties to realize and kind of figure out what I want [laughs]."

Relatedly, some men viewed heterosexuality, and particularly relationships between men and women, as socially and personally stabilizing. Harrison, for instance, framed his identification as straight in terms of "lifestyle" choices: "I'm married, I have kids, I'm not into that gay lifestyle." "Lifestyle," here, carries a great deal of weight. "In fact, the only force of nature, this is my own theory, that can settle men is a woman. If you're not married, you're going to go out there and go to Vegas once a year, play poker, stay up late, drink. But if you're married, you work, you settle down, you save." Harrison felt that heterosexuality was key for men's stability, so it is not surprising that he found value in identifying as straight himself.

This belief is incorrect, given that single men of all identities and men in same-sex relationships are perfectly stable too. Yet it still encouraged Harrison to identify as straight. Others contrasted the stability of marriage with women with the excitement of sex with other men. Cain described that sex with men was fun, but that "the experiences of marriage and having a family, that's also been rewarding. And long lasting, [it] has benefits. Whereas the other is so fleeting . . . they're both exciting in their own way, and they have different thrills." It is interesting that Cain used the word "thrill" to describe sex with men that could lead to discovery (in his own home or a dressing room) *and* forming a family. Cain had the best of all worlds by marrying a woman, having several children, and secretly having sex with men in dressing rooms, bathroom stalls, empty churches, and almost anywhere else that allowed for secrecy.

Kevin indicated a similar feeling. "I've always lived a straight life," he said, adding,

> I'm a husband and a father, and a grandfather, and I consider that part of a man's life as being straight. I enjoy my kids, I enjoy my wife, and enjoy my life, and I certainly wouldn't want to change it. I have no intention of leaving the wife for a guy or anything like that. It's just, the guy part is just something I do. Kind of like some guys drink too much, I just like guys. It's hard to explain.

For Kevin and others, sex with men was fun but not all that meaningful to their lives. Some, like Kevin, considered it a vice: something they probably should not do but also not anything that seriously threatened their lives or identities. Their families were important to them and provided a major reason for identifying as straight and masculine.

In sum, for most men, romantic partnerships with women, especially marriage and perhaps childrearing, were key to straight identification and masculinity. To them, straightness was a way of living and relating to the world. While they described attractions to or sex with women as related to heterosexuality and masculinity, romantic relationships with women were more central to their identities. If they were partnered to a woman, occasional sex with men was entirely compatible with straightness and masculinity.

They were fulfilled by their relationships with women or fatherhood, as they had been socialized to be in youth. Their feelings were real and valid, and also shaped by the straight institutions in which they had been socialized. Importantly, their narratives implicitly echo right-wing discourse about the importance of heterosexuality, conventional family arrangements, and masculinity for men.[20] They did not find the thought of partnering or raising children with a man nearly as desirable or fulfilling as doing this with a woman. This is despite the fact that many same-sex male couples are happily married and raise children.

* * *

Many people who talk to me about this research ask me how happy these men were in their romantic relationships with women. Did they long for a relationship with a man? Did they have sex with men because they were unhappy with their woman partner?

These are valid questions. None of the thirty-four married men I interviewed, nor the five with girlfriends, planned to leave their women partners. Most expressed satisfaction with their relationships. The main concerns they shared were common ones like money management or needing more personal time. Particularly noteworthy was the most frequent issue they reported: women partners not having a strong enough sex drive. Clearly, most still desired to have sex with their wives or girlfriends and were sad that their wives or girlfriends did not always feel similarly about them. Despite this complaint, most reported that they enjoyed their intimate relationships with women, were not unhappy, and did not long for monogamous romantic relationships with men.

Some men expressed deep care for their women partners by comparison to their feelings for men. As Ryan recalled, "I saw her [my wife] and I could just feel my, my heart did melt. And I've never had a man do that to me. Because I'll tell you what, if it hit me with a man like it did with my wife, it would probably bust my marriage up, that's how much I love her." Similarly, Mike shared about his wife that "she's the one that kept me here. Kept me grounded and things like that or I would've been probably crazy doing [something], probably dead in a grave somewhere now." Emphasizing his emotional fidelity, he made it clear that he had no intention ever to leave her: "I would never do that, like I said, to my wife or anything like that. . . . I would never do that to hurt her. Ever. Or my kids. . . . I've raised them very, very nice and they're very well-adjusted now. I just wouldn't do that. . . . [T]hat relationship is always going to be there. I don't think that'll ever go away. . . . I do love my wife. Still do." Mike did say that he would consider partnering with a man if his wife died or divorced him, but not in any other situation. Several other men expressed a similar sentiment.

Moreover, numerous men explained that they genuinely enjoyed having a woman partner. Despite concerns about their sex life, Eli said that he and his wife were "best friends," explaining that "we do so much together. . . . [W]e share the same hobbies, we share the same interests." Neil also enjoyed his relationship with his wife, pointing out the importance of their partnership in a rural context: "We get to spend quite a bit of time together because there's not a lot of other people around." His wife was not just company, he said, she was good company: "I like that she's intelligent, she can carry on a good conversation, she's a good cook, a good mother to our kids." This was especially important because his location is "very rural," adding, "I've got to drive about eighty miles to the closest Walmart."

Val, saying of his wife that "we definitely love each other and so forth and as we get older that's the overriding important thing," explained further: "She's just very supportive no matter what the situation is, does everything she can to be as helpful as she can, she's very lovely with my parents and with our kids and so forth. She would prefer to spend time with me than be alone or be with other people." Similarly, while Travis, a fifty-nine-year-old man in South Dakota, was frustrated that his wife was no longer interested in sex, he explained, "I've got friends that say why in the hell do you stay married to her. Well, I guess it's because I love her, and other than the fact that we don't have a sexual relationship we do have a good relationship." In short, for these men, marriage to women was far from simply instrumental. It was fulfilling too.

Along with love for their woman partners, several men discussed their enjoyment of children and the importance of the heterosexual family unit. Like many others, Aaron wanted to remain married in part because of his family: "In our society I think things are easier if there's an intact male and female parental situation. I think that is part of the reason I stay in my marriage. My wife and I do get along very well outside of the bedroom." Aaron believed that stable mother-father homes were important both for him and for the larger society. While he was frustrated that his wife no longer wanted to have sex with him, he nonetheless wanted to stay partnered to her in part to not disrupt the family they had formed:

That would be the biggest devastation I could see in my life, would be changing the family dynamic in my family. I have good kids, I have good grandkids, I have good in-laws, I have good kids-in-law, I dearly love my wife's family, and basically still getting along with my wife is why I'm so discreet. I come from a broken home, I know sometimes it has to happen, but [for] my family specifically it would be devastating to change it.

Having experienced his parents' divorce, Aaron felt that happy children needed the presence of a mother and father. It was important to him not to break up his family unit, as was true for other men I talked to. It is incorrect that man-woman relationships are the only types of relationships that facilitate social stability, since same-sex couples and women who intentionally plan to be single mothers also raise well-adjusted children.[21] It is, however, true that family instability, regardless of family type, can negatively affect everyone. Harrison and others sought to avoid this instability.

In summation, most men in relationships with women described their relationships with satisfaction. This reflected their embeddedness in rural and small-town straight culture, which expects men to marry women. They were not unhappy or looking for opportunities to leave women partners and enter into male-male relationships. They enjoyed their marriages or partnerships with women and wanted them to continue. They just also happened to enjoy sex with men.

It is worth acknowledging that men generally gain more emotional benefits from marriage than women do. The men I talked to reported real feelings of love and affection for their wives. Those feelings exist within social patterns that typically benefit men more than women. Although these men's extramarital sex with men might suggest that they are unhappy in their marriages, it is less surprising than might be expected that most expressed marital satisfaction. The way marriage works for many straight people is that men benefit more emotionally than women. While boys in early and middle adolescence often have fulfilling and emotionally intimate friendships, as they mature into adulthood, they learn that manhood means rejecting most forms of emotional intimacy and vulnerability.[22] This often prevents reaching out for emotional support.

The consequence is that men often have fewer, and less emotionally intimate, relationships with other men than women do with other women. Many men in relationships with women therefore turn to women partners as their main, or only, source of emotional support. Meanwhile, their women partners are more likely to have close friendships or emotionally intimate familial relationships outside of marriage. As a result, women may not require the same emotional energy from their male partners as those partners do from them. The result is that women often play a stronger emotionally supportive role in marriage than do men. Although I did not interview these men's women partners, and thus cannot say for sure whether these dynamics were true for them, the fact that these gender patterns are so ingrained suggests that these dynamics were likely present in many of these men's relationships, whether or not they were aware of them.

Religion

Given that rural communities and small towns tend to be more conservatively religious than urban ones, and that conservative religious beliefs are strongly tied to homophobia, it is unsurprising that religion influenced many men to identify as straight. About a third of the men I talked to indicated religion, primarily conservative Christianity, as a key reason for seeing themselves as straight. While most were not overtly prejudicial toward gay or bisexual men, many of those who were were also deeply religious. Religion was one of the few topics where some men expressed considerable conflict about their practices. Internalized homophobia related to religion, and the guilt associated with it, helped explain why many men identified as straight. These beliefs affected how they perceived sex with men and their identification as straight. While they viewed both sex with men and gayness as problematic, they were more easily able to reconcile the former within the context of their straight identity and life.

These men discussed consciously learning how to be straight in religious families, organized religious institutions, or religious social contexts. Consequently, most of the one third identified as straight in part to avoid the shame, guilt, or sin associated with gayness. For instance, James acknowledged that "currently I would say that I believe the gay life is something I would consider more of a struggle for me, something I don't want to live my life in. I would say that's just based off of my current Christian beliefs." While only about a third of the men indicated that religion shaped their straight identification, for these men, religion strongly affected them. They learned that gayness was inappropriate and even immoral. For these men, childhood religious beliefs, instilled by family and religious institutions, continued to influence how they perceived themselves. Shame and fear from their religious teachings were major reasons for identifying as straight.

For instance, when discussing his attractions to men, Will explained that "yeah, you try not to act on them. I mean, the way you were raised. Of course, I was raised in a Baptist home, and I think that had a lot to do with it. What you're taught is, you grow up, you marry, you have children, that's the life you live. There's no relations with a male." Similarly, Mark, a sixty-one-year-old who was raised in a deeply religious family, learned that gayness was one of the worst possible sins: "I think until I was probably fourteen or fifteen I never even heard the term 'homosexual.' 'Faggot,' 'queer,' yeah. But 'gay' hadn't been invented yet, didn't know the word 'homosexual.' The attitude that I picked up from people, [I] probably never even had a conversation, was that it was like the most awful thing you could do. Like one step below murder or something, open the chute and send you straight to hell." Mark internalized religious guilt and shame, as well as messages from his family that he should marry and raise children. Similarly, Harrison, who attended a "strict" Catholic school as a child, learned as a child that "there is nothing else but straight." As he further explained, "I was raised Roman Catholic and the Nobertines were very strict, and so [as an adult] I truly believe I'm in a state of mortal sin, and eventually I intend just to go to confession, be in a state of grace, and don't see guys anymore." He experienced substantial guilt and conflict about his practices.

Religious prohibitions against sex with men were not only reflections of childhood. Several men detailed current religious struggles with their sexual behavior, encouraging their identification with straightness. Notably, Ryan was much more conflicted about the thought of *identifying as gay* than about *having sex with men*. Recalling a time when he sought therapy to help reconcile his internal struggle over having sex with men, he explained, "The doctor said, 'If you're going to survive this, you're going to have to come out as gay.' And I couldn't do it. In fact I was planning my suicide because I couldn't do it. So there's got to be a straight side of me that wants that. That's been my struggle over the years." Like many others, Ryan found reconciling his religious beliefs with his sex with men easier than reconciling those beliefs with the idea of a gay identity.

Cain was one of the most conflicted of the men I interviewed. Cain enjoyed "thrilling" sex in locations where the risk of discovery was high: dressing rooms, his own home, and churches. Cain also experienced substantial struggles with religion:

I told you I had deep religious convictions as well. [It is] just like alcoholism runs in certain families, I don't think it makes you an alcoholic because alcoholism runs in your family. I do think there's an element of choice. It may very well be, I don't think it's really firmly established that there's a gay gene or whatever, but, even if that is true, I think there is still choice. It's somewhat disappointing to me that I don't have greater self-control. . . . I think it's related to my belief system, religious belief system. Which does not view this behavior, these acts as something a Christian should do.

Cain's religious beliefs, and the immense feelings of guilt and shame these created, encouraged him to identify as straight even as he voiced the thought that he might have "a gay gene." Similarly, George noted that sex with men made him feel "dirty":

[Religion] has affected me, I think that's really fuel on the fire of the guilt I was talking about. I'm the kind of person that after an encounter I feel really dirty and I want to just shower and get cleaned up. Go read the Bible or something, because I feel that it's a sin to do what I'm doing. I know that whether it's adultery or not, it's still a sin to do what I'm doing. But at the same time, I know that I'm not perfect and nobody is perfect, so I guess I can kind of justify it as, I only do what I can do in life. If I go to hell because of this I go to hell because of it. I would hope that I've done enough good, what I've done in my life being in the military and being in law enforcement and all the stuff that I've done to help others. I would hope that that would offset it, maybe? [laughs]

Notably, George recalled deeply masculine institutions like law enforcement and the military as a counterbalance to his sex with men. His framing of himself as a protector, a defining feature of masculinity, helped him reconcile his sex with men. Like George, Brian attempted to reconcile his sexual practices with his religious beliefs, shrugging off his psychological struggles with laughter and a sort of pragmatic fatalism:

You asked a little about church, and I think of myself [as] real religious. And to be honest with you, the biggest struggle that I have, sometimes I'm sitting in church and I'm thinking, "Have I committed a carnal sin?" Obviously I have, by allowing a guy to suck me off. I see jerking off with other guys as pretty much not a big thing, but when you get into Old Testament dogma, Leviticus 20:13, specifically, [laughs], it's pretty condemning. A man shall not lie with a man as he does with a woman, that kind of thing. And so that causes a great deal of guilt, and possibly because of that guilt I have not gone beyond [receiving oral sex] in any realm. So religion does play a factor in this whole thing. It is what it is, I'm pretty good at dealing with reality, so.

Brian's guilt at having sex with men was a reason he continued to identify as straight. Brian's masculinized suppression of his emotions seems to put him, notwithstanding his guilt, in a different category than Cain and George, who are both even more verbally conflicted about their sex with men. Religion influenced these men to live what they considered a straight life. It also led to strong feelings of guilt and shame about having sex with men. While some men offset this guilt with laughter and stoicism, others did not.

Notably, not all of the men I interviewed were religious, and many rejected religion. Some who had been raised in a religious context reported not being very religious as adults; Eli, for instance, explained that he was "a recovering Catholic." Others reported never having been very religious. While religion holds great importance for how many men perceive their sexuality and masculinity,[23] this is not the case for all men. It is important to recognize, however, that some religiously based ideals have become so widespread that most people perceive them as secular.[24] Many men's understanding of their straight identity reflects ideals rooted in religious discourse, such as ideals about marrying women and having children.

Marital relationships also often rely on gendered understandings of what husbands and wives are expected to do. Ideals about marriage and childrearing influenced how many men understood both their sexuality and their gender. Hence, whether or not they explicitly identified religion as a factor in how they perceived their sexuality and masculinity, it did likely influence them.

About a third of the men, however, directly discussed religion as the cause of anxiety and guilt. They internalized messages similar to those the Religious Right has expressed since the 1970s: deviating from heterosexuality and social norms relating to masculinity and femininity is dangerous and sinful.[25] Interestingly, much of the language in the Bible about gender norms is not original, and there are actually multiple versions of the Bible.[26] It is not necessary to support strict gender norms to be a Christian. Still, believing that homosexuality is a sin and fearing estrangement from religious communities and loved ones were important factors in explaining why many of the men I interviewed identified as straight and masculine. Notably, however, few enrolled in anything resembling conversion therapy, a discredited practice that unsuccessfully attempts to change sexual orientation.[27] Most men simply kept their practices hidden.

Masculinity and Rural and Small-Town Straight Culture

Being in a rural area or small town was a key part of how many of the men I talked to saw themselves as men. Over half used rural hobbies, occupations, or other elements to describe their masculinity. Some struggled to articulate this explicitly. Pat, for instance, nonchalantly answered a question about masculinity by saying, "Right now I'm standing outside on the front porch of the hunting cabin in this rural setting taking a leak." Rather than define masculinity, he alluded to it with particular tropes: urinating outside, a hunting cabin, and male-coded language. Their stories demonstrate that masculinity is a central part of rural and small-town straight culture.

Many noted that growing up in a rural area deeply affected their sense of masculinity: "I think it's put into us as a child over here. Boys are boys and girls are girls," explained Chris. Similarly, Sean said, "The masculinity part is a no-brainer, because like I said, it's rural, very conservative, very redneck." Lance, a fifty-four-year-old from Montana, described his community as "a farming, ranching community, as well as a lot of oil field work, so the guys out here are pretty hardcore, masculine types." David noted that both the rural area and the era in which he grew up affected his masculinity:

It was the way of life, that was the way you were. You were either that way or you were strange. I got to tell you, I think it would be really, really hard, particularly for a gay boy, to grow up in rural America, I think it would be tough. I think that's why a lot get out as soon as they can. It's better now than it was. Boy, when I was a teenager that was just a real no-no. . . . My dad and all his friends were officers and wardens and law enforcement and military, Boy Scouts, it was just the masculine side of life, everything we did. Yeah, just didn't have any femininity in my life at all.

Like David, many men who had been raised in rural areas noted numerous influences that facilitated identification with masculinity, including family members and other role models. As fifty-year-old Dan from Oregon tells it, "The way I was brought up, and the activities that I participated in were more of a masculine, they were more slotted masculine or feminine. There wasn't a question of what, it wasn't a question of like or dislike, it was just what guys did." Moreover, he continued, these expectations were enjoyable: "I enjoyed them. It has nothing to do with not enjoying them or just doing them, because I did enjoy them." Many men described their childhoods in a positive light. None identified any influences that provided socially acceptable options for male femininity or open gayness or bisexuality.

The physicality of rural labor in childhood helped build masculinity, particularly farm or ranch work. Jordan described himself as "a workaholic, I was born and raised on a farm, and we worked hard all of our lives. . . . [W]e had to get up at four in the morning and go change water before we went to school." Matt recalled, "My uncles had farms, so you'd be out there helping bale hay and stuff like that. . . . [W]e'd go over there for a weekend and help out. Things like that. . . . [Y]ou're always out doing manual labor, so you think of yourself as masculine." Tom similarly explained that "because I was on the farm . . . I've always done masculine things," while Donald reported, "I'm quite masculine. . . . I grew up in a ranching family and I enjoyed all the jobs that I did during the summer, farming and looking after cattle and horses. I enjoyed that a lot." Richard relatedly described how "my dad put me on a tractor, [I was] driving a tractor when I was six years old. And I learned how to drive a tractor. I do not ever recall a time that I did not know how to drive." Similarly, Bob remembered both work and play as a key part of his rural boyhood: "These two brothers I hung out with, we was real close friends, still are to this day. The older one was out chasing pussy and the younger one was all about me and him hunting and fishing and working on old trucks, helping our parents on the farm, things like that. Well, helping parents on the farm meant that we had more time together to do other things [like sex] [laughs]." Within a social framework that provided clearly demarcated boys-only spaces for work and friendship, Bob found it easy both to pursue "other things" and to disguise that pursuit. Generally, the men did not recall the hard work of their youth as onerous. Rather, they recalled it fondly. Childhood work in farming and ranching shaped how they saw themselves as men.

In adulthood, rural occupations also upheld masculinity. As Kevin explained, "I've always done blue-collar-type work, I live in a rural area, I've had a farm, I'm a farmer, farmed all my life." Chris, who currently lives on a ranch, said he had "worked on them my whole life off and on, farms and ranches." Neil described himself as

> kind of a cowboy I guess. I have some cattle so I work, I have a ranch, so a lot of my hobbies are associated with that. I spend a lot of time outside, fix the fence, I like to watch football, I like to listen to country music, I like to listen to rock music, I drive a truck, I shoot guns, I drink beer, drink whiskey. I like to go fishing. . . . I guess I just kind of grew up working on the ranch, doing stuff outside, playing football, playing basketball. Sports and working I guess.

Being a rancher was central to how Neil saw himself as a man, so much so that he felt most masculine "probably when I'm working cattle. That's a real man's job. It takes a lot of strength; it takes a lot of endurance." Being a rural man was so much a part of Neil's life that he was even unaware of it at times. For instance, he sent me a picture of his bare chest (I am not sure why), and the background showed that he was standing in a cornfield.

Several men also shared rural coming-of-age moments when they described their masculinity. As Donald said,

> Being manly was important to me. I wanted the men to accept me even though I was only a thirteen-year-old boy, [to know] that I could do a

man's work. And I was asked to do men's work [laughs] and I did. I even got to go to the bar when I was twelve for the first time. At the bar I had a little shot glass of beer. Not whiskey, but beer. . . . It was all just in good humor.

Donald recalled drinking with men for the first time as an indication that they accepted him as a man. Another common activity was hunting. "It's a cliché almost," Joey acknowledged, "but it would be getting my first deer. Killing my first deer, when I was thirteen. That's a real rite of passage here in the Midwest, hunting, for men, and I'm happy to say increasingly for young women." The link between hunting and masculinity remains despite women's increasing participation, perhaps in part because some men frame hunting as one way to be a provider. Richard, for instance, recalled,

> We were dirt poor, I mean literally dirt poor. My dad had [over five] kids and I was the oldest. And we lived really on a farm. When I was eight years old my grandfather gave me a single shot .22 rifle. And I remember many, many times coming home from school and my mother giving me five or six .22 bullets and telling me, "Go get dinner," and I'd take off out across the field out there and I'd shoot three to four rabbits. And I'd bring them back, mother would clean them, and that was dinner.

The symbolic nature of this gift, conferring masculinity from grandfather to grandson, hints at how the gift of a first gun can be an act of intimacy within families in rural areas and small towns. Even as a boy, Richard helped provide for his family in the late 1940s. For several men, rural lives were key to how they began understanding themselves as men when they were children or young adolescents.

However, even when activities like hunting, fishing, and shooting were simply hobbies, they were hobbies that defined the men I talked to as *rural or small-town* men. Many saw rural activities, in particular guns, hunting, and fishing, as central to how they perceived their masculinity. Jon described himself as "a big, tall, in-shape, good-looking, straight guy that likes to hunt, fish, camp, and I raise cattle for a living. I'm pretty much masculine."

STRAIGHT CULTURE | 121

Marcus explained that "I portray myself as very masculine. [I] wear jeans and boots and camouflage hats and sleeveless t-shirts, drive a truck, and like to shoot stuff." Travis also explained that "I like to shoot and hunt, and I'm a big hiker, and I think those are guy kind of things. I don't go to museums and I don't go to quartet music concerts, I don't spend time at art galleries and wine and cheese socials [laughs]." Similarly, Jack's description of his masculinity contrasts his outdoorsy activities with implicitly less masculine city life: "I consider myself pretty masculine. Appearance wise pretty masculine, the things I do, interests, all masculine, I like to shoot, I like to hunt. . . . [T]hose pretty much consume my life. . . . I don't wear suits, and ties, and khakis and all that. I wear boots, and I've always been an outdoors person, worked in the outdoors, and just have always identified with that, as pretty masculine." Outdoor work and hobbies, particularly the use of guns for hunting and shooting, were central to how he understood himself as a man. Hunting was a major reason why Jack lived in rural Oregon, and outdoor living distinguished him from urban men, who wear "suits and ties."

Hunting and fishing were so strongly identified with masculinity that, similarly to Bob's recollection of farm work and "other things" with childhood friends, they enabled male-male sex without compromising that masculinity. Describing outdoor activities as key to his masculinity, Pat mentioned his enjoyment of being in the forest where he could "act like I am hunting":

Yes, very masculine. I drive a pickup. I'm sorry I gave up all my hobbies, did that when I bought the little place I live at. But yeah, I like guns, I'm not good at hunting, but I like to go up in the woods and sit there and drink my half pint of Jack Daniels and act like I am hunting. I'd say very masculine. I like baseball. . . . I like masculine activities, I like to shoot weapons, rifles and pistols, drive a pickup, I like to go for walks in woods, love to own the ground, own farm ground, worked in the oil patch. . . . I'd describe myself, yes, as masculine, there's no question about it.

In addition to these masculine activities, Pat met men for sex at his hunting cabin. Rural masculinity ran through his hobbies, occupations, daily activities, and sex with men. Joey, the man who expressed approval at young women beginning to hunt, nonetheless saw himself as "a man's man" in part because he likes to "hunt and fish." He, too, hooks up with men in his hunting cabin: "I have a little deer hunting cabin, and he was in the area and we arranged well ahead of time, and he came and met me at my deer hunting cabin." Similarly, Val shared that he thought of "hunting, fishing, hiking, camping, [and] boating" when considering his masculinity, and noted that these activities bolstered his masculinity despite his having sex with men: "I guess when I'm looking for a guy to have sex with or having sex with a guy, I don't really spend time thinking about whether I'm feeling feminine or masculine. I feel masculine and I just concentrate on how to make the pleasure more intense and so forth, how to make it last. And overall maybe because we're doing a lot of masculine type things, hunting, fishing, camping, that sort of thing, I totally feel masculine." Val stated that rural hobbies helped him feel confident in his masculinity despite having sex with men, showing clear links between heterosexuality and masculinity.

Rural childhoods, rural occupations like farming and ranching, and outdoor activities such as hunting, fishing, and shooting were central to how many of the men I talked to understood both rural life and masculinity. For a majority, rural areas were key to how they understood themselves as men, a fact that reinforces how masculinity is a central aspect of rural and small-town straight culture. While there are similarities between straight cultures in rural and urban areas, they are also distinct due to the different ways in which men express masculinity.

For instance, while traits such as hard work, endurance, and providing for families are associated with masculinity in many areas, in rural areas and small towns they often take forms different from those in urban and suburban areas. Additionally, while men in all types of areas have sex with other men and identify as straight and masculine, the particular ways they understand their heterosexuality and masculinity differ by geographic context. For instance, many of the men I talked to mentioned gun-related activities when describing their masculinity, such as recreational shooting and hunting. Guns are more important to how rural and small-town men understand their masculinity than they are to urban men.[28] Many of the men I interviewed understood their masculinity in ways that reflected their rural and small-town context, and several distinguished themselves from urban men. This is similar to how Braden Leap, a sociologist at Mississippi State University, found that rural men understand themselves in opposition to representations of urbanity,[29] and how Miriam Abelson, a sociologist at Portland State University, detailed how masculine archetypes differ by geographic location.[30] In short, while straight MSM live in many types of places, the ways they understand themselves differ according to social context.

Straightness and Masculinity

Given that men's masculinity is a key aspect of rural and small-town straight culture, not surprisingly, many of the men I talked to viewed male masculinity and heterosexuality as overlapping considerably. All identified as straight and described themselves as masculine, facts that reflect the ways that heterosexual identification and masculinity reinforce one another.[31] Being straight meant being masculine. The men I talked to were invested in masculinity, and most felt that identifying as anything other than straight would have threatened their masculinity. In part to preserve their masculinity, they identified as straight.

Masculinity also reinforced their straightness, and several of the men I talked to contrasted their own masculine practices with feminine behavior, which many associated with gay men. For example, Jeff, a thirty-eight-year-old man from Idaho, explained that "the way I think about myself is straight. Part of that is because I guess I was always raised to believe that homosexuals were flamboyant, wild, pink hair, oversexualized, etc. And I'm masculine, straight acting, and entirely turned off by cross dressers, etc."

Bob colorfully described his masculinity when explaining why he identified as straight: "Pardon the language, but I'm not one of those burst into flames every time you walk out of the house kind of guys [laughs]." Many men, like Bob, described themselves as *behaving* in ways that were straight. They described that similarly to Dan: "It's my overall everyday persona, that's who I am most or all day." Being straight and being masculine were strongly connected. Having sex with other men did not compromise their masculinity or heterosexuality as long as their behavior in other respects reflected masculine norms. As Jon put it when explaining why he identifies as straight, "I'm a masculine guy that does guy things. Every once in a while I have sex with guys, but [not often]." Underscoring the link between rural masculinity and heterosexuality,

Tom indicated that he identified as straight "probably because of all the masculine things I've done in my life," such as farm work as a child.

Relatedly, many saw straightness as a verb, something they *did* most of the time, largely by maintaining partnerships with women, a key to being straight. As Chad noted, "I have a girlfriend who I love very much and, so we have a relationship, I function as a straight person, mostly, 99 percent of the time, I would say." Seamus shared that he is straight "probably because I'm married to a woman, and I only play around with guys every once in a while." Val echoed this, saying, "I'm primarily heterosexual. Definitely. I'm married and primarily have sex with women, but now and then I do enjoy sex with other men." Relatedly, Matt explained, "I act straight." Straight identification, then, referred not so much to these men's sexual attractions or behavior, but to their chosen way of living: having relationships with women partners or raising children.

Many of the men described their masculinity by stating that most people would not believe that they have sex with men. As Travis noted, "There's nothing effeminate about me [laughs]. I'm a man's man. I look it, I talk it, I work it, I am just a guy. Nobody would suspect that I have this other ulterior lifestyle because there is nothing that I have done, or show, or do. I mean, I'm just a guy." Being a "guy" meant acting masculine and presenting himself as straight. Similarly, George explained that

> I believe that I'm masculine enough to where nobody knows at all. I've seen YouTube videos of a guy coming out, or a video of a guy coming out and he says when I came out everybody said, "Oh, yeah, it's about time you came out; we already knew." I don't think anybody knows about me. Because I dress masculine, I'm a guy that goes out shooting guns, and I'm a masculine guy, but I have desires beyond some masculine activities.

George believed that he was so masculine no one would believe he could have sex with men. Indeed, he found the thought amusing, as did many other men. In line with others, Rand found it absurd that someone might know he has sex with men: "I'm a carpenter, a guy's guy, nobody would ever imagine that I do this [laughs]." Not being suspected of challenging community norms about sexuality and masculinity seemed to bolster the masculinity of several of the men I talked to, given that they held a secret almost no one else knew.

Perhaps unsurprisingly, along with affection and a sense of caretaking towards their women partners and children, for some men sex with or attractions to women was important to how they saw themselves as men. Many also said that they identified as straight in part because they had attractions to women, and that accordingly a gay (or even bisexual) identity was incompatible regardless of their sex with men.

As David explained, "I think it's my physical makeup, I'm an alpha male, I'm attracted to women." Rand noted that he felt most masculine when "engaged in wild sex with a woman while on top," while Jared reported that he felt "like a man the most" when he was "with a woman and I can satisfy her and then satisfy myself." Jared's sense of being in charge of his partners' and his own sexual satisfaction was not divorced from caring: "If there's some emotion tied to it that's even better, if there's a connection." Several felt that sex with women helped to define themselves as men. Keeping their sex with men secret from their women partners likely also bolstered their masculinity, in the sense that secrecy was a form of control. They could have sex with men without ever having to discuss this with their women partners, even if they were still having sex with their wives and therefore putting them at potential risk for exposure to sexually transmitted infections (STIs).

In any case, their sense of themselves as straight was central to how they understood their masculinity, and vice versa. Most explicitly or implicitly tied their heterosexual identification with their masculinity. They did this even as they knew that feminine straight men and masculine gay men existed. Masculinity was tightly connected to partnering with women, being a provider to their families, childrearing, working in rural occupations, or engaging in outdoor activities.

4

Why They Did Not Identify as Gay or Bisexual

The men I talked to identified as straight largely because of their embed-dedness in straight culture and desire to remain a part of a socially dominant group. It then makes sense that they actively chose not to identify as gay or bisexual. Key aspects of this choice include their atti-tudes about what it means to be gay or bisexual. Most felt that gay men were too feminine, urban, or incompatible with conventional marriage or family formation. Nonetheless, a majority supported equal legal rights, including same-sex marriage. This is in contrast to, for instance, deeply homophobic Republican elected officials who secretly have sex with men.[1] Yet many also expressed various types and degrees of homophobia, some subtle and some more obvious.

In this sense the men I talked to were like the majority of straight people, who support many forms of legal equality but not always infor-mal rights like the right to kiss in public.[2] There are, of course, many types of homophobia that exist alongside support for equal legal rights, and some men did express problematic beliefs. The men I talked to did not identify as straight only because of homophobia, any more than most straight men identify as straight only because of homophobia. Ho-mophobia did inform many men's beliefs about gay and straight identi-ties and did impact their choice of the latter. Ultimately, however, it was only one of many reasons for their straight identification. Clearly, the answers they gave are complicated.

Relatedly, most of the men I talked to knew that bisexuality was a possible identity but did not adopt that for themselves. Otto, for in-stance, admitted that "for a long, long time I thought I would probably be described as bisexual. But the more I read and understand, and asso-ciated myself more with identified bisexuals, that's not me, man. I'm not looking for a partner other than for sex." Many people are prejudiced against bisexuality, believing that bisexuals are confused or lying. This is untrue, yet many people believe it. Still, most of the men I interviewed knew that bisexual people existed and that they could have potentially identified as bisexual. They did not identify as straight simply because of prejudice against bisexual people or lack of awareness of bisexuality.

Most of the men I interviewed did not identify as bisexual in large part for three reasons. First, they considered bisexuality incompatible with having a woman partner. Second, they had no interest in romantically partnering with a man. And third, they thought identifying as bisexual would threaten their other relationships. The men I talked to carefully considered many aspects of their lives when thinking about their identity: their sexual practices, sexual attractions, romantic attractions, and current romantic partnership, among other elements. For a combination of these reasons, a straight identity in full or part made the most sense to them.

Romantic attractions and partnerships were especially important. Most were romantically interested only in women, and a majority were in relationships with women. Many therefore felt that bisexual identification did not make sense for them. While it is possible to identify as bisexual while being in a relationship with a woman, the men I talked to identified as straight because they considered relationships with women and embeddedness in straight culture most important for their identity. Their sexual encounters with men were mostly irrelevant.

Gay and Bisexual Men and Gay "Lifestyles"

Collectively, the men I interviewed felt that their understandings of gay and bisexual men and gay "lifestyles" contrasted with their sense of self in three important ways. First, they viewed gay men as feminine and themselves as masculine. Second, they thought that being gay or bisexual meant having or desiring a male romantic partner. And third, they perceived gay culture in urban terms: going to clubs, partying, living in gay neighborhoods, or associating mostly with other gay people. These activities contrasted with the rural lives that they perceived as necessarily both straight and masculine. Indeed, although all were aware of "bisexual" as an identity, most did not discuss bisexuality at length.[3]

Feelings of belonging in straight culture went hand in hand with feelings of not belonging in gay culture. The men I talked to were satisfied identifying as straight and masculine and expressing themselves that way. Few of them expressed much conflict over their identities. They felt that identifying as gay would mean sacrificing much of what they valued, including marriage and family. These attitudes about gay men and gay "lifestyles" are, of course, products of their socialization within rural and small-town straight culture. It is entirely possible to be masculine, marry a man, raise biological children, and live in a rural area or small town. The men I talked to, though, did not consider this as a possibility for themselves. Even if they had, such lives were not compatible with the particular aspects of rural and small-town straight culture they valued. As Ryan said, "There are people like me that don't want to give up my straight lifestyle but sure like getting together with a guy once in a while." For these men, occasional sex with men was compatible with the straight "lifestyles" they preferred.

Importantly, most felt that male-male romanticism was a hallmark of gayness or bisexuality. They therefore reinforced their straightness by avoiding romantic attachments to men. Ian, for instance, described what he called a "process of elimination" through which he decided he was straight: "I don't consider myself gay, I don't consider myself bi, I don't envision myself entering into a romantic relationship with a man, I only envision that happening with a woman. I don't consider myself gay, and for bi, my definition of bi is that you could enter into a romantic relationship with either male or female, and that doesn't describe myself either. Thus, I conclude I'm straight." Others felt the same way. As Jack explained, "I don't necessarily relate to the gay scene. I don't want to be with a man, as far as a relationship or anything like that. I just have these secretive desires for a male body." To Jack, lack of romantic desire for a man was a sign that he was straight: "I have no feelings like that [love] at all, and never have, for any man that I've been with, I guess. So it's just strictly physical with me."

Others explained that their focus on romantic partnerships with women prevented such relationships with men. As Peter stated, "I could never I don't think be in a relationship with a man, because there's something about being with a woman that just sort of has my whole interest." Aaron felt the same way: "I would have no interest in living with a man in a partnered relationship. My interest as far as a living partner would be only a woman." The men I talked to identified themselves in large part on the basis of their romantic attractions to and partnerships with women. As a result, nothing except "straight" made sense to them. These men were not unaware of bisexuality. The distinction they drew between romantic orientation and sexual interest led them to identify as straight because that identity better reflected their emotional desires and the partnerships they sought.

Many men also expressed the belief that gayness is inherently urban. As Harrison described it, a "gay lifestyle" involved "perhaps having a partner, going to clubs, being on Grindr all of the time, and Craigslist. Just perhaps living in a community and having most of your social circle be gay." These beliefs were not purely based on popular representations. For instance, Jeff explained, "I have one gay cousin, and he's feminine and flamboyant, the whole 'out and proud' thing, lives in San Francisco, and I wasn't interested in that at all. And so I guess I identified with the remainder of my heterosexual family." His cousin's gay visibility did not encourage Jeff to consider that identity as an option for himself because it did not appeal to him. Other men with gay friends or family members also expressed acceptance of their gay identities while disavowing those identities for themselves.

Other men also associated gayness with urban areas. Todd noted that "[with] a gay lifestyle there's more interaction with more people. It sounds silly [laughs], but there's more parties, there's more things going on, and more places to go and do different things than a straight life." He later elaborated, saying that "it's like an exciting lifestyle, and not boring," and that with a "gay lifestyle you're a little more apt to let your hair down and do wild, crazy things." Similarly, twenty-eight-year-old Brandon from Oregon explained that part of why he identifies as straight and prefers women is that he does not enjoy "a party-type lifestyle," given that "part of what I do is public service type of a job, and obviously I am not into that lifestyle because of what I do professionally and the values that I have."

Connor recognized bisexuality, but nonetheless considered himself straight: "If you say gay, that also goes into the lifestyle and culture a little bit more. Bi or straight just means a little culturally gay; you wouldn't be as into the party scene or the bars or anything like that." These men equated their rural and small-town identities with straightness and masculinity.

The phrase "gay lifestyle" deserves a little more analysis. Only fifteen men used the term "lifestyle," and most did not use the phrase with homophobic intent. Still, the expression "gay lifestyle" has homophobic roots in conservative anti-LGBTQ movements.[4] The organizations that promoted these movements spread rhetoric about "gay lifestyles." This term is packed with judgments about gay men's purported "promiscuity" and moral danger to society. This language has also led many straight people, including some men I interviewed, to think about gay people in terms of "lifestyles."

The term suggests that gay people "choose" their sexual attractions, even though attractions cannot be intentionally changed. The assumptions and stereotypes built into "lifestyle" are problematic. For instance, many gay men are masculine,[5] not all gay and bisexual men live in major cities, and most urban gay men do not party all the time or go to sex clubs. While some men recognized that parties and organized sex events are associated with particular subcultures within gay communities,[6] many did not. Several men who did not use the term "gay lifestyle" nonetheless echoed stereotypical beliefs about gay and bisexual men, showing that even without specific terminology, stereotypes persist.

The men I talked to did not discuss bisexual "lifestyles," even though they did think about and reject bisexual identification. While they did discuss bisexual identities and bisexual men, they focused more on distinguishing themselves from gay men and gay lifestyles. Clearly, they did not spend as much time considering the possibility of bisexual identity as they did considering gay identity. Yet this does not necessarily mean that they would have identified as bisexual had they considered it more. Instead it shows that their perceptions of gay men and gay lifestyles were the primary contrasts to how they identified themselves.

Homophobia

Even while distancing themselves from gay people, a majority of the men I talked to supported equal legal rights. They were not overtly homophobic in the sense of expressing hostility towards gay men or policies supporting gay equality. While some opposed equal rights or had mixed feelings, a majority supported them. However, some homophobia was evident in their attitudes about same-sex marriage and childrearing and in their explanations for why they preferred straight or bisexual men for hookups. As we shall see in chapter 6, when it comes to preferred hookup partners, many men preferred straight or bisexual men for hookups because they felt more "comfortable" around them than around gay men. Most did not state overtly homophobic beliefs when explaining this preference. Their explanations do indicate that sexual partners being straight or bisexual helped them feel as if simply having sex with men was not gay. These preferences are subtly homophobic but are different from beliefs about legal and social rights.

Of course, the question of whether the men I talked to as a group were homophobic is not a simple one. There are several types of homophobia. For instance, many straight people support equal legal rights but oppose informal social rights, such as same-sex couples holding hands in public.[7] Many of the men I talked to expressed subtle types of homophobia, though a majority did not express overt prejudice. Like other straight men, though, many did express homophobic beliefs that varied in type and degree, from subtle to more overt. All considered identifying and living as gay or bisexual incompatible with how they saw themselves. This was the case even as a majority expressed support for LGBQ legal equality.

Out of sixty men I talked to, fifty-eight answered questions about same-sex marriage and childrearing. Of these, forty-seven (81 percent) expressed support or neutrality toward same-sex marriage, and thirty-three (57 percent) expressed support or neutrality about same-sex couples raising children. Thirty-three expressed support or neutrality about both, fourteen expressed support or neutrality only about same-sex marriage, and eleven opposed or had mixed feelings about both. Neutrality included statements like "I don't care," "It doesn't bother me," and "I don't have any issues with it." I considered men opposed if they reported qualifiers to their support for equal rights.[8]

For instance, men who felt that same-sex childrearing was acceptable only for women, or only in cases of adoption or fostering and not assisted reproduction, I coded as opposition. Far more men had qualifiers for their support of same-sex childrearing than for their support of same-sex marriage. This reflects incorrect perceptions that LGBTQ people cannot effectively parent or should not reproduce. Indeed, many of the men raised concerns about the impacts of gay parents on children or stated that same-sex couples should only raise children if adopting or fostering. These are homophobic responses that reflect the importance they placed on the heterosexual nuclear family.

Nonetheless, many men reported liberal attitudes about LGBQ rights, and several expressed dismay at overt homophobia in their communities. Will, for example, visited the Castro district in San Francisco to see what life was like living as an openly gay or bisexual man and found it "very comfortable." When I asked him his identity, he said, "If someone's honest about it, I guess you would have to say bisexual, but I don't really live that life." He landed on "straight-leaning bisexual," despite being slightly more attracted to men than to women.

Later, over e-mail, he said, "I don't know if that makes any sense to you. I think, living a straight life is a much easier one than it would be to live a gay life. Maybe that's part of the reason, I am who I am." While acknowledging that homophobia may affect how he sees himself and lives his life, he nonetheless identified more as straight: "I'm not waving a rainbow-colored flag around anywhere, I can tell you that much." The dichotomy he saw between living a gay life or a straight life suggests that Will implicitly linked bisexual identification to gay identification, and therefore rejected both.

Several other men were quite liberal. Eli performed several same-sex wedding ceremonies for friends, worked in political activism related to LGBQ rights, and supported same-sex childrearing. As he said, "I think religious heterosexual couples will fuck your kid up more than anyone." Yet he considered himself "straight with lots of curiosity." Similarly liberal Jeremy explained that he "thought one of the proudest days in our country was when the Supreme Court made it [same-sex marriage] legal across the land." Adam, who also felt that same-sex marriage and childrearing were fine, said that "both my wife and I both have friends that are in same-sex relationships, we go out with them, we go to visit them." He also believed that "sex is just gender; there are so many different ways people identify themselves from pansexual to whatever it might be. It's hard to say what sex is. I think it's different for different people."

Sam joked about same-sex marriage: "I think it's cool and there's that famous comedian joke, why should gays be insulated from the same pain and heartbreak like the rest of us?" All of these men ultimately identified as straight, showing that their reasons for identifying as straight had more to do with embeddedness in straight culture than bigotry toward gay and bisexual men.

A distinct minority of men, however, were overtly homophobic. Some on the far-right end of the political spectrum opposed equal rights. Others were mostly supportive of equal rights but qualified their support. Cain was highly religious and politically conservative, rejecting the "gay lifestyle" on those grounds as well as because he did not see it as a good fit for him: "I just really hate that lifestyle. I really don't enjoy so much of the stuff that surrounds that." Other men also believed that gay people were problematic and should not have civil rights.

The most overt kinds of homophobia came in four different forms. First was active opposition to "gay lifestyles." Second was framing opposition to same-sex marriage or childrearing in terms of protecting families. Third was saying that LGBQ people should not reproduce but maybe should be allowed to parent children without a home. Fourth was saying that nondiscrimination laws oppress conservative straight people.

Similarly to other straight conservatives, the men I talked to who opposed equal rights did so because they felt that they were protecting the concepts of strong families and good parenting. As Ian phrased it, same-sex parenting is "not the ideal situation because children benefit from having both mom and dad in their lives. Mom can't be dad, dad can't be mom." Jordan believed "that a child needs the influence of a male and a female to be able to experience and see the difference." Paul also indicated that "the difference between regular marriage and homosexual marriage is that you don't have all the components of a family." He continued,

> Men bring certain things to a family, the mother brings other things to the family. And you just don't have the complete needs to raise kids if you don't have the masculine and the feminine influences. The man needs to teach any sons that may come along how to be men and the women need to teach their daughters how to be women, and a woman can't teach a boy how to be a man. And a man can't teach a girl how to be a woman. And you just kind of lose that.

Clearly all these statements are prejudicial. They also indicate how these men felt deeply attached to conservative gender beliefs. Many thought that to maintain social stability, straight couples should raise girls to be feminine and boys to be masculine. Anything that falls outside of that, according to them, is dangerous.

Several men reported prejudice that was different but related: that same-sex couples should be allowed to raise children only if they are adopting or fostering and are not seeking to have biological children. As Jon explained, "I think that children are best raised by their biological parents, so if a same-sex couple wanted to adopt some parentless child, I guess that would be fine," but he felt that "creating new children for same-sex couples is not okay." Neil also said that same-sex couples should be able to raise children through adoption, because "there are so many children in the world that are orphaned, that don't have parents, or they're in the foster care system, they don't have anyone to raise them, anyone to love them, any place to call home, so if two guys want to raise a kid, more power to them." However, he went on to say,

> I don't know if lesbians should be able to have a baby of their own because then they're using sperm from some guy, I don't know about that I guess. If they want to adopt a child I think that that's great, but I don't know about them making a baby with a guy's sperm. I suppose it's okay, but I think it would be better if they just adopted. If they can't biologically make a child together then they should adopt.

None said the same about straight people who experience fertility issues, which suggests that their primary concern was with same-sex parenting or reproduction.

Prejudice certainly affected the identity of conservative men. It is also important to remember that all of the men I talked to identified as straight because of their embeddedness in straight culture, especially their relationships with women. Prejudice played a strong role for some, but it was by no means the only factor. Their decision to identify as straight was based on pull factors, like wanting to preserve relationships with women and children, and for certain men also push factors, including prejudice.

A number of men who supported equality for political or ideological reasons nonetheless revealed underlying homophobic feelings. For instance, Lance supported same-sex marriage because of his libertarian ideals of small government, yet was uncomfortable with the idea: "I have a hard time reconciling it in my head that it's an actual marriage so to speak, but I guess in the terms of politics and the tax breaks involved and all that I think they should have a right to the same tax breaks and rights as any other human being. If they're partners and they're living together, why shouldn't they get the same tax exemptions and benefits that we do?" While seemingly progressive, men like Lance were homophobic in their perception of gay people, even as they supported legal equality for libertarian reasons.

A handful of men went further, taking questions about same-sex marriage and childrearing as an opportunity to complain about nondiscrimination protections for LGBTQ people. As Zach said, "The example that was up there in Gresham [Oregon] where that bakery, those people didn't want to bake a cake for those two women based on their religious beliefs. Well, then the government lets the people sue them. . . . [T]hey're trying to legislate people and ideologies and beliefs and I think it's gotten way out of hand."

Richard agreed: "If I'm in business, I can refuse to serve you, and I don't need a reason. . . . As far as gay marriage, I could care less whether they get married or not, okay, that's between them, but stop beating me over the head and stop passing a bunch of laws that I have to live under." These men explained discrimination in terms of individual liberty without considering how patterns of discrimination create social inequalities that disadvantage LGBTQ people.

Significantly, these problematic beliefs are not limited to the men I interviewed, and instead reflect anti-LGBTQ attitudes on the American Right more broadly. Many conservatives across America believe that discrimination should be a permitted and even celebrated form of free speech and religious expression.[9] Again, while prejudice was more apparent in some men's narratives than others, these men did not express attitudes that are much different from those of a majority of Republicans. Their conservative attitudes reflect and reinforce their embeddedness in straight culture.

Less overt homophobia was fairly common. A majority of men, for instance, preferred straight or bisexual men for hookups but did not express fear or dislike of gay people. Many said that they felt uncomfortable seeing or talking to gay people, avoided forming friendships with gay people, or felt that legal equality was necessary but that there could be some associated social issues. These are subtle expressions of homophobia similar to those of many straight people.[10]

Several men said they did not want to associate with gay people because they did not want anyone to suspect their sex with men. As Larry explained, "I would be less inclined to connect with someone who's openly gay. If I were to be seen with someone who's openly gay of course it would reflect on me, put some questions in people's minds about me or my friendship with them, and I don't have anything against gay people. My [close relative] is gay, so it's just the fear of me being found out." Men like Larry had reservations about associating with gay people despite having gay friends and family members. This type of subtle homophobia reflects their embeddedness in straight culture, but it does not cause it. Indeed, many straight men who do not have sex with men do not associate with gay people because they do not want others to perceive them as gay.[11] This is a part of how many straight men reinforce their masculinity and heterosexuality and is not limited to the men I talked to.

Several men supported legal equality but expressed concern about potential consequences. Connor, for instance, supported same-sex marriage and childrearing while revealing, more lightly, a belief that heterosexuality helped stabilize society:

> There's the argument that homosexuality is banned in every religion and country and society and everything. The one argument I want to put up when people say that is that I think it's because if it's allowed guys would just hook up with guys constantly [laughs]. My standup routine would be, "The only reason that any guy ever does anything is so he can impress women. So all the great inventions and all the work has been done just to get women, and if you don't have to get women, then it all just stops, you know?" [laughs]

Humor was one way men revealed subtle homophobia alongside otherwise progressive sentiments.

Other men distanced themselves from gay culture in ways that were not necessarily homophobic, either overtly or subtly. Neil, for example, was matter of fact in explaining that his everyday life made identifying as straight and masculine obvious: "Day to day, the majority of the time

I just kind of live in that straight world, straight persona. No one would ever think that I would be curious on the other side I guess, I don't think anyway. Kind of a macho guy, I guess. I like my job, and where I live, the rural area, [it is] very conservative, so it's kind of a straight world that I live in." For Neil and others like him, having occasional sex with men simply did not detract from embeddedness in their "straight world." Ryan had been less matter-of-fact about his same-sex sexual activity and had seen a therapist hoping to resolve his same-sex attractions: "I was in therapy for two years about ten years ago, trying to change that part of me, which was unsuccessful. My choice at the time, when I was in therapy, was either to pursue a gay lifestyle or to remain straight, and I could not identify as a gay man." Ryan had considered suicide and resolved his internal dilemma by deciding that, despite having sex with men, he is straight.

While most men felt that "straight" described them better than "gay," they felt this way for reasons more complicated than overt or subtle homophobia. As seventy-one-year-old Erik from Illinois explained, "I wouldn't marry a man but I don't have any ill feelings towards those that marry the same sex. I feel that if they're in love and they think they want to be or need to be married, I don't have a problem with that myself. I'm kind of on the live and let live, I guess you would say." A little less than half of the men I talked to expressed overt forms of homophobia, and others expressed various, often subtle types of homophobia. But still others were actively supportive of gay rights and saw gayness as an unfamiliar but harmless form of difference.

Overall, the role of prejudice varied depending on the man; it impacted some men more than others. All had more complex reasons for identifying as straight than prejudice, however. Even men with the most problematic beliefs indicated more nuanced reasons for identifying as straight. Many men were actually quite liberal about LGBQ rights, yet still identified as straight. While some detailed push factors for identifying as straight, such as prejudice, all of the men I talked to also explained pull factors, like preserving relationships with women partners and children. Thus, identifying as straight was primarily due to being embedded in straight culture, including the benefits of feeling a part of a socially dominant group and avoiding stigma. Evidence from nationally representative surveys supports this argument.[12] The National Survey of

Family Growth shows that straight MSM are not much different from other straight men in their attitudes about gays and lesbians.[13] It would not make sense, then, to say that straight MSM identify as straight solely due to prejudice.

Stigma toward Bisexuality

While all LGBQ people are marginalized compared to straight people, bisexuality is often stigmatized more than gayness and lesbianism, particularly for men. Stereotypes include beliefs that bisexuality is fake or that bisexual people are confused, incapable of monogamy, or too sexually active.[14] Nationally representative surveys show that while perceptions of bisexuality have improved since the early 2000s, a majority of straight Americans view bisexual people negatively or ambivalently.[15] They are also more likely to believe negative stereotypes about bisexual men than about bisexual women.[16] Bisexuals are, unsurprisingly, aware of these negative judgments.[17]

Many people, particularly men, likely identify as either gay or straight rather than bisexual in part because of this stigmatization. Moreover, bisexuality is often "erased."[18] There is little media representation of bisexual people, particularly men, and people are usually assumed to be gay or straight depending on their partner's sex.[19] Over 80 percent of bisexual people are in different-sex (man-woman) relationships.[20]

Many other people identify their sexuality on the basis of their current sexual or romantic partner rather than their attractions.[21] This means that many people view sexuality as binary. This is the case even though research has shown that both sexual and romantic attractions exist on a continuum.[22] The idea that bisexuality is illegitimate is common, and this shapes how people identify their sexuality.

Additionally, due to stigmatization, bisexual people face higher rates of many physical and mental health issues than gay, lesbian, and straight people,[23] as well as rates of substance use.[24] Whereas being open about one's sexual identity leads to better mental health and less substance abuse among gays and lesbians, for bisexuals being more open leads to worsened health outcomes.[25] This reflects widespread bisexual stigmatization. Fewer than one third of bisexuals have told most or all of the most important people in their life that they are bisexual, compared to over 70 percent of gay men and lesbians.[26] Perhaps for this reason, they are less likely to experience certain forms of discrimination than gays and lesbians.[27] Still, they are at heightened risk for health issues like anxiety and depression, as well as wage discrimination,[28] showing that the effects of bisexual stigmatization are profound.

While women and men are about equally as likely to identify as gay/lesbian, women are much more likely to identify as bisexual than men. Bisexuality is therefore also gendered. Women's likelihood of identifying as bisexual is rising over time, but men's is not.[29] This discrepancy may exist because women are not considered as socially important as men.[30] This gives them more flexibility to identify as bisexual than men.[31] In other words, women have less to lose than men do for identifying as bisexual.

For all these reasons, it is unsurprising that the men I interviewed did not openly identify as bisexual. Many differentiated between bisexual attractions or behaviors and bisexual identity. As Jon explained, bisexual "describes my behavior, but not my identity." Others, however, considered identifying as bisexual. Interestingly, Cain, one of the most overtly homophobic men, was more comfortable considering himself bisexual than many others. He explained that "privately I think probably I am more bisexual than I would like to admit. . . . I kind of feel like I am. I think some people deny that that even exists, but if anything I probably feel like that's what I am." Even as he considered the label, however, he also voiced anti-bisexual prejudice: "I don't know, technically, if there's such a thing as bi, I've seen some debate about that. Or if it's just denial, I don't know, but I think I'm bi." Nonetheless, Cain described himself as having a "straight lifestyle," even while acknowledging that the question of his sexual identity "is a bit difficult," because "I've always considered myself straight, but have gotten into what I would consider bi activity." This shows the distinction between identity and behavior.

Fifteen other men also used "bisexual" or some variant of "bisexual" as an additional or secondary descriptor in describing their identities, even while keeping that aspect of their identity private. Publicly they were straight. Privately, they still identified as straight, just not entirely. Again, this suggests that for many men straight identity reflected embeddedness in particular institutions and communities as much as, if not more than, it reflected prejudice. Joe alternated between describing himself as straight and describing himself as bisexual. Kevin identified as "straight" and "mostly straight" with "a percentage towards bi." Matt explained that he identified as "straight but bi, but more straight."

Many of the men I interviewed could hypothetically have identified as bisexual, given their sexual activity with both men and women, but nonetheless they felt that straight identity described them best. Bisexual stigmatization was a factor in some men's identification as straight, but by no means the only one. The men I talked to, as a group, embraced straight identification above all as a reflection of their embeddedness in straight culture and their desire to remain a part of a socially dominant group.

5

Helping a Buddy Out

How did the men I talked to interpret sex with men as compatible with heterosexuality and masculinity? The answers are complicated. Mike offers a key to this seeming paradox: "An alcoholic drinks, but everyone that drinks is not an alcoholic. My philosophy is, every gay person does this, but not everybody that does this is gay. And so you had to separate what was gay and what wasn't. I think a lot of it is all in your mind. If you're not gay, and you don't feel that you are, then it's not a gay thing. It's just helping a buddy out." This is one example of what I call "bud-sex": how rural and small-town, white, straight men interpret or engage in sex in ways that reinforce their heterosexuality and masculinity. What sexual practices "mean" differs across populations, historical periods, and social contexts. For instance, it was only in the late 1800s that oral-genital contact between men was legally considered "sex" in much of the United States.[1] Even in the 1990s, when President Clinton received oral sex from an intern, the public response showed there was disagreement about whether this was actually sex.[2]

While the sex these men have with other men involves acts similar to those between gay and bisexual men, the meanings they attach to these acts differ greatly. Gay and bisexual men perceive sex between men as tied to their identities. It both reflects and reinforces their gayness or bisexuality. Bud-sex, in contrast, minimizes the importance of male-male sex to straight men's identities. While both straight and gay or bisexual men may enjoy giving oral sex to other men, for instance, how they interpret that act has different implications for their identities.

While the men I talked to share overlap with other men who have sex with men,[3] they are also distinct. In particular, the importance of marriage to rural and small-town masculinity encouraged the men I interviewed to have sex with other men. They considered that less of a problem than having extramarital sex with women. Additionally, conservative beliefs about gender, which are more common in rural areas and small towns, encouraged sex between men as well. Women cannot be trusted for hookups, but men can be. These interpretations, tied to their rural and small-town contexts, helped make it easier to reconcile male-male sex with both heterosexuality and masculinity.

Bud-sex has three components. First is hooking up with other masculine, white, and straight or bisexual men. Second is having secretive, nonromantic sex. And third is interpreting male-male sex as largely unthreatening to masculinity, heterosexuality, or marriage. Men who engage in bud-sex often chose hookup partners who resemble themselves: masculine, white, and straight or bisexual. This helps the encounter feel relatively "normal." Some even described their sex as involving "normal" men in unexceptional circumstances offering aid, as Mike explained:

> This poor guy, he's married, his wife won't do it. So if his wife won't do him, we're just friends, we're buddies, we're not in a big crowd, there's not a bunch of people around, we'll just help you out. My wife doesn't do things, girls for some reason, you run into a lot of girls that don't do blowjobs, they just don't. . . . Basically it was, well, if your wife won't do it, come, I'll do it, or my wife won't do it, then we'll get together and just do it together.

This brings to mind other ways in which masculinity is tied to helping people: stopping to help change a flat tire, carrying something heavy up some steps, or opening doors for people when they have their hands full. Thinking of sex as a way for two guys to take care of each other's sexual needs therefore makes it seem entirely reasonable for two straight, masculine men. Through different types of interpretations of sex, such as this, bud-sex is made compatible with heterosexuality and masculinity.[4]

Mike was not the only man who explained this kind of sex with men as "helping a buddy out" or acting on "urges." By perceiving sex with men in these ways, the men I talked to felt they could relieve distracting desires without affecting other parts of their lives. They rejected common associations between sex with men, gayness, and femininity. They instead formed a unique understanding of sex with men as neither gay nor feminine by linking gayness and femininity with romance and emotion, while understanding their sexual encounters as unemotional and masculine. Again, Mike explained, "In my mind, I wasn't thinking this is a gay thing, this is just, I'm just helping my friend out. He just needs some helping, he's helping me out, and once it's over with it wasn't like call the next day, 'Oh, how are you,' no, it was over. Until the next time. It was over, they call it NSA now, no strings attached, so it was a no-strings-attached thing." This differentiation between the sex (masculine) and romance (feminine) helped them view sex with men as less threatening to their marriages than sex with women. This preserved a part of their lives (marriage) they saw as key to their straight, masculine identities.

The link between marriage and masculinity is particularly strong in mostly white, rural and small-town culture. People in rural areas and small towns are more likely to marry than their suburban and urban counterparts,[5] though this is mostly the case for white residents.[6] Even though in practice many people do not marry or eventually divorce, marriage remains an idealized type of relationship and life milestone in America. This is particularly so in rural and small-town America. Marriage was important to the men I interviewed, and they protected their sense of themselves as good husbands despite having secretive extramarital sex.

Bud-sex, with its unique understandings of gender and sexual identity, reflects and reinforces the men's embeddedness in straight culture. Sexual identity and gender depend on what sex acts *mean*, rather than on mere mechanics. Consequently, interpretations of sexual practices, not sexual practices in and of themselves, are crucially important. For the straight men I talked to, their interpretations both reflected and reinforced their embeddedness in straight culture. Bud-sex allows straight men to enjoy male-male sex without threatening either their heterosexuality or their masculinity.

Sex with Men: Straight, Masculine, and Helping Marital Bliss

Bud-sex encompasses three related but distinct interpretive elements. First is interpreting sex with men as "helping a buddy out" or acting on "urges." Second is viewing bottoming or giving oral sex as unthreatening to masculinity or straightness. Third is interpreting sex with men as less threatening to their marriages or partnerships with women than extramarital sex with women. Indeed, sex with men may even be necessary to address desires that would otherwise be distracting. Thus, counterintuitively, the men I talked to view sex with men as unthreatening to their identities or relationships with women, and perhaps even necessary to maintain them.

"Helping a Buddy Out" and Acting on "Urges"

Bud-sex involves unique interpretations of sexual behavior and masculinity. Bud-sex is not just a way to act on attractions or desires. It is "just helping a buddy out," as the quotation from Mike at the beginning of this chapter illustrates. Or it is a way to act on uncontrollable, unwanted "urges" or "impulses"—an aspect of sexuality that is generally understood as inherent to men. For the men I interviewed, these meanings bolstered their sense of themselves as straight, masculine men. Especially for men who reported attractions to other men, interpreting sex with men in complicated ways made it seem reasonable and even necessary for straight, masculine men to have sex with men. Both themes involve an interpretation of sex with men as a form of masculine, heterosexual bonding.

Whether by "helping a buddy out" or by relieving "urges," the men I talked to and their male sexual partners assisted one another in addressing sexual desires without affecting any other parts of their lives. Indeed, a handful felt that they had to have sex with men to maintain their heterosexuality and masculinity. Doing so relieved desires and allowed them to continue being devoted family men. Only a minority of the men I talked to felt that sex with men was "helping a buddy out" or a way to act on "urges," but for them it was crucial to how they understood their sexuality and masculinity.

Nine men in total agreed with Mike that sex with men was "helping a buddy out," and thus a form of straight, masculine, male-male bonding. "Helping a buddy out" allowed them to satisfy desires for men in a masculine way without affecting their marriages or other parts of their lives. Bob, for instance, explained that "growing up in a rural community, it was help your buddy out kind of thing, nobody's looking, and it was all kept under wraps, and nobody knew anything." As Mike elaborated, "It wasn't like, I'm attracted to you. I'm attracted to this, I'm attracted to that, it was just more of a get together and just guys being guys."

Cain understood his sexual activity as both acting on an urge and a form of mutual "helping": "I realize that this is an impulse that I have, and that I try to keep it in check. And I'm thinking an occasional bud or whatever to help me out, is what I need." Cain also reported enjoying helping other men: "What I've found of late is that I've really kind of drawn into the DILF [dad I'd like to fuck] kind of a role. Where [I am] particularly interested in kind of helping college guys explore." He also explained that "it was after I got married that I found myself being drawn in and attracted more so to maybe guys helping each other out."

A subset of men—many of whom, like Cain, were highly religious—considered sex with men a way to act on uncontrollable, unwanted "urges." Satisfying these urges helped suppress them, allowing both men to continue their lives otherwise uninterrupted. While similar to helping a buddy out, interpreting sex with men as an "urge" frames male-male sex as problematic but necessary. Counterintuitively, having sex with trusted men is critical so that urges can be resolved. Hence, Cain described sex with men as "taking care of the urge or the need of the day," explaining that "they're more, just satisfying needs. It's almost like sometimes, even if I jerk off just watching porn, or get off with someone, it's like now this is out of the way, now I can get my work done. It's almost like a chore, kind of a thing." Cain found sex with men pleasurable and necessary so that he could continue being a good husband and father. Ryan, who along with Cain was one of the men who reported the most conflict about his sexual practices, explained that "I definitely am compartmentalized, and that part of me that acts out on those urges is different than the other part of me. And I don't have classic split personality tendencies, but it's remarkable how we're two different people. . . . But if I go out and cruise at noontime and find somebody that I can have a quick encounter with, that's just, me getting my urge taken care of." Again, "taking care of" his "urges" helped Ryan continue being a good husband and father.

Many others who described sex with men as an outlet for urges likewise said they felt that there were two different parts of themselves. As Jeff explained, "I guess sexual relationships with my wife are about unity and passion, and they take a long time, and they're about fulfilling each other's needs. Whereas sex with men is strictly about my own needs, and I suppose I make sure the other guy gets off as a courtesy, but it's mostly about urges." Here, sex with women is different from sex with men, and has nothing to do with relieving urges. Instead it is intimate and meaningful to identity, unlike sex with men. Like Ryan, Dan felt that his urges did not define his everyday life: "I'm not looking for men when I'm out and about, I don't look at men, I'm not searching for that kind of person or even really thinking about it during the day. I don't know, it's kind of like an urge or something that I have, and I want to do that, engage in, with another man. . . . [I]t's not at the forefront of my everyday thinking." Like Dan, other men I talked to denied that sex with men was a defining part of their lives. It was simply either an act of male camaraderie or a necessary and occasional safety valve. As Lance explained, "I guess I feel the urge over time and after a couple of months goes by, I finally give in to it." For some highly religious men, and a few others, desires for men were unwanted urges with one solution: sex with men. Finding another man to help relieve these urges in a masculine way, one that would not threaten other parts of their lives or question their identity, helped maintain their heterosexual masculinity.

Bud-sex involves unique interpretations that seem contradictory, but rework male-male sex as compatible with heterosexuality and masculinity. Not all of the men I talked to saw sex with men as "helping a buddy out" or acting on "urges," but it was important for those who did. By interpreting sex with men in these ways, they framed it as necessary and compatible with heterosexuality and masculinity. "Helping a buddy out" and relieving "urges" both involve masculine bonding with men, while also framing sex with men as distracting or problematic but necessary. In connecting sexually with men similar to themselves, men are able to address their desires in a masculine way without threatening their identities or normal lives. Despite its seeming contradictions, bud-sex allows men to maintain their heterosexuality and masculinity. Indeed, however counterintuitively, several feel that sex with men is necessary to preserve their heterosexuality and masculinity.

Sex with Men: Neither Gay nor Feminine

Bud-sex involves unique sexual and gender interpretations of bottoming or giving oral sex. The men I talked to largely rejected the association between being penetrated, in either oral or anal sex, and being gay, bisexual, or feminine. By doing so, they are able to reinforce their masculinity and heterosexuality. The men I talked to had a wide range of sexual preferences: fifty-seven (95 percent) had oral sex, thirty-two (53 percent) had anal sex, and three (5 percent) mostly mutually masturbated with male sexual partners. Of the thirty-two men who had anal sex more than a handful of times, ten (31 percent) mostly bottomed, ten (31 percent) were versatile, and twelve (38 percent) mostly topped.

All but twenty men reciprocated in oral or anal sex in at least some encounters. Of those who did not usually reciprocate, seven (35 percent) did not have anal sex, five (25 percent) mostly bottomed, two (10 percent) were versatile by topping and bottoming with different men, and six (30 percent) mostly topped. Thus, there was a fairly even distribution of penetration practices. No men questioned their masculinity or straightness when another man penetrated their mouth or anus. Only fourteen (23 percent) felt that their penetration practices had some associations with femininity or gayness,[7] and for most of them, the association was a temporary feeling associated with a pleasurable sexual practice. It did not affect how they saw themselves as straight, masculine men. Few considered their penetration practices as especially meaningful to their identity or that of their sexual partners. In short, what was critical to their masculinity and heterosexuality was not what they did sexually, but how they interpreted it. Sex with men was pleasurable, but it did not threaten their masculinity or heterosexuality.

The vast majority of men did not associate their sex practices with either femininity or gayness. Indeed, they did not give the possibility much thought. For most, penetration was simply an opportunity for pleasure. As David explained, "I know that some people do, they view it as the guy doing the fucking is the bull and the other one is something else. But personally I don't see it that way at all, it's a mutual sexual satisfaction, however you get it. I don't feel any less of a man if I'm bent over and he's in me, at all. I just don't." David enjoyed bottoming with his gay FWB, and this did not affect how he saw himself. Despite being one of the few men who reported a long-lasting sexual friendship with a gay man, his straight identity was similarly unaffected by his friend's gay identity. Bob, who was uncomfortable with "flamers," also enjoyed bottoming, and found his enjoyment unproblematic. He liked masculine men to top him, but did not feel less masculine for doing so, even as he acknowledged that it might seem "kind of weird": "That's one of the things that I kind of even in my own mind kind of find weird [laughs]. This is more of a girly thing to be doing, but that never enters my mind. I don't think I'm any less by any one of those acts."

Matt, even as he invoked an association between "feminine" identity and the receptive role, also dismissed that association: "I see it in movies, I don't know. And then they switch, so neither one is basically the feminine one. . . . I just think it's hot, that's all." Like Matt, several men said that gay male pornography had helped them see sex in terms of pleasure rather than identity. Many provided short, straightforward answers to questions on this topic, conveying nonchalance about their sexual practices. Jose simply said, "No. I just feel like it's something that I'm interested in. It doesn't bother me at all." Billy similarly shared, "I don't think it makes any [difference] one way or the other. I never thought of it."

The penetration practices of the men I talked to reflected their sexual tastes at any given time and were not meaningful for how they understood themselves as men. Jordan explained that "I find that very masculine men including myself love to give, and we love to receive [laughs]. I think for a lot of people it doesn't have anything to do with masculinity or femininity at all." In Connor's words, "I think of it as more of a pleasure thing" rather than an expression of identity.

The men I talked to perceived themselves as masculine and straight. Consequently, most interpreted penetration practices as neither feminine nor gay. Sean also stated that "when I have been penetrated I don't feel like any less of a man afterwards." Sex with men was simply a pursuit of pleasure. Particular acts did not have meanings associated with gayness or femininity. As Travis stated, penetration is "just part of the sex. I don't think it puts, I don't think it makes you feel one way or the other, it's just a part of getting off."

A number of men shared that giving or receiving oral or anal sex with men was similar to what they did with their women partners. Ernie felt that being penetrated is not related to femininity in part because he engaged in similar practices with his wife: "I consider myself very masculine but I love to suck cock. . . . I've had my wife use a dildo on me before, it doesn't make me feel less masculine so I don't [know] why it would be any different otherwise." Relatedly, Brandon felt that giving oral sex to a man was similar to giving oral sex to a woman: "I do the same thing to women is kind of how I see it. I wouldn't say I feel less straight when I'm doing it." Interestingly, even as the men I interviewed did not consider penetration related to femininity or gayness, several also likened giving and receiving between two men as similar to sex between men and women. Zach did not find penetration concerning or meaningful for how he understood himself, noting that "I don't think it's an either or, I think that it's just part of what you do in the process of enjoying one another and it's just part of the act." Adam felt that sex, no matter what form, was just a matter of pleasure:

> I don't necessarily see either one whether you're passive or active, it's just a matter of self-gratification and if you are gratifying someone. It's just, it's a mutual feeling that you share in the fact of the enjoyment of it. So it's like I love making my wife happy sexually and I have no problem making a guy feel good sexually. So I don't see either one being feminine or masculine, it's just gratification. . . . [and] I don't see it in terms of straight or gay or anything else.

In sum, most men did not view their penetration practices as especially meaningful for their sexual identity or masculinity. Instead, they felt that their practices were simply a way to experience sexual pleasure.

What was key for the men I talked to was not what they did sexually, but how they interpreted it. Most did not associate their penetration practices with femininity or gayness. Of the minority who did, most viewed the feeling of femininity or gayness as temporary (in the moment) and not meaningful for how they perceived their straight identity or masculinity. This is similar to those men who viewed bottoming as a temporary reprieve from the pressures of masculinity. These interpretations helped them understand their sex practices as compatible with heterosexuality and masculinity.

Bud-sex involves viewing sex with men as fun, perhaps even necessary to address desires, but not threatening to masculinity or heterosexuality. Sex is simply a pursuit of sexual pleasure or needs, not an expression of gender or sexual identity. The men I talked to identified as straight and masculine, and generally preferred their male sex partners to identify similarly. It follows suit that they would interpret their sexual practices in ways that would reinforce these identities rather than challenge them.

Not Cheating: Extramarital Sex with Men

By viewing sex with men as less threatening to marriage than sex with women, the men I talked to preserve their sense of themselves as good husbands. Being a husband was a key aspect of their identities, given that marriage is important within rural and small-town straight culture. Of the thirty-nine men who were in relationships with women at the time I interviewed them, thirty-six (92 percent) considered extramarital sex with men not to be cheating or to be less threatening than extramarital sex with women. Thirty-three of thirty-four married men (97 percent) felt this way, as compared to three of five men in nonmarital relationships with women (60 percent). Similarly, Alicia Walker, a sociologist at Missouri State University, found that many straight women who have sex with other women do not interpret that sex as cheating.[8] This finding suggests that many straight people view same-sex sex as irrelevant to their identities or marriages. Nonetheless, the men I interviewed who were in monogamous relationships knew that their partners would not approve of them having sex with men, so they kept it secret.[9]

The men I talked to offered two interrelated reasons why they perceived sex with men as less threatening to their marriages than sex with women. First, they felt that sex with other straight or bisexual men did not contain the same potential for emotional attachment as sex with women. Thus, sex with men would not threaten their marriages the way extramarital sex with women might. Relatedly, many said that their wives' loss of interest in sex left them no choice but to have extramarital sex. The men I talked to expressed varying degrees of guilt about extramarital sex. Whether for the sake of relieving urges or as a way of meeting sexual needs no longer met by their wives, however, most felt that sex with men was less threatening to their marriages than sex with women.

In both scenarios, the casual nature of sex with men was important. As Peter explained, "I guess I would say I view it differently because I would never hook up with another woman while I was married. I think it's because that would seem, I couldn't do that very casually. . . . [T]hat just feels like I'm looking for a relationship and not sex." Similarly, Marcus said, "I like to think that if I was with a girl I would be cheating, but if I was giving a guy a blowjob, that's not that big of a deal. It's a guy, there's no emotional attraction or nothing emotional there at all." Tom explained, in language that reflects the way many of the men I interviewed talked about the pleasures of penetration, that "I really don't think about it. For me, being romantic and emotional is more cheating than just having sex." He continued, "I kind of think of it as, I'm married to a nun," necessitating sex elsewhere. Other men, like Chris, acknowledged similar thoughts:

> I guess I just don't look at male sex as cheating, just it's something to do once in a while to just get some release. . . . I guess the attitude I have developed myself is if it's with a man it's not but if it's with a woman it is. Why I don't know. . . . I don't see any emotional views with anybody else. I've got my emotional here at home and I keep them separate. I don't quote unquote fall in love with another guy or anything like that. Friendship yes, but that's it.

Sex with other men was not romantic, and therefore not viewed as cheating. It was largely instrumental, casual, and free of expectations beyond the sex itself.

There were a few men, however, who acknowledged emotional attachment to some male partners. Jack, who was divorced for reasons unrelated to his sex with men, reflected on years of hooking up with men during his marriage:

> I do not view it as cheating. Except for when emotion should happen to be involved, and maybe that's the fear that I had with my buddy that I called it off. If we had been getting to develop feelings, then yes, it would have been cheating. If it was with a woman, if I was having an affair with a woman on the side while being married, I absolutely would call it cheating. But with a man to me, it's more just physical, get your nut off, and go on. Never see him again, so no, I do not believe it's cheating, in the situation, in the context that there's no emotion involved, I do not think it's cheating.

Sex with men was not cheating for Jack when it did not involve emotion. Even though most of the men I talked to said that sex with men naturally involved no emotional attachment, many did take steps to prevent romantic bonds that could have affected their partnerships with women.

Numerous men emphasized that because they were not going to leave their wives, sex with men was fairly irrelevant to their marriages. As Cain explained, "I think one way I have resolved it is that I'm not cheating on my wife. I don't have the intention of leaving her. . . . [and] I don't find myself tempted to do anything with a woman, other than my wife." He continued, "I would never cheat on my wife with another woman. It's like being with a guy every so often helps me kind of maintain, in fact sometimes it even seems like it helps me become a better lover to her, but that's maybe part of my rationalization, I don't know. . . . [I]t takes that edge off. And, kind of satisfies my, my interest or longings or, desires or whatever." According to Cain, sex with men helped him maintain his marriage. Ryan shared similar sentiments: "Even when I have an encounter now, I'm not cheating on her. I wouldn't give up her for that." Ryan, like the rest of the men I talked to, knew that most people would perceive extramarital sex with men as cheating. Still, *he* felt that it was not. By remaining committed to their wives or women partners, the men I talked to were able to understand their sex with other men as unproblematic or as less of a problem than extramarital sex with women.

Similarly, a handful of men said that they believed their wives would, if they ever found out, feel differently about them having sex with men than they would about them having extramarital sex with women. Extramarital sex with women might have led to romantic ties. It might also have indicated that men's wives were deficient in some way. Lance explained that "I view it [sex with men] as not cheating because there isn't a love aspect to it; if there was, I think I would call that cheating." Sex with women, on the other hand, "I would view that as cheating, I couldn't imagine if the situation came out explaining that one to my wife and being able to reconcile it. Whereas if it was a man, I think I could reasonably work it out."

Similarly, George explained, "My wife knows that I have done things with guys before, before we were married, [and] she knows that I've done things with guys since I've been married." He continued, "She has adamantly said that it isn't as bad to be with a guy as it is if I were to be with a girl, because then it's a self-confidence issue on her part that she's not satisfying me." George's wife, while unaware of his current sex with men, did not see his past sex with men as especially threatening. Joey echoed this, explaining that men are not "competitors" to his wife:

A lot of guys say things are not good in their marriage, or their wife has health problems and so on, and they go on to say but I don't want to cheat on her, which is why I'm doing this [laughs]. And I understand exactly what they're saying. And an affair with another woman, that happened once to us, and it was my fault, a long time ago, but it was very, very damaging, long-term damage, and I don't want to ever do that again. Now the obvious question is what if my wife finds out I'm doing this. Well, certainly it would be a sit-down kind of discussion topic, but I think it would be far more acceptable than if I had an affair with a woman. I can't fully explain that. I just think women have this real radar for other women, other competitors, and they're not going to see a male in the same way as they would see another woman competitor.

Val also described that he believed his wife would evaluate sex with men as less problematic than sex with women.

I don't look at it as cheating, I look at it as having a more complete sex life. I think if I were having it with other women then it definitely would be cheating. . . . I think that if I were to hook up with another woman and my wife knew about it she would be devastated by that. She would have a real problem with it and I would ultimately feel pretty guilty about it as well. I feel like my female [need] belongs to her. As far as with a man, I don't think she sees that as competition so long as it's not what I'm exclusively doing. I think she understands that it's something totally different than a man and a woman getting it on together and it's something that I need. So I don't think she has as much of a problem with it so long as there's no disease involved and so forth.

Men satisfy different sexual needs than women, according to Val, and consequently his sex with men would not threaten his wife. Whether or not they had first-hand experience of extramarital affairs with women, several men felt that their wives would see other women sexual partners as competitors in ways they would not see men. However, most who felt this way still kept their encounters secret. Whether or not they were right about how their wives or women partners might feel, these beliefs helped them feel as though sex with men was not as threatening to their marriages as sex with women.

For men in sexless marriages who chose men rather than women, "hooking up with a man is self-preservation. Hooking up with a woman is self-satisfaction," as Pat put it. He has sex with men because "I really didn't want to cheat on her." Within this formulation, sex with men is necessary to relieve urges, but not specifically urges for other men. Instead, their urges are simply expressions of a "normal" masculine sex drive. Brian, similarly, was not very interested in sex with men, but felt that it was the best option given that his wife no longer was interested in sex:

> Within the last year though I have gotten a few blowjobs from guys, simply because the wife's going through menopause and she's basically not interested, and when she is interested it's half-hearted, kind of thing. And I did actually pursue some women maybe a year and a half ago, but I always felt like I was cheating on her, so I never had sex with any women. More of an emotional back and forth, couple e-mails, that kind of thing, and then I always felt guilty, so I'd break it off.

Sex with men was not as enjoyable as sex with women, Brian explained, but it was better than nothing: "Within the past year though, I could actually say fifteen months, I've had a couple of blowjobs from guys. Simply, I felt like my balls were going to explode, and wife just genuinely was not interested. And it's almost like you might be starving to death and you'd rather have a steak but you stop at McDonald's because it's nearby, so that kind of thing. I don't think it's cheating." Brian also maintained that "basically, men are physical, women are physical, emotional, mental, spiritual, a mixture of all sorts of things. . . . I think me with a female would sort of like be cheating, not sort of, would be cheating on my wife. But me with a guy, that's just kind of busting a nut, it's just physical, jerk off, go, that kind of thing."

Adam shared similar thoughts: "I don't feel like I want to cheat on my wife with a woman to have sex. I know other men that are in the same situation and it became something that just happened." He continued: "My wife really doesn't necessarily enjoy sex, and I don't feel like I want to take up an affair or relationship with another woman. I don't feel right about that, so my sexual experience with other men is basically out of need to have some personal gratification." Adam explained that sex with women is "not cheating," because "men are a lot less complicated and it's just easier, it's like, it's sex but there's no attachment. I don't think women can do that."

These comments demonstrate that bud-sex relies on specific beliefs about gender. Women, and relationships with women, involve romantic attachment. In contrast, men, and sexual activity with men, are perceived as unemotional. When feelings are involved between male sex partners, those feelings are nonromantic and do not threaten other aspects of either man's life.

Several of the men I talked to perceived sex with men as not cheating because only sex with women counted as cheating. They framed this as being like finding a loophole in their marriage contract. Hooking up with men was, by default, "not cheating. Probably because it's with a person of the same sex," Seamus said. "And I would think that cheating is more with a person of the opposite sex." As Mike too acknowledged, "Once I got married and stuff, I promised her that she would be the only girl, and she has been." Sex with men was not considered cheating because cheating necessarily involves sex with another woman. Mike and others did not necessarily feel good about their secretive sex, but they felt that it was less threatening to their marriages than sex with women. Kevin echoed this:

> To me, meeting up with women would be cheating on my wife. And when I meet up with guys, I justify it by saying, well it's only fun between me and the other guy, it's not like I have another woman. . . . [I]f you cheated on your wife you would cheat [with] another woman. Having sex with another woman would be cheating on your wife. And I have a feeling that with another guy, doesn't. I'm sure she or other people would argue on that, but that's just the way I feel.

Given Kevin's understanding that cheating was necessarily between a man and a woman, he felt that what he was doing was not cheating. Brett also felt this way, and used his experience hooking up with two women to distinguish extramarital sex with men and women:

> I think whether it's right or wrong, my perception of having a guy is a little less like cheating than it was with a woman. And not everyone

would see it that way, the average South Dakotan would probably think that having sex with a guy is much worse than having sex with another woman. But maybe I was rationalizing my behavior in thinking that well, no, if we jack off with a guy or suck him off that's not quite as bad as having sex with another woman. I don't know why. I guess the traditional view of sanctity of marriage is you don't have sex with another woman. But marriage vows and such, at least in the old days, didn't address sex with another guy. It was just ignored as if it didn't exist. It was suppressed. Maybe that's why it didn't seem so wrong to me, I don't know.

Having had extramarital sex with both women and men, Brett felt as though sex with men was less problematic for his marriage: "I've met up with fifty-plus guys, I've met up with only two women. One encounter was quite positive, the other was not. And I think maybe the one experience was not as gratifying is it was a little too close to home, it seemed more like cheating, whereas I never really had that problem, never had that feeling at least, with another guy." Because Brett felt more easily able to separate emotion from sex with men than with women, he considered it fairly unproblematic for his marriage. Further, as he noted, it was not a violation of any vows, unlike the times he had sex with women.

In sum, most of the men I talked to who were partnered with women viewed extramarital sex with men as not cheating or as less threatening to their relationships than sex with women. They remained emotionally committed to their women partners and had no plans to leave them. They felt that sex between men was much less likely to involve romantic intimacy than sex with women, and was thus less problematic. They thereby resolved potential feelings of guilt, preserving their marriages or nonmarital partnerships with women. Equally importantly, they also preserved their understanding of themselves as straight, masculine, rural or small-town men. By viewing sex with men as unthreatening to their marriages, they also viewed it as fairly unthreatening to their straightness and masculinity. In short, the belief that extramarital sex with men is compatible with heterosexual marriage is a central element of bud-sex.

It is important to remember that most of these men considered it impossible to have an open relationship or tell their wives about their sex with men. Their partners, family members, friends, and living contexts constrained the choices available to them. They navigated their life constraints and came to the conclusion that secretive sex with men was the best option. Under these conditions, bud-sex flourishes, allowing men to address desires without affecting other parts of their lives, including their partnerships with women. Bud-sex also safeguards men from homophobia, whether from loved ones, from their broader community, or within themselves.

An additional note: I did talk to a few men who secretly had sex with men and still had sex with their wives. Many men no longer had sex with their wives, and thus did not increase their risk for STI transmission, but some did. Secretive sex with men paired with continued sexual involvement with unknowing women partners is obviously problematic. Few of the men I talked to addressed this problem directly. Given how easy it is to contract and transmit STIs, it is disturbing that men would threaten their wives' physical well-being, even if unintentionally. For the men who still had sex with their women partners, bud-sex was implicitly masculine in that it involved the pursuit of risk yet with little anxiety about consequences of that risk. This conflicts with the heterosexual masculine protector role that several described, but few acknowledged this.

6

Guys like Me

Most of the men I talked to had sex with men like themselves: masculine, straight or secretly bisexual, and white. This is not happenstance. Sex between similar men is fundamental to bud-sex. Partnering with similar men helps make the encounter seem more "normal" and thus compatible with straightness and masculinity. For the men I interviewed, having sex with men like themselves reflects and strengthens their embeddedness in rural and small-town straight culture. White, masculine, straight men reflect the composition of the rural and small-town communities in which these men find comfort and belonging.

Sexually partnering with men unlike themselves and unlike the men in their social contexts would have seemed more out of place and thus threatening to their identities. Hence the very institutions that encouraged their masculinity and heterosexuality also shaped their desires for particular kinds of men. Sex with fellow white, masculine, and straight or secretly bisexual men helped them feel more secure in their heterosexuality and masculinity. Being with men like themselves helped make the encounter seem more "normal" to them. It made sex a part of, rather than a departure from, rural and small-town masculine male bonding.

On sensitive topics like sexual partnering preferences, it is important to examine practices, especially when they diverge from stated preferences. I asked these men about their preferences for particular types of men as well as who they actually hooked up with. Overall, twenty-six (43 percent) stated a preference for other straight or bisexual, white, masculine men. Eleven (18 percent) stated preferences for two of those characteristics, and twenty-one (35 percent) stated preferences for one of those characteristics. When the men stated a preference for just one characteristic, that characteristic was usually masculinity. Only two men (3 percent) said they preferred gay, feminine men of color.

Yet, in practice, most men hooked up with men like themselves a majority of the time. Almost all usually had sex with men who shared two of three characteristics related to race, expression as masculine or feminine, and sexual identity. More than half (thirty-five, or 58 percent) reported that a majority of their male sexual partners were straight or bisexual, white, masculine men. Nearly a third (nineteen, or 32 percent) reported that a majority had two of those characteristics, and only five men (8 percent) reported that a majority of their sex partners had only one of those characteristics. Only one man reported that a majority of the men he had sex with had none of these characteristics (they were gay, feminine men of color). In short, while many men did not report preferences for sexual identity or race, their practices suggest otherwise.

It is impossible, of course, to know their exact sexual partnering histories, especially with regard to sexual identity. Many of their sexual encounters were brief or involved little conversation, and I did not interview their sex partners. For the purpose of understanding bud-sex, though, their partner's identities are unimportant. What matters is how men *think* their partners identify. Knowing or thinking that their sexual partners were straight or bisexual—and most importantly, perceiving them as masculine—helped put the men I spoke with at ease.

A disclaimer: the quotations in this chapter are hard to read. More than a few draw on stereotypes about feminine men, gay men, or men of color. Many stigmatize male femininity, express subtle (or overt) homophobia, or indicate racist ideas. I do not draw attention to every problematic statement because a majority are problematic in some way. It is important to keep in mind the problematic ways these men rationalized preferring certain types of partners over others.

Masculinity

The vast majority of men (fifty-one; 85 percent) said they preferred hooking up with other masculine men, and fifty-three (88 percent) said they hooked up with masculine men a majority of the time. This was true even of those who reported no sexual attractions to men. Masculinity was overwhelmingly the most important element in their partnering practices. This fact illustrates historical shifts in the relationship between gender and sexuality in America. In the late nineteenth and early twentieth centuries, many masculine men penetrated feminine men without feeling as though this affected their masculinity or "normal" sexuality.[1]

That is, a century ago, *gender expression as masculine or feminine* and *penetrating or being penetrated* were organizing elements for how men's sexuality was understood. The concept of sexual identity was not yet widely used at that point.[2]

Today, the *biological sex* of sexual partners is the organizing element for sexuality. Yet there is also a widespread perception that femininity is linked to male-male sex.[3] Hence men who engage in bud-sex distance themselves from femininity. They normalize their sexual encounters as masculine, and compatible with heterosexuality, in part by partnering with other masculine men.

While the men I talked to had a wide range of physical preferences, most defined masculinity in terms of mannerisms, demeanor, clothing choices, hair style, and voice rather than body build. Many said that if they wanted to have sex with someone feminine, they could simply have sex with their women partners. For most, it was important that women were feminine and men were masculine. Jack was one such man: "Totally masculine, I'm not into femininity at all. I mean that's what I got women for, in my mind. It's a turn off to me, femininity in a man is a turn off. That's what attracts me to men, the masculinity. And it's a turn off in a woman if she's masculine." Jeremy, too, stated that "I either want to be with a woman or I want to be with a man. I don't want to be with a man who exhibits extreme feminine characteristics." Most of the men I talked to were not interested in feminine men or masculine women. Hence, traits that suggested male femininity were undesirable. This meant paying attention to a variety of characteristics: how men carried themselves, mannerisms, grooming, voice, perceived attention to self-presentation, etc. George explained:

> I don't want a sissy femme guy at all. . . . Somebody that has more of those tendencies where, you can tell from when you look at somebody whether they're more masculine kind of guy versus more of a femme kind of guy, the way they talk, the way they walk, the way they act, things like that. I'm not talking about whether they're into sports or not . . . I'm just talking about the way they carry themselves.

Even while they paid close attention to masculine demeanor, an important part of masculinity involved not being overly attentive to one's own appearance. For instance, as Larry explained, he was interested in men who were "very masculine. Just demeanor, I am attracted definitely to someone that's not chiseled, they don't have to have a perfect body, they don't have to be manscaped, I like just good old hard-working type guys, not gross or sloppy by any stretch, but I definitely am attracted to more of a man's man type of person." Similarly, Jack said that "a masculine man is what turns me on. . . . I like hair, I don't like shaven anywhere, but I don't like so furry that they're a gorilla or something, there's a sweet spot in there, but definitely shaved nuts or whatever does not do anything for me. I like the deep voice of a man, I like legs, nice hairy legs, just masculinity all the way around." Many of the men I talked to expressed discomfort about feminine men, whom they perceived as artificial. Ryan, for instance, explained, "We've all met flamers, men or boys that. . . . have a certain kind of talk, and very effeminate mannerisms. And, masculinity's what attracts me, not that. . . . I'm not comfortable around femme." Ryan, like others, felt that feminine men behaved unnaturally and masculine men behaved naturally. He explained that he thought of "flamers" as men who "just act like they're really uncomfortable being guys, and they want to overact as female." This is of course not true. Still, Ryan's, Jack's, and Larry's statements reveal that "normal" rural and small-town masculinity depends on the lack of obvious femininity.

Like Ryan, a number of men expressed discomfort around feminine men. A handful elaborated on this, giving specific reasons why, most of which hinged on their association of femininity with emotion. Marcus, for example, offered that

it's hard to explain. But I would say, a guy that I would consider more like me, that just gets blowjobs from guys every once in a while, doesn't do it every day. And I know that there are a lot of guys out there that are like me. They're manly guys, and doing manly stuff, and just happen to have oral sex with men every once in a while [laughs]. So, that's why I kind of prefer those types of guys. . . . It seems that, in my mind, that a more masculine guy wouldn't harass me, I guess, hound me all the time, send me a thousand e-mails, "Hey, you want to get together today, hey what about today, hey what about now." And there's a thought in my head that a more feminine or gay guy would want me to come around more.

A number of men said that feminine-acting men were undesirable in part because they feared such men might become too emotionally attached. Their desire to avoid potential emotional attachment echoed their wariness about hooking up with women. These sentiments draw on stereotypical ideas about gender. Ryan, Jack, Larry, and others did not simply avoid feminine men. They actively sought out masculine ones. In the United States, masculinity is typically understood as less emotional, more pragmatic and instrumental. Hence, pursuing sex that did not have the potential for romanticism, and with equally masculine men, reinforced, rather than compromised, their masculinity.

Many men found *rural* masculinity, specifically, attractive. As Dan explained, the kind of man he liked was "I would say more masculine. . . . The outdoors kind of guy, man's kind of man, that likes to do man things, hunting and fishing and things of that nature that point towards a male, masculine man. . . . I would prefer somebody of my own kind of persuasion, of more masculine activities, more outwardly looking, acting masculine and performing in that way in everyday activity." Dan and others were not seeking to romantically partner with other men. Yet many nonetheless preferred men with hobbies and dispositions that reflected a rural masculinity. For men who were specifically seeking out casual sex, rather than relationships, this preference might seem irrelevant. What difference would it make if a man liked fishing or hunting? For men who are open to sexual friendships, however, it is important that their male sex partners have the potential to be buddies. Most people pick friends whose tastes and activities reinforce their own sense of identity. Men who engage in bud-sex are no different in this respect. As Bob explained, he preferred an "outdoors man, I like to go swimming, kayaking. I love to hunt, love to fish, somebody that I can do those things with and not have it all be about the sex." He contrasted the men he liked to

> these guys that sit around and play computer games and all that crap all day long, and bitching, complaining, that gripe worse than a bunch of old widow women, "you see the way that bitch did this," and then that gets back into those guys that are kind of flamers, they're like, "Oh, Charles, did you see the way he was dressed? That's just totally gaaay." And that's just the way they talk, what in the fuck, nobody talks like that, that's just a

stereotype and some people run with it. Maybe it works for them, I don't know, but it don't work for me, to me it's a huge turn off. I got to go the other direction when I see that kind of stuff happening.

Bob's statement demonstrates the association of rural masculinity with normalcy. "Flamers" and guys that complain "like women" are imitating a stereotype rather than speaking naturally: "Nobody talks like that." This statement is stigmatizing toward feminine men. Still, Bob and men like him prefer men whose "normal" behavior reinforces their own masculinity. These are men with whom they can form nonromantic, sexual friendships.

A sense of rural settings as secure and normal stands out in other ways too. Mike, for instance, preferred rural men for unprotected sex, without asking for STI tests. He did so because he felt that rural men were "too stupid" to constitute a risk:

I can pretty well feel people out. And when I have phone conversations and I ask questions or I'm texting or whatever the case is, and I ask questions and stuff, I don't feel that they would have any reason to lie. It all depends on where you're from, if you're coming from the city, absolutely not. Because if you're up in the city, there's all kinds of opportunities and all kinds of things going on, God only knows what you're involved in. And things like that. . . . I don't just go, when I talk with guys and stuff like that I don't just, I set it in advance.

Mike continued, explaining what he does to establish trust with his male sexual partners.

You don't just call me and say, "Hey, let's do it," and I leave and do it. No, sir, I have conversations, I have text messages, I say call me, and things like that because I want to hear your voice. And sometimes I know you can hear it in a person's voice, and different things like that. When I found a bunch of country boys [laughs], a bunch of rednecks and country boys here in [rural] Illinois is what you deal with. And, honestly, they're too stupid to do other things [laughs]. They are, they're too stupid to think of that stuff, even. So, no, I'm never worried about that. . . . That's why I get with these guys, these country boys, they ain't partying with nobody.

The apparent disdain in describing his sex partners as "stupid" is belied by the affection behind that description. Even though by definition he and the rural men who topped him without condoms were engaging in risky sex, he attributed risk to an urban, not a rural, setting. He felt more comfortable with rural men because he considered other straight, masculine, rural (and often white) men to be safer than other types of men.

Despite their desire for secrecy, many men, including Bob and Marcus, were open to or interested in forming sexual friendships with men. Mutual interests were important when there was potential for a sexual friendship. Bob, for instance, preferred having friendships with male sexual partners, and even publicly visible ones. Residents in his rural setting perceived these friendships as nonromantic and nonsexual. He preferred "someone, what you do in the daytime is what people see one way and then when the lights go out, it's a whole complete different ball-game." In describing this someone, he explained that

> he would be masculine. Very much so. . . . In appearance, in his attitude, in demeanor, knowing what they want and not pussy-footing around about things. Kind of a take charge kind of person. . . . [I'm an] outdoors man, I like to go swimming, kayaking. I love to hunt, love to fish. [I like] somebody that I can do those things with and not have it all be about the sex. . . . I just like the outdoorsy kind. . . . Guys I hooked up with about women, we don't even talk about that, women are never part of the equation. It's all about hunting and fishing and fucking [laughs]. That's the way my friend explained it, he said that's the way I am too, it's all about fishing, hunting, and fucking, and not necessarily in that order [laughs].

Marcus, in contrast, said he sought out straight and bisexual men because "we can talk about women or, there's been times where we've watched hetero porn before we got started or whatever, so I kind of prefer that." Both Bob and Marcus were seeking out men they saw as similar to themselves, who could be friends. As Bob said about one sexual friend, "He's a redneck. He's a cattle farmer with his dad and his uncle, he does all that outdoors stuff. . . . hunting and fishing. He's masculine in every way." Many of the men who described themselves using elements of rural areas also preferred those elements in potential sexual partners. They sought out rural, masculine, straight or bisexual male sexual partners. These are men who reflect and reinforce their own identities, and the communities to which they belong.

When explaining their preferences for masculine men, many of the men I talked to conflated masculinity with heterosexuality, just as they did when describing themselves. For instance, in describing his most recent male sex partner, Joey said he was "very much heterosexual. He had a pickup and a fishing boat and a family, [and] it's kind of cliché but certainly masculine. There would be no indication from his mannerisms that he was gay or had any kind of bisexual nature."

Joey was far from the only man for whom masculinity and heterosexuality were overlapping categories. Paul shared that he preferred a man who was "either straight or bi" because "I typically think of a gay man as the swishy feminine, and that's not what I want. If I want feminine I'll have a female." Many others also discussed preferred sexual partners as though femininity and gayness were almost identical. This was the case even among those who also acknowledged that gay men could be masculine. As Cain said, "I'm really not drawn to what I would consider really effeminate faggot types." Asked to explain the type of guy he likes, he offered this example: "I did hook up with one twenty-year-old guy, and we met at a little convenience store. He wanted me to get in his truck with him. Nobody would ever suspect that this dude would like to play with guys. And he's got like a shotgun hanging in his truck, in the rack, and he's a hunter type, and he in fact was dressed in like camo, kind of stuff." Unlike Bob and Marcus, Cain mostly did one-time hookups, though he was seeking a "regular bud" to keep his "urges" in check. His preference for men with overt markers of rural masculinity was common among the men I interviewed. Unlike most other men, though, Cain was not shy about being homophobic and using the word "faggot."

It is remarkable that the straight men I interviewed are more interested than gay men in masculinity and all things "man." While gay men tend to prefer masculinity in sexual partners,[4] there is also more variation in preferences among gay men. While the phenomenon is seemingly paradoxical, the men I interviewed reinforced their own sense of themselves as straight by investing in masculinity—their own and others'. This helped the men I talked to feel that their sex with men was "normal" and compatible with straightness. While it may seem gay or bisexual for a man to seek out masculinity in other men, it is also counterintuitively very "straight" as well.

Heterosexuality and Secretive Bisexuality

Overall, thirty-five of the men I talked to (58 percent) stated that they preferred straight or bisexual male partners, and forty (67 percent) reported that a majority of their partners were straight or bisexual. Estimates from a nationally representative survey, the 2011–2017 National Survey of Family Growth (NSFG), show that approximately 62 percent of men who had sex with men in the previous year identified as gay, 27 percent as bisexual, 10 percent as straight, and 2 percent as "something else."[5] Only about 8.2 percent of American men have had sex with another man in their lives, according to a different survey.[6] A far smaller percentage have had sex with a man in the preceding year: only 2.7 percent of men aged fifteen to forty-four, according to NSFG estimates. Thus, a majority of the men I talked to likely either sought out straight and bisexual men or misinterpreted how their partners identified.

Nonetheless, some men deliberately hooked up with gay men, often because there were few alternatives. Regardless, in many cases, gay partners' masculinity or whiteness helped the men I talked to feel more comfortable. These characteristics compensated for their sexual partner's gayness. However, a few men reported that they preferred gay men because they were better at giving sexual partners sexual pleasure or because gay men were more secure in their sexuality and masculinity than straight or bisexual men. These characteristics, a few men said, helped them feel more comfortable. Most of the men I talked to, however, did not feel this way.

There were four main reasons why a majority of the men I talked to preferred straight or secretly bisexual men. First was the belief that gay men are feminine. Second, and relatedly, was the desire to avoid romantic/emotional attachment. The men I talked to felt as though that would be more of an issue with (feminine) gay men than (masculine) straight or secretly bisexual men. Third was a belief that such men would be more likely to also want secrecy. And fourth was feeling more comfortable around straight or bisexual men than gay men. Many of the men I talked to felt that because straight and bisexual men were interested in or partnered with women, they had a similar "straight lifestyle." Indications of this included sexual identity, masculinity, and relationships with women.

Many men felt that having a wife or woman partner helped guarantee discretion. As Cain said, "Well, I like the masculine-looking guy who maybe is more bi." As he noted when discussing a recent sexual partner, "He mentioned having a girlfriend, and that's kind of a type that I would find more appealing to me." Cain felt more comfortable around these types of men because, he explained,

> I'm not out, and so someone who is out, I'm sometimes a little bit hesitant about what they may say to others or talk. Because somebody else down low is probably going to be a bit more respectful and not out somebody. . . . I typically like to be around guys that also have women in their lives. They're down low, it's kind of a boys' club kind of a thing, it's not like the effeminate gay club, I don't know how to describe it, but that's kind of where I am.

Cain felt that straight and bisexual men were better able to keep a secret than gay men. His statement about them being in a "boys' club" suggests the extent to which he sees himself and these other men as being similar. He conflated these characteristics with masculinity and sexuality: "And again if they're very effeminate I'm probably not going to be attracted. . . . I'm slightly more turned on if I know it's a straight or married dude, particularly if they're younger. . . . I'm thinking the kind of guy that's looking for a man and woman is going to be more of a masculine kind of a guy . . . not the effeminate type." Many others echoed these themes of secrecy and similarity. As Jack explained,

> He would be in the same boat as me. He would be straight, preferably married or definitely partnered up with a female, with one thing on his mind, getting his rocks off with me. . . . [T]hey are in the same boat as me, and they're not going to out me, and that is very important to me. In the society I live in, these are very, very hidden, deep feelings that nobody knows about. So I feel more secure with a married man because of that very reason, because that's all they want, just to get off with me and then go back to their lifestyle like it never happened.

Assurance of secrecy was key for Jack, as was preventing romantic attachment. Men in a situation like his were likely looking for the same sexual and emotional dynamic, he figured. Brian offered similar thoughts:

> I don't really want some guy calling me at all hours of the night or something like that. If the guy's married, then that's his first commitment. . . . I think like me, they like jerking off and then going on their way. I wouldn't say all three of them would march in a Pride parade or go to a gay club or something along those lines, I think all three like me are just trying to bust a nut since the wife's not doing their job. . . . I'm married, they're married, that just about virtually guarantees secrecy. Nobody wants a divorce.

Brian's comment about wives "not doing their job" indicates a sense of male entitlement to women's bodies. Regardless, in seeking out fellow married men, the men I talked to repeatedly mentioned their desire to maintain secrecy and avoid unwanted emotional attachment. Like others, Brian felt that feminine or gay men would be too likely to become attached and perhaps ruin his marriage. He felt this way even though many gay men enjoy casual sex. Nonetheless, a number of men I talked to said they believed gay men were more likely to become emotionally attached and should thus be avoided.

Others indicated a preference for bisexual or straight men because they felt that such men were more comfortable company. This preference reflects their feelings of belonging in straight culture and not belonging in gay culture. Moreover, most of the men I talked to were not used to interacting with openly gay men and did not necessarily understand them. Bud-sex involves hooking up with men who have a similar worldview and disposition. As Marcus said, "I don't think that I've ever met up with anybody that considered themselves gay at all." Regardless of the statistical unlikeliness of this, the point is that in his own perception of himself, Marcus said that he

> prefer[s] either straight or somebody that calls themselves bi. . . . Straight guys, I think I identify with them more because that's kind of [how] I feel myself. And bi guys, the same way. We can talk about women

or, there's been times where we've watched hetero porn before we got started or whatever, so I kind of prefer that. . . . I'm not attracted, it's very off-putting when somebody acts gay. And I feel like a lot of gay guys just kind of put off that gay vibe, I'll call it, I guess, and that's very off-putting to me. . . . I'm kind of talking about those people that you see and you don't have to hear them talk, you just look at them and you know that guy's gay. . . . I would say that they definitely look more feminine than a straight or bi guy.

For Marcus and others, a "gay vibe" means femininity. Seeking out men similar to themselves in disposition means seeking out men who identify as straight or bisexual, especially men partnered to women. Bud-sex involves sexual partners who perceive and respond to the world, and to sexual encounters, similarly. This includes partners who do not have a gay vibe, even if they are gay or bisexual. As Joe said, "Like me, he'd be open. He wouldn't be gay, he wouldn't obviously be gay, he'd be saying, 'Look, here it is, take it, that's as far as I can take it.' . . . [I prefer] bisexual because he would be of the same mind that I am. He would understand what I'm feeling and would respond probably similarly. So we could engage with common knowledge, that's why." Joe wanted men who were "open" to sex with men but closed to the possibility of romantic entanglement. He saw bisexual men as "of the same mind" in terms of masculinity, sexual interest, emotional availability, and outlook.

For these reasons, many of the men who met sexual partners online asked them their sexual identities before proceeding with meeting them. Ian, for instance, noted that "usually one of the questions I ask is like, 'Do you think of yourself as gay, straight, bi, something else?' Just to help get an idea of what this person is about, how this person picks, what this person gets into." He explained that one reason he did so was that he prefers men who are "probably similar to me, maybe possibly bisexual, but that's kind of pushing it. Mostly, straight." Joey similarly specified, "I'd be looking for a similar kind of guy who doesn't do this a lot, but on occasion with another, as I say, sane, married, or divorced guy—but a man who has identified all his life as heterosexual."

The men I talked to said that they typically preferred men who only occasionally hooked up with other men outside their marriage or partnership to a woman. They usually felt more comfortable with men who identified as straight or bisexual, especially if they were partnered to a woman. They believed that these types of men would have a similar worldview and way of engaging in sexual encounters. Whether preferring one-time hookups, purely sexual relationships, or sexual friendships, the men I interviewed tended to seek out guys similar to themselves.

This is a central component of bud-sex. This pattern is subtly homophobic, because it is exclusionary and draws on stereotypes about gay men. Otto acknowledged this but explained that he nonetheless preferred straight men: "Preferentially over a gay [man], if there's a straight guy that identifies like me, I would go I guess that way. I really honestly don't feel like I'm homophobic at all. I guess it would be just more, I don't know, more like me."

Whiteness

The majority of the men I talked to also preferred to hook up with white men, either to the exclusion of men of all other races or in addition to men of certain other races (often Latino, sometimes Asian) over others (usually black). They did hook up with men of color, but less often than they did white men. Thirty-five men (58 percent) stated preferences for white men, either alone or in combination with other races. Notably, fifty-five (92 percent) said that a majority of their partners were white. Although white people tend to explain same-race sexual or romantic partnering as coincidental,[7] over half of the men I talked to stated racial preferences. This indicates the extent to which their whiteness is intertwined with their sense of themselves as both straight and masculine. Of the men I interviewed, fifty-eight identified as white, one identified as "Hispanic," and one identified as multiracial[8] and said most people perceive him as white.

The gap between stated preferences and actual partnering practices is due in part to living in areas where the majority of residents are white, which rural areas in the Midwest, Mountain West, Pacific Northwest, and far Northern California typically are. It likely also reflects a preference for white men even among men who did not report such a preference. This preference corresponds to their desire to partner with men like themselves in other respects. As with straightness and masculinity, whiteness in sexual partners helped the men I interviewed feel more normal.[9] Their narratives suggest that they feel more comfortable with white men like themselves, even as they were also open to hooking up on occasion with men of color.

Many of the men I talked to who stated preferences for white men had trouble articulating why they did. This is typical when white people describe preferences or practices that are related to race.[10] Those who did offer explanations reported that it was more normal for them to partner with white men, said they felt more desire for men who looked and acted similarly to themselves, or noted that they could better relate to other white men.

Joey, in particular, offered a remarkably clear analysis: "I think it's just an embedded comfort level, I think a man of a different race would add sort of another complexity, another layer, and kind of to the psychology of it, and ideally it's just a focus on physicality, I don't want to deal with any extra psychology involved." Joey's statement perfectly details the relationship between whiteness on one hand and claims to masculinity and heterosexuality on the other. Having sex with a man of color would complicate his ability to shrug off the sexual encounter as normal and irrelevant to his identity.

While few men were so clear when explaining their preferences, themes of feeling normal, comfort, and a lack of "extra psychology" were echoed in what they did say. Erik noted that he prefers white men because "I guess it's what I would feel most comfortable around." Ian similarly acknowledged that he prefers white men "because I'm Caucasian, and I can better relate to [them] as a result." For many of the men I talked to, men racially similar to themselves were ideal. Kevin, struggling to explain his preference, said, "I would say I prefer white guys, but I mean I'm not a racist or anything like that. . . . I guess because I'm white, and I guess you'd say more normal for me to be with white guys." Paul, recognizing that "that's my hang-up with race," differentiated between men of color and the white American norm: "Well, he'd be white like myself. Just because that's my hang-up with race. Just because he'd be more like me. Culturally, whereas I see other races as not coming from the same culture and having differences there, I guess I think of, when I talk about other races, I think of immigrants who are just, still not into the American culture all the way yet. Western European–type culture is what I would be looking for, or American." Even though there are tens of millions of US-born people of color, Paul nonetheless perceived them as culturally different. This sense of greater comfort with white men was evident in Todd's narrative as well. Even as he acknowledged that "black guys, I've been with a few and they're nice," he said that "without sounding racist," he felt "more comfortable with a white guy" because "sometimes I think it should only be white-white." This statement is, despite the qualifier, racist.

The importance of whiteness as a marker of normalcy can also be seen in the hierarchy of sexual partners evident in most men's sexual preferences or sexual histories. Like Todd, many of the men I interviewed explained that the more racially similar potential hookup partners were, the more interested they were in hooking up with them. Latino or Asian men were, after white men, often the next most desired or common sexual partners, as Joe noted: "I'm white. The closer to white you get, Hispanic's okay, but the further from me you get, if you get to the black side, I'm just not in. My mind does not compute on that spectrum."

David described similar racial preferences at more length:

> White. Let me put it this way. Probably not a black guy. He could be Latin, possibly even Asian, but I would lean primarily towards white guys that are more or less like me, Anglo-European, that kind of thing. [I am] not turned off by others, and I would probably have sex with a black guy under certain circumstances, [but] I'd have to know him real well, have known him for a while, it wouldn't be like a "let's meet and do something." They wouldn't be my first choice, at least not the first time.

David's feeling that he would have to know a black man "real well" even while he is often comfortable in casual encounters with fellow white men reflects feelings of comfort around white men similar to himself. As Ian similarly explained, "Not to be racist or anything, but there are just certain physical aspects that in general I don't find attractive. In general, I would say I am typically more interested sexually in people that are Caucasian. Maybe Asian. Not very often someone that's African American." Even though most of the men I talked to tried to phrase their statements in ways designed to make them sound un-racist, their statements are, of course, racist.

When explaining preferences for white men, some men specified that they enjoyed men who were racially white but with darker skin tones. While most simply described their racial preferences as white, others were more specific. Harrison contrasted his preferences for men with those for women: "For women it would be white, German Irish, northern European. For a man it would be Southern European, Italian, Spanish, Middle Eastern." Beliefs about purity versus exoticism explained these differences: "The archetypical feminine woman is like a Renaissance lady from northern Europe. Like I said, I'm Irish German. I guess she's the Madonna. Then the guy, I want the opposite, dark, swarthy, hairy, just the opposite. Something that is completely foreign to the women I've interacted [with]. The men are completely foreign to the women I'm attracted to." Northern European ancestry is purer, according to Harrison, and men from Southern Europe or elsewhere in the Mediterranean region are less pure, more exotic, and therefore sexually desirable. Yet, notably, they are often still racially white. Harrison explained that he hooked up with white men about half the time and "Hispanic" men the other half, since they also matched his preference for darker, hairier men.

Similarly, Brandon noted that while "race is not necessarily an attracting factor," he explained that what he looks for is "tan, so Hispanic or even a mixed white person who tans well. I'm not really attracted to the pale skin or anything. So not necessarily race but more like a tanner tone of skin I guess." The preference for "tan" skin precludes many black people. Brandon's partnering history demonstrates this: Brandon estimated that about half of his sexual partners were white and the other half were "Hispanic," with one who was Asian.

Several men used racial/ethnic stereotypes to explain preferences for white men. Tom volunteered that "sometimes Mexicans can be a little impatient and a little rude, has been what I've found." Also invoking a nebulous quality of personality, Connor offered a more nuanced—and urbanized—hypothetical when surmising that "maybe just for the fantasy of it I'd have a black guy if it was a professional, serious type of black guy, not a hip-hop guy. I mean if you're going to make up a fantasy . . . then might as well go for the exotic thing." Due to his belief that professional black men were rare, Connor considered them "exotic." Aaron similarly indicated that cultural stereotypes about black men explain why he did not find them attractive:

I wouldn't have anything against a black person as a sexual partner just on the basis of their blackness . . . [I]t's not because of race, it's more because of lifestyle or attitude or whatever. It's like I don't understand things like the thug lifestyle, that sort of thing. But just specifically I wouldn't have anything against any race as far as an ideal sexual partner, it's just kind of, if there was absolutely nothing in common outside of the bedroom, that's where it wouldn't fit my ideal partner.

To Aaron, black men had little in common with white men; they were too enmeshed in the "thug lifestyle." This stereotypical description of black men draws on specifically urban archetypes, making black men seem even less appealing to him. Similarly, Lance noted that men of color were too different from him: "I've had very limited exposure to other races and the few that I did were not really compatible personality-wise." Jared too shared the fact that he prefers white men because "I would say they tend to have more personality, maybe more character. More I guess, I would say maybe a higher sex drive." Regardless of specific characteristics they attributed to race, many of the men I talked to felt that men of color, especially black men, were dissimilar from themselves. These beliefs are racist and reduce men of color to stereotypes.

Some men did not state racial preferences yet described features related to race that they found attractive, such as blue eyes. Cain explained the type of guy he likes using an example: "What we did, we drove to a graveyard in town that was remote, and we sucked each other off in his truck. I had him over to the house before. But again, he's that rugged, twenty-year-old guy, fucking eight-inch [cock], and he has black hair. And I'm trying to think if he has blue eyes, which that's also a big turn on to me, if a guy has blue eyes." Cain preferred young, masculine, white men who could demonstrate their masculinity through markers of rural activities like hunting.

Even many of the men I interviewed who did not state racial preferences for white men still stated that a majority of their male partners were white. This indicates the extent to which whiteness helped the men I talked to feel more "normal" when hooking up with other men. Their rural and small-town surroundings, in which a majority of residents were white, do account, in part, for why many hooked up with white men a majority of the time. Still, their mobility suggests that partnering with white men is due to more than just demographics: fifteen (25 percent) of the men I talked to reported hooking up with other men when traveling out of their town for work.

Further, a majority reported a willingness to travel at least some distance to hook up with men or reported hooking up with men while out of town for reasons unrelated to work (for instance, to see relatives or go on a vacation). Rural and small-town surroundings, therefore, do not represent the entire picture. For instance, Jack consciously sought to hook up away from where he lived, to safeguard his privacy: "I would always make sure [hookups] happened far away from home, from where I lived." Yet most of Jack's sexual partners were white, even when he hooked up in cities that had larger populations of men of color.

Additionally, many men reported that they hooked up with men who were passing through the areas where they lived. Billy, for instance, noted that "I don't even mess with guys here in town, normally travelers that trip through the area. Or I'll take a trip through Portland on the weekend, and I'll just go fucking nuts, sucking guys' dicks." Thus, despite men of color traveling to areas where the men I talked to lived, and despite the fact that the men I interviewed traveled to areas with more men of color, most still hooked up with white men a majority of the time.

In sum, the majority of the men I talked to hooked up with or stated preferences for men like themselves: masculine, straight or secretly bisexual, and white. Hooking up with men similar to themselves made the sex feel more normal and, thus, compatible with masculinity and heterosexuality. It is also possible that many of the men I talked to avoided black men in part because black men in America are often portrayed as hypermasculine, and so the men I talked to may have felt as though their own masculinity would be in question had they hooked up with a black man.

Overall, partnering with other similar men is a key element of budsex, which helps redefine sex with men as compatible with straightness and masculinity. This echoes findings in nationally representative samples, which show that LGBQ people are much more likely than straight people to have interracial partnerships. This finding even includes straight-identified people who have had past same-sex partners.[11] Identifying as straight makes it less likely that a person will enter into interracial partnerships. This is the case in part because straight people are less likely than LGBQ people to challenge sexual norms.

Why Whiteness?

There is more to be said about partnering practices based on race. By hooking up with men who looked the part of the masculine American archetype—rural or small-town, white, and straight or secretly bisexual—the men I talked to were able to interpret the sex they had with other men as inconsequential to their identities. Hooking up with men similar to themselves, and by extension men common in the areas where they lived, allowed the men I interviewed to reinterpret sex with men as unthreatening to their masculinity and heterosexuality. This in turn preserved their feelings of belonging in rural and small-town white, straight culture. Hooking up with white men a majority of the time is in part due to the demographics of the areas where the men I interviewed lived. It also, however, reflects how rural and small-town white, straight culture shaped the men's desires for other white men.

Nationally representative data from the 2011–2017 National Survey of Family Growth suggests that whiteness is particularly important for straight white men who have sex with men. Among straight men who have had two or more male partners, there is a statistically significant relationship between their own race and the race of their most recent male sexual partner.[12] Straight white men were much more likely to hook up with a man of their same race than straight Latino or black men or gay/bisexual men of any race. While same-race partnering is the general rule for most races and sexualities,[13] it is notable that straight white men had by far the highest rate of same-race partnering. This again suggests that whiteness helps make the sexual encounter feel more normal and thus compatible with heterosexuality and masculinity.

Their Own Racial Perceptions

A related but harder-to-answer question is to what extent sex with men was related to the racial identities of the men I interviewed. While only two men identified as something other than white, two other men identified as white yet reported a complex understanding of their racial identity. Just as they identified as straight and masculine despite sex with men, they identified as white despite nonwhite ancestry. Sean, for instance, said, "I'm mostly Caucasian although I do have some Hispanic in me, and maybe some black, some African American in me. That part has not been confirmed, but there's rumors about my grandmother. And I have some features that indicate maybe that's true, and I do have darker skin than most Caucasian men do . . . but I identify myself as Caucasian. But I definitely would never be accepted into the Aryan Nation [laughs]." I interviewed Sean over the phone and do not know what he looks like. According to his account, he is not immediately perceived as white in rural Oregon. He also explained, "I would say I'm heterosexual for the most part, but occasionally I like to expand my horizons, I guess." Interestingly, the way Sean perceived his masculinity was just as complicated:

> Masculinity, I'm a typical, I got to say I look like a biker, I ride Harley, I like guns, I shoot guns, I own a farm, a small farm in addition to my work. I drive pickup trucks, just very typical for someone like me. I'm very strong, fairly athletic, I lift weights, I got big arms, big biceps and chest muscles and stuff, and so that's my masculinity and that's what everybody sees of me. But, in a feminine side of me, I actually secretly am a cross-dresser, I like to wear women's lingerie, kind of dress like a woman a little bit. . . . I have a few pairs of panties that I carry around with me in my backpack. I've gone to some other guy's houses a couple times wearing those.

Sean reworked his multiracial heritage, occasionally feminine gender practices, and sex with men as compatible with identification as white, masculine, and straight. Being straight, white, and masculine is "normal" in his rural context, so it is unsurprising that he identified with those categories.

Richard, similarly, identified himself as being "as masculine as John Wayne," adding, "My views of my own sexuality would be that I'm straight, but I do happen to enjoy certain aspects of sex with another man." In that sense he was like most other men I interviewed. He also, however, reported that he had a "quarter" Native American ancestry. He too described his racial heritage as complex but nonetheless identified as white: "I'm a dyed-in-the-wool Caucasian. My ancestry is German, English, Native American, and a little bit of nigger in the woodpile. So, pretty well a mixed bag there. But Caucasian, European Caucasian."

Richard's description of his black heritage is racist and offensive. His identification as "European Caucasian," despite his black and Native American ancestry, underscores his efforts to identify with what he perceives as what is normal: whiteness. Neither Sean nor Richard are "wrong" to identify as white, since whiteness is a socially constructed concept.[14] Instead, their identification as white reveals their attempts to identify with what seems normal to them. They provide additional evidence that many men seek to identify with normalcy, despite characteristics and behaviors that may have otherwise challenged feelings of being normal. Notably, Jose, who identified as "Hispanic" and said most people perceived him that way, also preferred white men and hooked up with them a majority of the time. This behavior further suggests that living in rural areas and small towns in which a majority of residents are white shapes these residents to desire other white people.

Conclusion

What if male heterosexuality and masculinity are not always what they appear to be? I have been exploring this question by talking to men who identify as straight yet have sex with other men. None considered sex with men an important part of how they understood themselves. They did not identify as straight because they were closeted gay or bisexual men. Instead, they identified as straight because they saw themselves as straight, masculine men and did not want to change that identification. They had complicated gender and sexual identities but ones that they believed made the most sense for them, given other aspects of their lives. Sex with men was largely irrelevant to their identities. Their stories are filled with irony and paradox, and are complicated. The results are messy, which is exactly why this subject is so interesting. It is complex and nuanced, and for that reason we can learn a lot from it.

Men who seem unusual because of disconnects between how they identify and how they behave show that sexual identity is not just an individual trait mirroring attractions or behaviors. It also reflects being a part of certain institutions and communities. The men I interviewed knew they could *potentially* identify as gay or bisexual, but they had little interest in doing so. They were embedded in straight culture and wanted to stay that way. This was partly the case because they enjoyed the benefits of identifying with a socially dominant group. It was also partly psychological, in that they derived comfort from being part of a dominant culture.

Identifying as straight also protected them from discrimination and kept them from experiencing rejection from loved ones. And part of their reason for identifying as straight is that they felt as if identifying as anything else would threaten how they understood themselves as men. In other words, these men were invested in masculinity, ironic as that may seem, given that they had sex with men. They identified as straight in part to preserve their sense of themselves as masculine.

Just as interestingly, many of the men I talked to were not particularly attracted to other men. They had sex with men because they wanted sex outside of marriage and felt that sex with men was not cheating or was less threatening to their marriages than extramarital sex with women. To them, women could not be trusted for hookups, but men could. Ironically, the importance they placed on marriage encouraged them to have sex with other men. So too did their beliefs that men and women were natural emotional partners, which therefore made casual sex with women risky or even impossible. Again, these men's stories are filled with irony and paradox, and yet they are genuine.

The concept of "straight culture" connects past research on sexuality and gender, as well as this book's findings. Most people are embedded within institutions and communities that uphold social norms that encourage heterosexuality for everyone, femininity for women, and masculinity for men. While straight cultures look and operate differently depending upon context, most of them perpetuate gender inequality, expectations of heterosexuality, and the assumption that there are only two "opposite" genders, in different ways and to varying extents. Thus, even many people who have same-sex attractions or sexual behaviors—like the men I talked to—identify with heterosexuality because they are a part of straight culture. Hand in hand with being embedded in straight culture are feelings of security being part of a dominant group, as well as comfort knowing they will never experience stigma on the basis of their sexuality.

These Men Are Psychologically Okay

Should we be concerned about the psychological well-being of men who have sex with men yet identify as straight? The men I talked to experienced varying levels of internalized prejudice. Still, they identified as straight mostly because they were embedded in rural and small-town straight culture. They reported satisfaction with their communities, which were composed mostly of other straight people. Those with women partners said they loved their partners and had no plans to leave them. They found great meaning in being a partner or a father. Most felt that their sense of themselves as men was tied to their straight identity.

The happiness of these men contrasts with portrayals of them as miserable and secretly gay or bisexual, as in *Brokeback Mountain*. A more accurate cultural reference is Oliver in the film *Call Me by Your Name*. This 2017 film was directed by Luca Guadagnino and is based on a novel written by André Aciman. In it, Oliver experiences a summer of passion with another man, Elio, but nonetheless decides to marry a woman and (presumably) identify as straight. He enjoys sex and romance with Elio but is also embedded in straight culture. The men I interviewed were similar in that they enjoyed the sexual (and sometimes, temporarily romantic) company of men, but not in a way that would affect other aspects of their lives. This seemingly contradictory behavior did not make them miserable, either.

In terms of mental health or substance abuse, straight MSM are not much different from other straight men, according to research from several nationally representative samples.[1] In other words, they are not being torn apart by a "mismatch" between how they identify and how they behave. It is therefore unwise for others to try to force them to identify as gay or bisexual, and the costs of doing otherwise can be severe. Ryan, for example, saw a therapist who suggested that he come out as gay, and he found this so upsetting that he considered suicide. Eventually Ryan decided to continue identifying and living as straight and was happy that he did.

Clearly, mental health professionals should encourage men who secretly identify themselves as gay or bisexual to disclose their sexual identity, with the hope that they will have an opportunity to share this information with their loved ones. Mental health professionals should also, of course, challenge internalized prejudice among men of all identities. Asking men who identify as straight to come out as gay or bisexual, however, may cause more psychological harm than good, despite the best of intentions.

Ideally our social world would be without pressures and constraints that shape people to identify themselves in particular ways. Sadly, we do not live in a perfect world. How people understand and express their gender and sexuality is deeply affected by social context. Inequalities in our social world affect the options that are available to individuals when it comes to living their lives, as well as how people understand themselves. The fabric of society needs to change so as to not unfairly favor heterosexuality for everyone, masculinity for men, and femininity for women. People should be free to identify and express their sexuality and gender in ways they find most comfortable.

As we work towards this goal, we need to acknowledge that many people today are embedded within straight culture due to expectations of heterosexuality that structure almost every institution and social context. We need to eliminate prejudice and expectations of heterosexuality, not shame straight MSM for having an "incorrect" identity. Criticizing straight MSM for their identity makes it seem as though individuals are the problem when in fact it is larger structural forces that shape how people identify and act. Imposing identities on the men who are quoted in this book, or on any other individuals, benefits no one. Doing so is not good for straight MSM, as they do not want that. It is also not good for LGBTQ people, who would be forced to deal with men who do not want to be a part of their communities. In short, it is essential to acknowledge and respect individuals' identities. At the same time, it is necessary to challenge social mechanisms that perpetuate gender and sexual inequality.

Theoretical and Practical Implications

Acknowledging the existence of straight cultures helps reveal more about heterosexuality, which until recently has been neglected in research. Heterosexuality is many things at once: an identity, an institution, a way of relating to the world, and a culture. Like all cultures, it has institutions that undergird it and communities that are connected to it. Most straight men do not have sex with other men, of course. Those who do, however, like the men in this book, show how and why many men come to identify as straight and masculine. Sexual identity is not just a shorthand for attractions or sexual practices. It also reflects embeddedness in some communities and institutions over others.

For this reason, straight MSM are not queer. The men I talked to happily aligned themselves with heterosexuality and masculinity. Their sex with men did not detract from this. There is nothing inherently transgressive about male-male sex.[2] Yet collectively, their experiences "queer" understandings of sexuality and gender. They show that men's sexuality and masculinity are flexible over the course of one's life. They also show that heterosexual identification reflects being embedded in certain cultures rather than biological destiny. *Attractions* reflect biological influences,[3] but *identification* as straight and masculine is in large part a social product. The men I talked to became straight and masculine through socialization in institutions that undergird straight culture. They maintained these identities through life decisions, like forming families with women partners and preventing romantic attachments to other men. Heterosexuality and masculinity are affected by social processes, just as are all other identities.

A key conclusion, then, is this: heterosexuality should be considered less a reflection of attractions and sexual behaviors and more an indication of how people live. This includes belonging to certain institutions, having relationships with particular people, feeling that it is necessary to identify as straight to be masculine, and of course enjoying being part of a socially dominant group. A shorthand for all these things is "straight culture."

Another set of complicated questions arises about marriage. In the United States, children are taught that marriage is a loving union between two people, typically (although these days not exclusively) a man and a woman. If that is true, why would one spouse "cheat" on the other? Why would the cheating partner not communicate with his or her spouse about the desire for extramarital sex? Is the spouse pretending to not know what is going on, or does the spouse actually not know? If they know, why do they not say anything? If they do not, how could they never notice anything? I cannot answer these questions, but they are worth considering. Only 36 percent of married or cohabiting Americans are very satisfied with their sex life.[4] Perhaps unsurprisingly, then, about one out of every six Americans has had extramarital sex, and around 3 percent of people do so each year.[5] Interestingly, there are major differences by age cohort. People in their fifties and sixties are more likely than younger people to report extramarital sex.[6] Men are more likely to "cheat" than women.[7] The findings from this book help explain these numbers. Communication between spouses clearly needs to improve, and not just when it comes to the category of men that I interviewed.

Extramarital sex is complicated. On one hand, extramarital sex may actually help marriages where the main issue is that one partner no longer wants sex and the other does. Even women who have extramarital sex with men say this.[8] On the other hand, if the spouses do still occasionally have sex, the noncheating one is being put at risk for STIs without his or her knowledge. If the spouses are no longer having sex, however, the main issue is the lack of communication and honesty. This must be considered alongside the benefits of extramarital sex: the partner wanting to have sex having it, the partner who does not want sex not feeling pressured to have it, and the otherwise happy marriage continuing.

It would perhaps benefit many marriages if they could be open. Both partners could communicate their needs and have their sexual desires met elsewhere if necessary. Open relationships are not necessarily a threat to marriage. Under certain circumstances, they could actually help preserve them. Regardless, the findings from this book and other research show that spousal communication needs to improve, in terms of both sexual and nonsexual issues. Relationships need not be sexually open, but they do need to be undergirded by clear communication and mutual respect.

A Few Final Notes

Many of our assumptions about straight men who have sex with men are flawed, partly because their sex is secretive. The more we study them, the better we will understand the choices men make when navigating sexual identification, masculinity, and sexual preferences.

The men I interviewed seem exceptional for having a disconnect between how they identify and how they behave, since sexuality is such an interesting topic. But how exceptional are they really? It is very common for people to describe themselves one way but do something that seems to contradict that identity or description. We see this in all aspects of social life. Our social world is filled with contradictions and disconnects between how people describe themselves and what they actually do. The men I interviewed are actually quite typical.

ACKNOWLEDGMENTS

I could not have completed this project without the support of my mentors, colleagues, and loved ones. C. J. Pascoe provided unforgettable professional and intellectual mentorship. C. J. also reminded me of the importance of work-life balance, which helped me work hard during the week and recharge on the weekends by hiking the many beautiful trails in Oregon, Washington, and far Northern California. Thank you also to Kristen Barber, Raoul Liévanos, and Peter Alilunas for their feedback. Kristen, thank you for providing mentorship from the beginning of this project to the very end. I also want to thank Clare Evans, who taught me complex quantitative multilevel data analysis skills and helped me develop as a scholar through her teaching, mentorship, and collaborations on our coauthored papers. Thank you also to Liahna Gordon, my undergraduate mentor at California State University–Chico. It is because of Liahna that I became a sociologist in the first place. I would not be the scholar I am without all of these mentors.

I also want to thank those who helped turn this book into a reality. Thank you to Ilene Kalish at NYU Press for supporting this project from its proposal to the completed book, and for providing feedback that helped clarify main points. Thank you also to the other folks at NYU Press who worked hard to put together this book. Additionally, I wish to thank two outside editors, Tedra Osell and Connie Rosenblum, for their work on drafts of this book that made its writing much more accessible and its main points clearer. Thank you also to the anonymous reviewers of this book manuscript, who provided helpful feedback.

Many thanks also to the institution that funded my postdoctoral work: the Sexualities Project at Northwestern (SPAN). Thanks to SPAN, I had two years of funding support to turn this project into a book. Héctor Carrillo and Gregory Ward, the codirectors of SPAN, both helped me professionalize and become a more effective scholar.

Of course, I also want to thank the sixty men I interviewed, who opened up to me about their personal lives. For many, I was the only person they ever told about their experiences. Thank you to these men for trusting me.

Many thanks also to my loved ones, in no particular order: Mom and Dad, Kari, Shon, Tanya, Lauren, Ashley, and Janeth. I would not have completed this project without their love and support.

METHODOLOGICAL APPENDIX

Recruiting men for this project was challenging. Many men who reached out to me were hesitant to take part in the study because of how secretive they were. Countless others, surely, never reached out for the same reason. When someone did contact me, I established trust by answering his questions over e-mail as well as by walking him through the consent form and identity-protection procedures approved by my institution, such as never releasing any identifying information. This helped to put men who were initially nervous at ease. Several men also said that they had researched me online and saw my academic e-mail address as proof that I was a legitimate researcher.

In any study, it is important to make sure answers are valid. I trusted what these men told me for several reasons. First, the time commitment involved with the interview probably deterred any would-be jokesters. A one- to one-and-a-half-hour interview is a sizable investment of time. Second, the fact that I did not pay the men meant that there was no financial motivation for them to make up answers. Third, there are few documented cases in qualitative social science research in which someone gave an interview and was later found to have given mostly false statements, in part because of the first two reasons.

Fourth, I went through transcripts to make sure that the men I interviewed did not give statements that contradicted ones they had made earlier in the interview. Their statements were consistent, including to questions I asked them about their past and about the timeline of events. It is almost inconceivable that someone could participate in an interview for laughs and then give fake statements over one to one and a half hours that never contradicted one another. The only times answers did not "match" were in the places where men discussed racial preferences and their actual racial partnering histories. This makes sense because most white people report these kinds of disconnects to avoid sounding racist.

Fifth, many of the men said they participated for one of two reasons. Many said they had earned master's or doctoral degrees and remembered having a difficult time recruiting participants. Their knowledge of the research process, including institutional and federal rules about protecting data, made them more comfortable sharing information. Additionally, many said that being able to talk to someone about this often-taboo subject was a relief and almost a sort of therapy. Simply allowing these men to talk about a part of their lives that they could discuss with almost no one else was appealing for many of them. This is, relatedly, why many of the men I interviewed were clear and thoughtful in their responses. They had thought a lot about their lives and wanted to talk honestly about them.

The most challenging aspect of the research was simply finding willing men. While recruiting between 2014 and 2017, I received 654 responses from Craigslist advertisements. The fact that so many men e-mailed me, but did not follow up, shows how secretive and difficult-to-access these men are. This 654 figure does not include men who were ineligible to participate (for instance, if a man e-mailed and said he identified as gay). It also does not include snarky comments, like the following:

E-mail 1: This is a ruse to find hookups, right?
E-mail 2: Oregon pollster? Sound[s] like someone hoping to twist some figures to promote the gay agenda. . . .
E-mail 3: Wow. There's an angle I haven't seen in a while. Nice try but your act has been done before.

E-mails like this were common. Intriguingly, several people who responded to my ads thought I was not actually a researcher but someone with a sexual kink. They lost interest when they found out I was not role playing and was just a researcher who needed to interview men. That makes me wonder how many people pretend to be researchers as part of an elaborate sexual role-playing fantasy.

Of the 654 contacts, 36 scheduled interviews but later either canceled or never followed up. Two of them called me on the phone before hanging up just minutes into the conversation. Relatedly, twenty-six men refused a telephone interview or sought more privacy. Another three only agreed to participate with compensation, which I could not provide. Lastly, at least thirty-six men asked me for sex in return for participation or sent pictures of their penises, and never followed up on an offer for a nonsexual interview.[1] (I should also make it clear that I never had sex with any of the men I interviewed.)

TABLE A.1. Participant Characteristics[a]

Characteristic	Frequency	Approximate Percent of Sample
Attraction:		
Only men	2	3.3%
Mostly men	6	10%
About equally men and women	13	21.7%
Mostly women	32	53.3%
Only women	7	11.7%
Age:		
Adult teenager	1	1.7%
20s	4	6.7%
30s	9	15%
40s	6	10%
50s	19	31.7%
60s	14	23.3%
70s	7	11.7%
Relationship status with women:		
Married	34	56.7%
Nonmarital relationship	5	8.3%
Divorced or widowed, currently single	9	15%
Single, never married	12	20%
Education:		
Less than high school	1	1.7%
High school	3	5%
Some college, an associate's, or trade school	23	38.3%
Bachelor's	16	26.7%
Master's	12	20%
PhD or professional degree	5	8.3%
Race/ethnicity:		
White	58	96.7%
Latino	1	1.7%
Multiracial	1	1.7%

[a] Percentages for age and race/ethnicity do not add to 100 due to rounding.

TABLE A.2. Participant Information*

Name & Age	Relationship Status to Women	Self-Identity	Level of Attraction
Rex, 19	Partnered, never married	"Straight male, but I'll take just about anything."	Mostly women
Ernie, 21	Married	Straight	Mostly women
Glenn, 26	Single, never married	Straight	Mostly women
Brandon, 28	Dating, never married	Straight	Mostly women
James, 28	Single, never married	Straight	About equal
Peter, 32	Married	Straight & mostly straight	About equal
Neil, 34	Married	"Straight, with a little curious side."	Mostly women
Jose, 35	Single	"Straight but curious"	Mostly men
George, 37	Married	Straight	About equal
Larry, 37	Partnered, never married	Straight	Mostly women
Jeff, 38	Married	Straight	Mostly women
Marcus, 38	Married	Straight	Only women
Jon, 39	Married	Straight	About equal
Mitch, 39	Single, never married	Straight	Mostly women
Joshua, 40	Partnered, never married	Straight	Mostly women
Ian, 42	Single, never married	Straight & mostly straight	Mostly women
Connor, 43	Single, never married	Straight	About equal
Bob, 46	Married	Straight	Mostly men
Seamus, 47	Married	Straight	Mostly women
Jeremy, 49	Single, never married	Straight	Mostly women
Cain, 50	Married	Straight & bisexual	About equal
Dan, 50	Single, divorced	Straight	Mostly women
Mike, 50	Married	Straight	Only men
Eli, 52	Married	"Straight with lots of curiosity"	Mostly women
Jack, 52	Single, divorced	Straight, "with some bi tendencies"	Mostly men
Otto, 52	Married	Straight	About equal
Rand, 52	Single, divorced	Straight	Only women
Will, 52	Single, divorced	"Straight-leaning bisexual"	About equal
Lance, 54	Married	"I guess more often than not heterosexual. I just experiment with the bi occasionally."	Mostly women
Brian, 55	Married	Straight	Only women
Harrison, 55	Single	"It's fluid but I would say straight or bi. Straight."	About equal

TABLE A.2. *(cont.)**

Name & Age	Relationship Status to Women	Self-Identity	Level of Attraction
Paul, 55	Married	Straight	Mostly women
Adam, 57	Married	Straight	Mostly women
Sam, 57	Single, divorced	"Mostly straight with a little bit of bi"	Mostly women
Todd, 57	Single, divorced	Straight & gay	About equal
Sean, 58	Partnered, never married	"Heterosexual for the most part, but occasionally I like to expand my horizons"	Mostly women
Billy, 59	Married	Straight & bisexual	Mostly women
Tom, 59	Married	Straight	Mostly women
Travis, 59	Married	Heterosexual	Mostly women
Matt, 60	Married	"Straight but bi, but more straight"	Mostly men
Ryan, 60	Married	Straight & mostly straight	Mostly men
Mark, 61	Married	Straight & bisexual	Mostly men
Chris, 63	Married	"Straight with I guess bi interests"	Mostly women
Jared, 63	Married	"Straight, bicurious"	Mostly women
Joe, 63	Married	Straight & bisexual	Only women
Brett, 64	Married	Bisexual & straight depending on context; more bisexual	About equal
Jordan, 64	Married	Straight	Only men
Aaron, "mid-60s"	Married	"Romantically straight and sexually bi"	Mostly women
Joey, 66	Married	Heterosexual	Mostly women
Trevor, 66	Single, widowed	Straight	Only women
Chad, 67	Partnered, divorced	Straight & mostly straight	Mostly women
Vince, 67	Single, never married	Straight	Mostly women
Kevin, 69	Married	Straight & mostly straight, with "a percentage towards bi"	Mostly women
Zach, 70	Single, widowed	Straight	About equal
Erik, 71	Single, divorced	Straight	Only women
Val, 72	Married	"Primarily heterosexual"	About equal
Pat, 73	Married	Straight & bisexual	Mostly women[a]
David, 74	Married	Straight	Mostly women
Donald, 74	Single, divorced	Straight	Mostly women
Richard, 75	Single, divorced	Straight	Only women

[a] I reinterviewed Pat after several years, and his attractions had shifted from only women to mostly women.
* This table intentionally excludes additional information, which may pose a threat to confidentiality. All information is what the participants reported at the time of the interview.

NOTES

INTRODUCTION

1 Data are from the National Survey of Family Growth (NSFG) 2011–2017, a nationally representative survey. See U.S. Department of Health and Human Services 2018 for more information. The NSFG is conducted continuously and is released in waves: 2011–2013, 2013–2015, and 2015–2017 were available at the time I wrote this book. I combined these waves and recalibrated weights according to guidelines in technical documentation. The combined NSFG dataset includes data from men aged fifteen to forty-four not currently residing in an institutional setting. In most statistical estimates, I excluded men from analysis if they (1) reported a history of sex work, (2) reported nonconsensual sex with men and exclusive attractions to women or reported being unsure about their attractions, (3) identified as straight and reported nonconsensual sex with men, or (4) reported only two lifetime male sexual partners and reported that their first same-sex sexual experience happened when they were under the age of fifteen. Thus, estimates from the NSFG are for straight men who had had consensual sex with multiple male sexual partners when they were aged fifteen years or older. All estimates are weighted with person, strata, and cluster weights.

2 Preliminary studies for this project I published in peer-reviewed journals, including *Gender & Society* and *Sexualities*. See Silva 2017 and Silva 2018.

3 See for instance my projects examining nationally representative data, including Silva 2019 and Silva and Whaley 2018.

4 Dameron 2019.

5 Hensley, Tewksbury, and Wright 2001 and Kunzel 2008. Notably, there is little social science research about straight men having sex with other men in prison.

6 Oselin and Barber 2019.

7 Top: inserting in anal sex. Bottom: receiving. Versatile: topping and bottoming, with the same man or with different men. Most MSM are to some degree versatile, though many prefer to top or bottom. These preferences are not necessarily related to how masculinely or femininely a man expresses himself, nor to body type.

8 The 2011–2017 National Survey of Family Growth (NSFG), which surveyed American men aged fifteen to forty-four not currently residing in an institutional setting (U.S. Department of Health and Human Services 2018). The 95 percent confidence interval was 551,582 to 860,068. Estimates should be evaluated with caution due to small sample sizes.

9 The 95 percent confidence interval was 162,713 to 300,550. This is likely an under-estimate, given that same-sex sexual practices and attractions are substantially underreported even in anonymous surveys (Coffman, Coffman, and Ericson 2017). Greater survey privacy results in much higher estimates of sexual minorities (Robertson et al. 2018). Further, the survey I used, like most others, did not ask about mutual masturbation. For both of these reasons, the actual population of men who have sex with men is likely much higher. Additionally, as I show through interviews, growing older encourages many men to have sex with other men. Thus, the percentage of straight men who have had sex with other men may increase with older ages. This is difficult to analyze with surveys, however, because most do not comprehensively analyze sexuality, especially beyond middle age. Numbers I provide are best estimates based on representative survey data but should be viewed with caution, since the sample size of straight men who reported no nonconsensual sex with men and two or more male partners in the 2011–2017 NSFG (n=59) is small.

10 The estimate was 27.85 percent, and the 95 percent confidence interval was 16.63 percent to 42.77 percent.

11 Carey 2016.

12 Hochschild 2016.

13 Adamy and Overberg 2017.

14 Lynch 2019.

15 Adamy and Overberg 2017. Importantly, however, many areas that were formerly rural gain population because they are so economically successful; they go from being rural to being semi-urban or urban. These places are not reflected in statistics about rural areas. Additionally, there are many innovative businesses in rural areas that benefit local workers and the economy (Wojan and Parker 2017).

16 Trying to repeal the Affordable Care Act, preventing background checks on gun purchases, and cutting taxes on wealthy people and paying for it by slashing important government services is not helpful for most Republicans living anywhere. But many people continue to vote Republican in part because they feel that Republican politicians and judges will protect white people's status, or because of resentment against people of color or immigrants (Hooghe and Dassonneville 2018; Metzl 2019; Mutz 2018). Republican officials do in fact often work to disadvantage people of color: Republicans have created almost all the laws that suppress voter turnout (Hakim and Wines 2018), and these laws disproportionately affect black and Latinx people (Ansolabehere and Hersh 2017; Horwitz 2016; Lapowsky 2018; Mock 2016; Newkirk 2018). This is one reason why Donald Trump won in 2016. Republican judges also give longer sentences to black defendants than Democratic judges do (Cohen and Yang 2018), one of many examples of how Republican officials often disadvantage people of color. It is no coincidence that 83 percent of Republican voters are white, compared to 59 percent of Democratic voters (Pew Research Center 2018). Republican officials often work for the interests of white people and against the interests of people of color (Serwer 2017).

Hostility toward women, among men *and* women, is also a key predictor of Republican support (Maxwell and Shields 2018; Valentino, Wayne, and Oceno 2018). So too are men's fears about being emasculated or about women gaining social equality (Cassino 2018; Knowles and DiMuccio 2018). A majority of Republicans are homophobic, too: only 41 percent of Republicans support marriage equality, compared to 65 percent of independents and 77 percent of Democrats (Greenberg et al. 2019). Most Republicans claim to not be racist, sexist, or homophobic, but Republicans are much more likely than Democrats and independents to embrace these ideologies (Cox, Lienesch, and Jones 2017a, 2017b; Maxwell and Shields 2018; Milbank 2016; Valentino, Wayne, and Oceno 2018; Vandermaas-Peeler et al. 2017). Republicans are also more likely than Democrats to report skepticism of higher education (Pew Research Center 2017; Brown 2018), experts (Motta 2017), and even science (Cohen 2018). Republicans often rationalize these attitudes by saying they have "traditional beliefs" and support "religious freedom" in cases of discrimination, or because they oppose so-called political correctness.

17 Florida 2016; Gamio 2016; Gould and Bryan 2018.
18 United States Census Bureau 2016.
19 Mishel 2019; Priebe and Svedin 2013.
20 Schilt and Westbrook 2009.
21 Seidman 2002.
22 Lesbian, gay, bisexual, and queer. I use "LGBQ" when discussing research or topics directly addressing sexuality. I use "LGBTQ"—"T" standing for transgender—for studies and topics that discuss sexual *and* gender minorities, including transgender and nonbinary people.
23 Savin-Williams and Vrangalova 2013.
24 See Ghaziani 2014a for an explanation of how researchers can identify sexual cultures. See also Mohr and Ghaziani 2014.
25 Mallory, Brown, and Conlon 2018.
26 Peters 2017.
27 Warbelow and Diaz 2017; Mason, Williams, and Elliott 2017.
28 Flores and Park 2018.
29 Ofosu et al. 2019.
30 "Accelerating Acceptance" 2018.
31 Pear and Peters 2018.
32 Greenhouse 2019.
33 Cha 2019.
34 Robert Wood Johnson Foundation 2017.
35 Fidas and Cooper 2018.
36 CareerBuilder 2017.
37 McCarthy 2020.
38 Brown, Romero, and Gates 2016; Conron, Goldberg, and Halpern 2018.
39 Gattis, Sacco, and Cunningham-Williams 2012.
40 Gonzales, Przedworski, and Henning-Smith 2016; Lick, Durso, and Johnson 2013.

41 Gonzales and Ehrenfeld 2018; Hatzenbuehler, Keyes, and Hasin 2009; Hatzen-buehler et al. 2010; Hatzenbuehler et al. 2012; Kail, Acosta, and Wright 2015; Meyer 2013; Raifman et al. 2017; Raifman et al. 2018.

42 Sun and Gao 2019.

43 Mittleman 2018, 2019.

44 Downing and Rosenthal 2020.

45 Henning-Smith and Gonzales 2018.

46 Seidman 2009.

47 Doan, Loehr, and Miller 2014.

48 Bailey et al. 2016.

49 Löfström 1997. See also Patil 2018 for an explanation of how colonialism and imperialism helped form the foundation for heterosexuality.

50 Subcultures of men who had sex with men, as in London (Norton 2006) or colonial Mexico (Tortorici 2007), emerged between the seventeenth and eighteenth centuries, but these were different from the sexual identities that would take root over a century later.

51 Adam 1985; D'Emilio 1997.

52 Boag 2003.

53 D'Emilio 1997.

54 Adam 1985; Faderman 1991.

55 Boag 2011; Johnson 2013.

56 Boag 2011.

57 Rosenburg 2016.

58 Howard 1999.

59 Foucault 1988; Katz 1995.

60 Canaday 2009.

61 Capó 2017.

62 Rosenburg 2016.

63 Rosenburg 2016.

64 Heath 2009.

65 Wilcox 2001. Relatedly, this helps to explain why religiosity is a key motivator behind anti-LGBQ bigotry (Sherkat et al. 2011; Whitehead 2010). It also helps explain why the religiosity of schooling contexts in youth is associated with sexual identification (Wilkinson and Pearson 2013).

66 Chauncey 1994.

67 Kimmel 1996; Rotundo 1993.

68 Rotundo 1993.

69 Chauncey 1994; Rotundo 1993.

70 Chauncey 1994; Kimmel 1996; Rotundo 1993.

71 Kimmel 1996; Rotundo 1993.

72 Chauncey 1994.

73 Chauncey 1994.

74 Katz 1995.

75 Chauncey 1994.

76 Chauncey 1994.

77 Rupp 2012.

78 Faderman 1991; Smith-Rosenberg 1975; Vicinus 1984.

79 Katz 2001; Rotundo 1989.

80 I say "genital contact" rather than "sex" because many at this time did not perceive mutual masturbation or oral-genital contact as sex (Katz 2001).

81 Diamond 2003.

82 Katz 1995.

83 Katz 1995.

84 Freud 1975 [1908].

85 Jackson 1999.

86 Ingraham 1994, 2008; Jackson 1999, 2006; Rich 1980.

87 Ingraham 2008.

88 Bailey et al. 2016.

89 Sexual identification can also differ between countries, due to a complex mixture of social, cultural, and economic factors (Cantú 2009; Carrillo 2017; Carrillo and Fontdevila 2014).

90 Rust 1992.

91 Adam 2000.

92 Kitzinger and Wilkinson 1995.

93 Charlton et al. 2016.

94 Egan 2012, 2019.

95 England, Mishel, and Caudillo 2016; Gates 2014; Savin-Williams and Vrangalova 2013.

96 England 2016.

97 Silva and Evans 2020. See also Gates 2017; Mustanski et al. 2014; Cohen et al. 2018; Compton and Bridges 2019.

98 Budnick 2016.

99 Walker 2014.

100 Carrillo and Hoffman 2016, 2018.

101 Duffin 2016.

102 Some researchers have used latent class analysis (LCA) or latent profile analysis (LPA) to identify unmeasured subgroupings within a population. Conventional regression models are variable-centered, examining the association between particular independent variables and the dependent variable of straight identification. In contrast, LCA and LPA are person-centered forms of analysis that use variables to find groups of people who are distinct from other groups on the basis of those variables (Grzanka 2016). Kuperberg and Walker (2018), for instance, use LCA to examine straight-identified college students whose last hookup partner was the same sex. Their analysis suggests that there are distinct subtypes characterized by differences in religiosity, homophobia, and circumstances of the hookup. My own research (Silva 2019) has shown that about half of men and

women with substantial same-sex sexuality are neither overtly homophobic nor very conservative in terms of gender attitudes.

103 Silva 2019.

104 Many LGBQ people are socially or geographically isolated from other LGBQ people, so their LGBQ identification reflects how they see themselves as different from straight people. It does not necessarily reflect embeddedness in a culture that is LGBQ. That said, feelings of connection to LGBQ cultures may also emerge from media representations or participation in online communities (Gray 2009). In short, while identification as straight reflects embeddedness in a straight culture, the same is not necessarily true for identification as LGBQ. Identification as LGBQ reflects feelings of difference from straight people, and sometimes but not always embeddedness in a different type of culture. Straight culture, because it is hegemonic, structures most aspects of social life.

105 Indeed, within much of the West, understandings of purportedly normal gender and sexuality are racialized as white.

106 Some explore geographic variation in identification or identity expression, including Gray's (2009) ethnography of rural queer youth in Kentucky, Brown-Saracino's (2015, 2018) investigation of women's LBQ identities across four American cities, and Carrillo's (2017) exploration of Mexican men who had sex with men who migrated to the United States. Others examine smaller, niche subcultures or communities, such as Hennen's (2008) detailing of the unique gay subcultures of bears, fairies, and leathermen: bears are large, hairy men who act conventionally masculine but also form emotionally intimate relationships with other men; fairies embrace femininity; and leathermen perform exaggerated masculinity and often recast middle age as a desirable attribute. Orne (2017), relatedly, examines queer men's sexual networks in Chicago during a time of assimilation and gentrification.

107 Ingraham 2008:23.

108 Dean 2014.

109 Whereas some of Dean's (2014) participants engaged in transgressive practices to challenge inequality, like not correcting some people's misperceptions of them as gay, the men I interviewed engaged in transgressive practices (sex with men), but this did not challenge inequality because few to no people knew about it.

110 Seidman 2002.

111 Ward 2015:5.

112 Schalet 2011.

113 González-López 2005.

114 Avishai and Burke 2016; Burke 2016; Diefendorf 2015; Gerber 2011.

115 Armstrong, England, and Fogarty 2012; Hamilton and Armstrong 2009.

116 Davis 2015; Fausto-Sterling 2000.

117 Hart et al. 2019; Magliozzi, Saperstein, and Westbrook 2016.

118 Westbrook and Schilt 2014.

119 Westbrook and Schilt 2014.

120 Stone 2019.
121 This is certainly the case with most straight cultures, though many LGBQ people and institutions (sadly) operate in similar ways, reflecting their socialization within straight culture.
122 Beck 2019.
123 Diaz 2018.
124 Eliot 2009; Fine 2010; Marwha, Halari, and Eliot 2017; Rippon 2019; Tan et al. 2016; see also MacLellon 2017.
125 Kersey, Csumitta, and Cantlon 2019; Reardon et al. 2019; Stoet and Geary 2018.
126 Frederick et al. 2018.
127 Armstrong, England, and Fogarty 2012.
128 Loofbourow 2018.
129 Hamilton and Armstrong 2009; Miller 2016.
130 Herbenick et al. 2015.
131 Loofbourow 2018.
132 Smith et al. 2018.
133 Lee 2017; Roscigno 2019.
134 Langer 2017.
135 Marcin 2018.
136 Relman 2020.
137 E. Martin 1991.
138 R. Martin 2018.
139 See also Roughgarden 2004 for an explanation of how cultural ideas about "natural" sex/gender differences are challenged by many animal species.
140 In the workforce, having children lowers women's wages (Budig and Hodges 2010; England et al. 2016) but not men's (Killewald 2013). This is the case in part because managers see fathers as more responsible, whereas they see mothers as a drain on company resources. It is also the case in part because in society broadly, women are generally expected to take off more time from work than their male partners to care for children. Relatedly, there is a wage gap between men and women that exists at all education levels (Gould and Kroeger 2017; Carnevale, Smith, and Gulish 2018), as well as a wealth gap (Chang 2015). This is not simply due to women selecting lower-paid occupations: data from 1950 to 2000 shows that the average pay of an occupation decreased as women comprised more of the workforce in that occupation (Levanon, England, and Allison 2009). This means that work women do is seen as less valuable than work men do, and as a result, women are paid less. Additionally, from childhood through adulthood, girls and women are rated as less competent than boys and men even for the same or better performance or qualifications (Lavy and Sand 2015; Mitchell and Martin 2018; Moss-Racusin et al. 2012). Even in movies women are portrayed as less valuable: on average male characters talk more and are more central to the film's plot than female characters (Ramakrishna et al. 2017).
141 Martin and Kazyak 2009.

142 Martin 2009; Solebello and Elliott 2011.

143 Gansen 2017; Pascoe and Silva 2019.

144 Myers and Raymond 2010.

145 Miller 2016; Pascoe 2011.

146 Leonhardt and Quealy 2015; Livingston 2018.

147 Halberstam 2005; Herring 2010. Many people have this bias, including law-makers and judges, and it affects rural LGBTQ people's lives through laws, policies, judicial rulings, and lack of attention to their unique needs (Boso 2013; Jerke 2011). Both Boso (2013) and Jerke (2011) show how urban stereo-types affect judges' rulings in cases involving LGBTQ people. For instance, many judges in family cases have ruled that rural LGBTQ parents should not have custody because rurality and LGBTQ life do not go well together, thus legally legitimizing community prejudices. Similar dynamics have emerged with disputes over the legality of firing LGBTQ people in rural areas (Boso 2013). Courts could instead apply heightened scrutiny for rural LGBTQ people to protect them, but most have not done so (Boso 2013). There are also many LGBTQ people in small cities (Forstie 2020), some of which have gay bars (Mattson 2020). See also Rosenberger et al. (2014) for information about rural American gay men's sexual practices, health behaviors, and community en-gagement.

148 Movement Advancement Project (MAP) 2019.

149 Stone 2018.

150 Stone 2018.

151 See also Brekhus 2003 and Brown 2008.

152 Kosciw et al. 2018.

153 Movement Advancement Project 2019.

154 Prince, Joyner, and Manning 2019.

155 Gray, Johnson, and Gilley 2016.

156 Gray 2009.

157 Abelson 2016; Stein 2001.

158 Robert Wood Johnson Foundation 2018.

159 Parker et al. 2018.

160 Farmer et al. 2016 and Wienke and Hill 2013; see also Price-Feeney, Ybarra, and Mitchell 2019. Studies such as Cain et al. 2017 and Lyons, Hosking, and Rozbroj 2015 have found that rural gay and bisexual men fare worse than their urban counterparts, but their samples are not representative (though they are large). Using a representative sample, Poon and Saewyc (2009) found that rural sexual-minority adolescents in British Columbia were at heightened risk for several health issues compared to their urban counterparts. The survey was conducted in 2003, however, so it is unclear whether these differences still exist.

161 Gray, Johnson, and Gilley 2016; Oswald and Lazarevic 2011.

162 Robert Wood Johnson Foundation 2018.

163 Gates 2017; Newport 2018.

164 Fellows 1998. Additionally, some gay men move from rural areas to urban areas, and then move back to rural areas (Annes and Redlin 2012a; Vermes 2020). See also Vermes 2020 for information about rural LGBTQ pride events.

165 See also Dentzman et al. 2020 and Leslie 2017 for an examination of LGBTQ farmers.

166 See for example Swank, Fahs, and Frost 2013 and Gottschalk and Newton 2009.

167 Brown-Saracino 2019; Ghaziani 2019; Gieryn 2000. See also Ghaziani 2014b.

168 Bederman 1996; Chauncey 1994; Kimmel 1996; Rotundo 1993.

169 Pascoe and Bridges 2015.

170 West and Zimmerman 1987.

171 Schrock and Schwalbe 2009:281.

172 Bird 1996; Pascoe 2011.

173 Barber 2016; Diefendorf 2015; Heath 2019; Pascoe 2011.

174 Connell 1987, 2005; Connell and Messerschmidt 2005; Messerschmidt 2015.

175 Connell 1987.

176 Bridges and Pascoe 2014.

177 Bridges and Pascoe 2014; Lamont 2015; Munsch and Gruys 2018.

178 Abelson 2019.

179 Abelson 2019.

180 Silva 2019.

181 O'Connor, Ford, and Banos 2017; Weaver and Vescio 2015.

182 Falomir-Pichastor, Manuel, and Mugny 2009; Nagoshi et al. 2019; Willer et al. 2013.

183 See also Diefendorf and Bridges 2020, Duckworth and Trautner 2019, and Worthen 2020.

184 Campbell and Bell 2000:540.

185 Pini, Brandth, and Little 2015.

186 Leap 2017.

187 Morris 2008; Kazyak 2012; Little 2015. See also Brandth 2019 and Tyler and Fairbrother 2013.

188 Barber 2016.

189 Bridges 2014.

190 Bye 2009; Courtenay 2006.

191 Mencken and Froese 2019.

192 Gahman 2015.

193 Igielnik 2017.

194 Annes and Redlin 2012b; Kazyak 2012.

195 Kazyak 2012.

196 Abelson 2016, 2019.

197 Lichter and Brown 2011.

198 Desmond 2006:393.

199 There is a vast expanse of rural, far Northern California several hours north of San Francisco. Many residents see themselves as culturally distinct from the rest

of California, and some even call for secession to form the State of Jefferson. Unlike the rest of the state, the population of the far north is mostly white and conservative. See Branson-Potts 2018 and Wilson 2017 for a regional profile or listen to "The Revenge of Rural America" episode on the *It Could Happen Here* podcast.

200 United States Census Bureau 2016.

201 Bump 2014; Economist 2016.

202 I limited recruitment to rural spaces and small towns that share fairly similar characteristics because I do not analyze specific regional differences in how the men I talked to identify and express their gender and sexual identity.

203 These areas have not experienced large-scale migrations of Latinx populations, as have some rural areas of the South (e.g., Texas) and parts of the rural Southwest, nor do they have large populations of rural black people stemming from legacies of slavery, as in the South (Jakubek and Wood 2018). While people of color are present in the rural spaces and small towns I examine, they are a minority.

204 There are many definitions of "rural" in both law and research. See Woods (2009) for an explanation of how it is difficult to define rural, and how scholars have navigated this.

205 Lichter and Brown 2011; Woods 2009.

206 Office of Management and Budget 2010.

207 Included in the OMB's definition of "metropolitan area" are regions, like counties, that have multiple small towns that together comprise fifty thousand or more. For instance, a county in which the three largest towns have between twenty and thirty-five thousand people each is technically a metropolitan area. I did not exclude men who lived in areas like this, since I was interested in spaces that were rural or small town rather than suburban or urban. Further, the structure of Craigslist made it impossible to target only rural areas and not small towns. There were few differences between men from rural areas (e.g., living in the countryside) and men from small towns (e.g., living in a town of thirty-nine thousand located in a county with several towns smaller than that).

208 I also advertised information about the study in a Grindr profile, but only for a short time. Grindr is a popular location-based app among MSM. Most men who contacted me on Grindr either did not follow up or identified as gay or bisexual, reflecting Grindr's target population. I received few serious inquiries on the app, so I deleted it. Through Grindr, I connected with Mark and Jon.

209 It was fortuitous that I completed interviews in late 2017. On March 23, 2018, Craigslist banned personals ads. This was in response to the US Congress passing the Allow States and Victims to Fight Online Sex Trafficking Act just two days prior, which made websites liable for any users who utilized them for sex trafficking or sex work. Critics pointed out that this bill actually makes sex trafficking worse by pushing it underground, where it is more difficult to trace, and renders sex work more dangerous by taking control away from independent sex workers. Regardless, websites such as Craigslist deleted forums where users could seek anonymous sex. It is therefore impossible to replicate this research.

210 This project expands on, and differs from, the few existing studies of straight MSM. It is the first to examine how rural and small-town straight MSM themselves understand their gender and sexuality. The interview methods I used in this project complement content analyses that Ward (2008, 2015), Reynolds (2015), and Robinson and Vidal-Ortiz (2013) used, as well as online interviews that Carrillo and Hoffman (2016, 2018) conducted. Perhaps counterintuitively, straight men who post ads looking for sex with men may not always engage in it. As Robinson and Moskowitz (2013:562) found, many straight-identified men view Internet cruising, posting, and e-mailing as "self-contained erotic acts" that do not transition into offline behavior. Online ad representations may therefore inaccurately reflect the narratives of straight MSM and will at best capture only snippets of their lives, given that researchers cannot ask them questions. Hence, while content analysis of Craigslist ads is well situated to analyze how straight MSM discursively construct straightness and gender in online settings, it is not necessarily helpful in analyzing how they understand their own narratives. Similarly, online interviews guarantee anonymity and may increase participation, but may also discourage the sharing of nuanced data due to the time it takes participants to type answers, so I interviewed men in person or over the phone. For other research about straight MSM, see Reback and Larkins 2010.

211 I uploaded all transcripts to the qualitative data analysis software NVivo to apply codes, repeating the process as I coded additional transcripts and created new codes. I created all codes during analysis rather than at the beginning of the study. My approach resembled that which Deterding and Waters (2018) suggest: I first developed broad codes, and later more specific codes once I was more familiar with the data. Further, as Emerson, Fretz, and Shaw (1995) explain, I developed ideas after collecting and analyzing data, and this shaped how I collected further data (for example, by adding new interview questions). This approach is common in qualitative research. As the sole researcher, I created and applied all codes.

212 Balay 2018.

213 Relatedly, the sexologist Alfred Kinsey, as well as his colleagues Wardell Pomeroy and Clyde Martin, found that many men in the rural western part of the United States had had sex with other men, which they documented in their pioneering 1948 book about men's sexuality. As they explain,

> There is a fair amount of sexual contact among the older males in Western rural areas. It is a type of homosexuality which was probably common among pioneers and outdoor men in general. Today it is found among ranchmen, cattle men, prospectors, lumbermen, and farming groups in general—among groups that are virile, physically active. These are men who have faced the rigors of nature in the wild. They live on realities and a minimum of theory. Such a background breeds the attitude that sex is sex, irrespective of the nature of the partner with whom the relation is had. Sexual relations are had with women when they are avail-

able, or with other males when outdoor routines bring men together into exclusively male groups. Such a pattern is not at all uncommon among pre-adolescent and early adolescent males in such rural areas, and it continues in a number of histories into the adult years and through marriage. Such a group of hard-riding, hard-hitting, assertive males would not tolerate the affectations of some of the city groups that are involved in the homosexual [community]; but this, as far as they can see, has little to do with the question of having sexual relations with other men. This type of rural homosexuality contradicts the theory that homosexuality in itself is an urban product. (457–59)

214 Carrillo and Hoffman 2018.

215 Ward 2015.

216 Robinson and Vidal-Ortiz 2013; Ward 2015.

217 Ward 2015.

218 See Bridges 2014 for how many young, white, urban, straight men construct hybrid masculinities that are "softer" than those generally considered conventionally masculine.

219 See Abelson 2016, Gray 2009, and Kazyak 2012 for how LGBTQ people in rural areas are typically less visible than those in urban areas, and tend to emphasize similarity to other community members to be accepted.

220 Leap 2017.

221 Movement Advancement Project 2019.

222 Abelson 2016; Kazyak 2012.

223 Specifically, MSM with two or more male sexual partners. I analyzed this using the National Survey of Family Growth 2011–2017 (U.S. Department of Health and Human Services 2018). This mirrors my findings elsewhere: Silva (2019) and Silva and Whaley (2018).

224 Han 2015; Snorton 2014.

225 Han 2015; Phillips 2005; Robinson and Vidal-Ortiz 2013; Snorton 2014.

226 Barnshaw and Letukas 2010; Miller, Serner, and Wagner 2005; Schrimshaw, Siegel, and Downing 2010; Wolitski et al. 2006.

227 Ford et al. 2007.

228 Centers for Disease Control 2019.

229 Adam 2016; Mustanski et al. 2019; Saleh and Operario 2009.

230 Ford et al. 2007.

231 Duffin 2016; Martinez and Hosek 2005.

232 Hunter 2010.

233 Choo and Ferree 2010; Cho, Crenshaw, and McCall 2013; Crenshaw 1991; Collins 2015; Grzanka 2014; McCall 2005.

234 Choo and Ferree 2010; Cho, Crenshaw, and McCall 2013; Collins 2015; Grzanka 2014; McCall 2005.

235 Choo and Ferree 2010.

236 Bourdieu 1985, 1989; Sallaz and Zavisca 2007.

237 Bonilla-Silva 2003:104. Hagerman (2016) shows that socialization is not necessarily uninterrupted, however, but its effects are still profound.

238 Bonilla-Silva, Goar, and Embrick 2006; Bonilla-Silva 2016.

239 Williams and Emamdjomeh 2018. See Krysan and Crowder 2017 and Havekes, Bader, and Krysan 2016 for a detailed examination of the causes of neighborhood segregation.

240 Cox, Navarro-Rivera, and Jones 2016.

241 Bonilla-Silva, Goar, and Embrick 2006.

242 Pierce 2016.

243 Livingston and Brown 2017.

244 Livingston and Brown 2017.

245 Livingston and Brown 2017.

246 Seidman 2002.

247 England, Mishel, and Caudillo 2016.

248 Caplan 2017; Lourie and Needham 2017.

249 Another reason older men participated more is that they had more free time. Most were retired and not taking care of children, making it easier to find time to interview.

250 Lindau et al. 2007; Lochlainn and Kenny 2013; Malani et al. 2018.

251 Galinsky, McClintock, and Waite 2014.

252 Waite et al. 2009.

CHAPTER 1. WHY THEY HAVE SEX WITH MEN

1 For instance, about 3.6–4.1 percent of men have a slight amount of attraction to other men (Savin-Williams and Vrangalova 2013), but only some of them identify as "mostly straight" (Savin-Williams 2017), whereas others simply identify as "straight." Indeed, only seven men I interviewed identified as "mostly straight" in full or part, and of these seven, five identified as both "straight" *and* "mostly straight." Men who identify as straight, including the men I interviewed, differ from men who identify as "mostly straight" (as well as bisexual, gay, and queer) due to their embeddedness in straight culture.

2 Carrillo and Hoffman 2016, 2018; Siegel and Meunier 2019.

3 Herdt 1987.

4 Seto 2017.

5 Anders 2015.

6 Savin-Williams 2017.

7 As chapter 2 shows, some men were also concerned that they themselves would become too attached to other men and worked to ensure this did not happen.

8 See Diefendorf 2015 for an exception.

9 Aguilar 2017.

10 Stewart 2018.

11 Stewart 2018.

12 Levin 2018.

13 Jones 2018.

14 A handful reported past open relationships with women partners. These usually involved sex with women other than their primary partner, or threesome arrangements in which another man had sex with their women partners but the men I interviewed did not have sex with that man (or threesomes in which another woman was involved). Very few reported having ever told past woman partners about sex with men.

15 Open relationships are generally understood to allow sex with people other than one's primary partner; polyamorous relationships generally refer to romantic connections with more than one person. It is possible to be both open and polyamorous.

16 Barker and Langdridge 2010; Brewster et al. 2017; Fleckenstein and Cox 2015; Rubel and Bogaert 2015; Schippers 2016.

17 Levine et al. 2018.

18 Frederick et al. 2018.

19 Armstrong, England, and Fogarty 2012.

20 E.g., Diamond 2009.

21 Not all of the men I interviewed were able to describe their proportion of sexual attractions to women and men before and after they experienced them shifting. Most used imprecise language like "a little" or "a lot," even after follow-up questions. I note exact proportions when men did report them.

22 Ward 2015; Zeeland 1995.

23 Some suburban Latino straight and bisexual MSM have shared similar beliefs (Fontdevila 2019).

24 This is aside from practices that necessarily involve another penis.

25 Flood 2008; Pascoe 2011.

26 Jeremy saw my research advertisement when he traveled to one of the regions I targeted for research.

27 Hamilton and Armstrong 2009.

28 Reiner 2017.

29 Carrillo and Hoffman 2016, 2018.

CHAPTER 2. FRIENDSHIP, INTIMACY, AND LOVE BETWEEN MEN

1 Stacey 2004.

2 This distinguishes them from many of Humphreys's (1970) participants, who stopped at public restrooms for quick, casual, one-time hookups.

3 Pascoe 2011; Way 2013.

4 Katz 2001; Rotundo 1989.

5 I use this term to describe someone the men I interviewed met for sex more than once.

6 See, for instance, the website Urban Dictionary.

7 Overall, thirty-three reported FWBs and/or deeply intimate friendships.

8 Reynolds 2015; Robinson and Vidal-Ortiz 2013; Ward 2015.

9 None of the men I interviewed were on pre-exposure prophylaxis (PrEP) to prevent themselves from contracting HIV, either.

10 Coincidentally, the same number of men (eleven) reported intimate friendships and loving relationships. Not the same men, necessarily, but the same number of men.

11 Diamond 2003.

12 Adam 2000. Interestingly, however, some straight men in the Philippines form secret romantic relationships with gay men (Cerna and Cosido 2020).

13 Diamond 2009; Rust 1992.

14 Silva 2019.

CHAPTER 3. STRAIGHT CULTURE

1 See table A.2 for full self-identification information. Some did claim an identity in addition to "straight," or qualified their straight identification with another description. Nonetheless, all identified in full or part as straight. Men with more complicated understandings of their identity usually did not tell others about that, but they honestly portrayed themselves as straight: that is indeed how they identified, at least in part.

2 Abelson 2016; Kazyak 2012; Leap 2017.

3 Abelson 2016; Gray 2009; Kazyak 2012.

4 Movement Advancement Project 2019; Robert Wood Johnson Foundation 2018.

5 Pascoe 2011; see also Rich 1980.

6 Bourdieu 1985, 1989; Sallaz and Zaviska 2007.

7 Martin 2009.

8 Solebello and Elliott 2011.

9 Martin 2009.

10 Gansen 2017.

11 Myers and Raymond 2010.

12 Pascoe 2011.

13 Pascoe and Silva 2019.

14 Messner 1992.

15 While some people consider hunting and fishing sports, the men I talked to discussed them as hobbies. As a result, I detail hunting and fishing in later sections about rural culture, rather than here.

16 Messner 1992.

17 See also Hudson 2013 for a literature review about men who have sex with men, and who are also married to women.

18 Leonhardt and Quealy 2015.

19 James saw my research advertisement when he traveled to one of the regions I targeted for research.

20 Stone 2019.

21 Boertien and Bernardi 2019; Bos et al. 2016; Brewaeys and Bos 2018; Cheng and Powell 2015; Golombok et al. 2016; Manning, Fettro, and Lamidi 2014.

22 Pascoe 2011; Way 2013.

23 Diefendorf 2015.

24 Gerber 2011.

25 Fetner 2008; Stone 2019.

26 Perry 2019.

27 Waidzunas 2015.

28 Mencken and Froese 2019.

29 Leap 2017.

30 Abelson 2019.

31 Schilt and Westbrook 2009. See also Robinson and Spivey 2007 for how ex-gay movements use discourse about the importance of masculinity, and men's control over women, to advance their homophobic and antifeminist agenda.

CHAPTER 4. WHY THEY DID NOT IDENTIFY AS GAY OR BISEXUAL

1 Avery 2016.

2 Doan, Loehr, and Miller 2014.

3 That said, sixteen saw themselves as both straight and bisexual at the same time. These sixteen men told other people that they identified as straight, and to themselves they identified as both straight and bisexual (or as some variant of bisexual). This shows how complex their sexual identity is. Those men who were sexually attracted to women tended to explain that this made a gay identity incompatible: thirty-two said they were "mostly" attracted to women, and seven that they were exclusively sexually attracted to women. Arguably, neither "bisexual" nor "straight" fully describes men who are *mostly* attracted to women. For these men, a "bisexual" identity would have fully described their sexual behaviors, partially described their attractions, and not at all reflected their embeddedness in straight culture. "Straight," the term they preferred, partially described both their sexual attractions and sexual behaviors, and fully described their embeddedness in straight culture. The men I talked to identified as straight because they felt that their sexual attractions to, and sexual encounters with, men were not as important to their identity as their romantic partnerships with women and their embeddedness in straight culture.

4 Fetner 2008; Stone 2019.

5 Ocampo 2012. Obviously, however, it should be perfectly acceptable for men to be feminine, and feminine men should not face social stigma.

6 Hennen 2008; Orne 2017. Of course, there should not be stigma attached to casual sex, and gay men who engage in it should not face homophobic judgments.

7 Doan, Loehr, and Miller 2014.

8 For instance, if they said that same-sex marriage or childrearing should be legal due to libertarian ideals for small government but that they did not support it, I considered that opposition.

9 Greenberg et al. 2019.

10 Doan, Loehr, and Miller 2014.

11 Dean 2014.

12 In my study analyzing the 2013–2015 National Survey of Family Growth, a nationally representative survey of men aged fifteen to forty-four, I found that, when I

analyzed subgroups within populations, about half of all straight men with substantial same-sex activity and/or attraction were neither overtly homophobic nor conservative in terms of masculinity attitudes (Silva 2019). This was the case even though homophobia as a variable was strongly related to straight identification for men with substantial same-sex activity and/or attraction when considered as an undifferentiated group (Silva 2019).

13 The 2011–2017 NSFG interviewed men aged fifteen to forty-four and asked them their level of agreement with the statement "Sexual relations between two adults of the same sex are all right." Options included "strongly agree," "agree," "disagree," and "strongly disagree." "Neither agree nor disagree" was presented as an option only if the respondent insisted. I compared the responses of straight men (1) who had two or more male sexual partners and (2) who had not. I excluded men who reported nonconsensual sex with men. To amplify my findings, I analyzed these responses using multiple statistical techniques, and "weighted" the results to make them representative. I excluded "neither agree nor disagree" responses when analyzing variables categorically because fairly few respondents chose this option. I included these responses when comparing means. When the means were compared, straight men who had had sex with men were actually more liberal in their attitudes about gays and lesbians than straight men who had not had sex with men (t-statistic: -2.41, $p < .05$). When attitudes about gays and lesbians were examined categorically, there were not statistically significant associations. (Statistical estimates should be evaluated with caution given small sample sizes.) Despite the NSFG's many imperfections—it only surveyed men through their forties and asked only one attitudinal question about LGBQ issues in the latest survey—it is one of the best data sources available. Few other surveys ask about sexual behavior, sexual identity, and social attitudes (Wolff et al. 2017). I cannot say for sure how well the NSFG represents my respondents. While not a perfect match to my interview study, the NSFG does supply further evidence that prejudice is not the only reason for straight identification. It did also ask three attitudinal questions about masculinity. Masculinity attitudes included the following: "Men only need to see a doctor when they are hurt or sick"; "A man should not show pain"; "Men have greater sexual needs than women." When the means were compared, straight men who had had sex with men were more liberal than other straight men in their attitude about going to see a doctor when hurt or sick (t-statistic: -2.38, $p < .05$). It was not statistically significant when examined categorically. Straight men who had had sex with men were more liberal on the attitude about men's sexual needs when examined categorically (the design-based F-statistic was 4.52, $p < .01$), but not when comparing means.

14 Dyar and Feinstein 2018.

15 Herek 2002; Dodge et al. 2016.

16 Dodge et al. 2016.

17 Beach et al. 2019.

18 Hayfield 2020.

19 Bisexuality is also underrepresented in scholarly research: Monro, Hines, and Osborne 2017.
20 Parker 2015.
21 Rust 1992.
22 Savin-Williams and Vrangalova 2013.
23 Dyar et al. 2019; Lew, Dorsen, and Long 2018; Ross et al. 2018.
24 Paschen-Wolff et al. 2019; Taggart et al. 2019.
25 Feinstein et al. 2018.
26 Parker 2015.
27 Parker 2015.
28 Mize 2016.
29 England, Mishel, and Caudillo 2016.
30 Mize and Manago 2018.
31 England 2016.

CHAPTER 5. HELPING A BUDDY OUT

1 Katz 2001.
2 In 2018 former White House intern Monica Lewinsky began discussing her sexual encounters with President Clinton in light of the #MeToo movement (Bever 2018). Her account suggests that while she was not forced into sex, "the road that led there was littered with inappropriate abuse of authority, station, and privilege" given that she was an intern and he was the president.
3 While bud-sex is similar to the sexual behavior of other straight men who have sex with men, it is also unique. Through content analysis of Craigslist ads and military or fraternity bonding rituals, Jane Ward (2015) argues that many straight white men in urban, suburban, and military contexts frame their sex with men as a way to bond with other similar men. Carrillo and Hoffman (2016, 2018) refer to the racially diverse and primarily urban and suburban group of men they recruited online as "heteroflexible," given that most were primarily or exclusively attracted to women.
4 See also Ward 2015.
5 Leonhardt and Quealy 2015.
6 Livingston 2018.
7 I focus on men's thoughts about their own practices. For instance, I do not analyze men's thoughts about anal sex if they had not experienced it.
8 Walker 2014.
9 Only two men, Joe and Rex, were in open relationships with women.

CHAPTER 6. GUYS LIKE ME

1 Chauncey 1994.
2 Chauncey 1994.
3 Hennen 2008.
4 Sánchez and Vilain 2012.

5　U.S. Department of Health and Human Services 2018. Estimates add up to 101 percent due to rounding. From these estimates I excluded most men who reported a history of sex work or nonconsensual sex with men.

6　Twenge, Sherman, and Wells 2016.

7　Bonilla-Silva 2003.

8　As Brian said, "I'm a little bit of everything. I've got European blood, both Anglo and Latino, and I've got a little bit of African blood within me, so I'm a mutt. I look mostly Caucasian, though."

9　This pattern is similar to how Jane Ward (2015) theorizes.

10　Bonilla-Silva 2003.

11　Horowitz and Gomez 2018.

12　That is the only question the NSFG asked about the race of men's male sexual partners. The F-statistic was 8.50, $p < .001$, based on 394 cases. This should be viewed with caution given small sample sizes. This, like all other analyses, was weighted to adjust for the sampling design. The NSFG provided only four categories for race/ethnicity: white, black, Latino, and "other." It was not possible to determine the racial/ethnic identities of men the NSFG categorized as "other," which is why I analyze only white, black, and Latino men.

13　Lin and Lundquist 2013; Lundquist and Lin 2015.

14　Many people perceived as white today were not always considered fully white. People from Southern and Eastern Europe, as well as Jewish people, were typically considered not "really" white until the 1930s or 1940s. See Roediger 2005, Rothstein 2017, and Zimring 2015 for more on how this happened.

CONCLUSION

1　Caplan 2017; Gattis, Sacco, and Cunningham-Williams 2012; Krueger and Upchurch 2019.

2　Indeed, today some masculine, gay-identified, and mostly white men align themselves with white nationalism or other far-right movements (Minkowitz 2017; see also Halberstam 2011 for a historical examination).

3　Bailey et al. 2016. See also Diamond 2009 for an explanation of how an interplay between environmental factors and biological influences can shape attractions.

4　Horowitz, Graf, and Livingston 2019.

5　Labrecque and Whisman 2017.

6　Wolfinger 2017.

7　Labrecque and Whisman 2017.

8　Walker 2017.

METHODOLOGICAL APPENDIX

1　The number is likely higher than thirty-six, but due to technical e-mail issues, I was not able to track some correspondence from 2014–2015.

REFERENCES

Abelson, Miriam J. 2016. "'You Aren't from around Here': Race, Masculinity, and Rural Transgender Men." *Gender, Place & Culture* 23 (11): 1535–46. https://doi.org/10.1080/0966369X.2016.1219324.

———. 2019. *Men in Place: Trans Masculinity, Race, and Sexuality in America.* Minneapolis: University of Minnesota Press.

"Accelerating Acceptance 2018." 2018. Los Angeles: GLAAD. https://www.glaad.org.

Adam, Barry. 2000. "Love and Sex in Constructing Identity among Men Who Have Sex with Men." *International Journal of Sexuality and Gender Studies* 5 (4): 325–39.

Adam, Barry D. 1985. "Structural Foundations of the Gay World." *Comparative Studies in Society and History* 27 (4): 658–71.

———. 2016. "Neoliberalism, Masculinity, and HIV Risk." *Sexuality Research and Social Policy* 13 (4): 321–29. https://doi.org/10.1007/s13178-016-0232-2.

Adamy, Janet, and Paul Overberg. 2017. "Rural America Is the New 'Inner City': Small Counties Fare Worst by Key Measures of Socioeconomic Well-Being." *Wall Street Journal,* May 27.

Aguilar, Jade. 2017. "Pegging and the Heterosexualization of Anal Sex: An Analysis of Savage Love Advice." *Queer Studies in Media & Popular Culture* 2 (3): 275–92. https://doi.org/10.1386/qsmpc.2.3.275_1.

Anders, Sari M. van. 2015. "Beyond Sexual Orientation: Integrating Gender/Sex and Diverse Sexualities via Sexual Configurations Theory." *Archives of Sexual Behavior* 44 (5): 1177–1213. https://doi.org/10.1007/s10508-015-0490-8.

Annes, Alexis, and Meredith Redlin. 2012a. "Coming Out and Coming Back: Rural Gay Migration and the City." *Journal of Rural Studies* 28 (1): 56–68. https://doi.org/10.1016/j.jrurstud.2011.08.005.

———. 2012b. "The Careful Balance of Gender and Sexuality: Rural Gay Men, the Heterosexual Matrix, and 'Effeminophobia.'" *Journal of Homosexuality* 59 (2): 256–88. https://doi.org/10.1080/00918369.2012.648881.

Ansolabehere, Stephen, and Eitan D. Hersh. 2017. "ADGN: An Algorithm for Record Linkage Using Address, Date of Birth, Gender, and Name." *Statistics and Public Policy* 4 (1): 1–10. https://doi.org/10.1080/2330443X.2017.1389620.

Armstrong, Elizabeth A., Paula England, and Alison C. K. Fogarty. 2012. "Accounting for Women's Orgasm and Sexual Enjoyment in College Hookups and Relationships." *American Sociological Review* 77 (3): 435–62. https://doi.org/10.1177/0003122412445802.

Avery, Dan. 2016. "20 Republican Politicians Brought Down by Big Gay Sex Scandals." *NewNowNext*, December 30. http://www.newnownext.com.

Avishai, Orit, and Kelsy Burke. 2016. "God's Case for Sex." *Contexts* 15 (4): 30–35. https://doi.org/10.1177/1536504216684819.

Bailey, J. Michael, Paul L. Vasey, Lisa M. Diamond, S. Marc Breedlove, Eric Vilain, and Marc Epprecht. 2016. "Sexual Orientation, Controversy, and Science." *Psychological Science in the Public Interest* 17 (2): 45–101. https://doi.org/10.1177/1529100616637616.

Balay, Anne. 2018. *Semi Queer: Inside the World of Gay, Trans, and Black Truck Drivers*. Chapel Hill: University of North Carolina Press.

Barber, Kristen. 2016. *Styling Masculinity: Gender, Class, and Inequality in the Men's Grooming Industry*. New Brunswick, NJ: Rutgers University Press.

Barker, Meg, and Darren Langdridge. 2010. "Whatever Happened to Non-Monogamies? Critical Reflections on Recent Research and Theory." *Sexualities* 13 (6): 748–72. https://doi.org/10.1177/1363460710384645.

Barnshaw, John, and Lynn Letukas. 2010. "The Low Down on the Down Low: Origins, Risk Identification, and Intervention." *Health Sociology Review* 19 (4): 478–90. https://doi.org/10.5172/hesr.2010.19.4.478.

Beach, Lauren, Elizabeth Bartelt, Brian Dodge, Wendy Bostwick, Vanessa Schick, Tsung-Chieh (Jane) Fu, M. Reuel Friedman, and Debby Herbenick. 2019. "Meta-Perceptions of Others' Attitudes toward Bisexual Men and Women among a Nationally Representative Probability Sample." *Archives of Sexual Behavior* 48 (1): 191–97. https://doi.org/10.1007/s10508-018-1347-8.

Beck, Julie. 2019. "How Many People Have to Die before We're Done with Gender Reveals?" *Atlantic*, November 11. https://www.theatlantic.com.

Bederman, Gail. 1996. *Manliness and Civilization: A Cultural History of Gender and Race in the United States, 1880–1917*. Women in Culture and Society. Chicago: University of Chicago Press.

Bever, Lindsey. 2018. "What Monica Lewinsky Learned from #MeToo." *Washington Post*, February 26. https://www.washingtonpost.com.

Bird, Sharon R. 1996. "Welcome to the Men's Club: Homosociality and the Maintenance of Hegemonic Masculinity." *Gender & Society* 10 (2): 120–32. https://doi.org/10.1177/089124396010002002.

Boag, Peter. 2003. *Same-Sex Affairs: Constructing and Controlling Homosexuality in the Pacific Northwest*. Berkeley: University of California Press.

———. 2011. *Re-Dressing America's Frontier Past*. Berkeley: University of California Press.

Boertien, Diederik, and Fabrizio Bernardi. 2019. "Same-Sex Parents and Children's School Progress: An Association That Disappeared over Time." *Demography* 56 (2): 477–501. https://doi.org/10.1007/s13524-018-0759-3.

Bonilla-Silva, Eduardo. 2003. *Racism without Racists: Color-Blind Racism and the Persistence of Racial Inequality in the United States*. Lanham, MD: Rowman & Littlefield.

———. 2016. "Reply to Professor Fenelon and Adding Emotion to My Materialist RSS Theory." *Sociology of Race and Ethnicity* 2 (2): 243–47. https://doi.org/10.1177/2332649216628300.

Bonilla-Silva, Eduardo, Carla Goar, and David Embrick. 2006. "When Whites Flock Together: The Social Psychology of White Habitus." *Critical Sociology* 32 (2–3): 229–54. https://doi.org/10.1163/156916306777835268.

Bos, Henny M. W., Justin R. Knox, Loes van Rijn-van Gelderen, and Nanette K. Gartrell. 2016. "Same-Sex and Different-Sex Parent Households and Child Health Outcomes: Findings from the National Survey of Children's Health." *Journal of Developmental & Behavioral Pediatrics* 37 (3): 179–87. https://doi.org/10.1097/DBP.0000000000000288.

Boso, Luke. 2013. "Urban Bias, Rural Sexual Minorities, and the Courts." *UCLA Law Review* 60 (3): 562–637.

Bourdieu, Pierre. 1985. "The Social Space and the Genesis of Groups." *Theory and Society* 14 (6): 723–44. https://doi.org/10.1007/BF00174048.

———. 1989. "Social Space and Symbolic Power." *Sociological Theory* 7 (1): 14–25. https://doi.org/10.2307/202060.

Brandth, Berit. 2019. "'Tough and Tender'? Agricultural Masculinities and Fathering Activities." *NORMA: International Journal for Masculinity Studies* 14 (4): 223–38. https://doi.org/10.1080/18902138.2019.1654725.

Branson-Potts, Hailey. 2018. "In California's Rural, Conservative North, There Are Big Dreams for Cleaving the State." *Los Angeles Times*, March 17.

Brekhus, Wayne. 2003. *Peacocks, Chameleons, Centaurs: Gay Suburbia and the Grammar of Social Identity*. Chicago: University of Chicago Press.

Brewaeys, Mathilde, and Henny Bos. 2018. "Bewust Alleenstaande Moeders: Ouder-Kindrelaties, Sociale Steunnetwerken En Het Welzijn van Hun Kinderen." *Pedagogiek* 38 (2): 189–222.

Brewster, Melanie Elyse, Blake Soderstrom, Jessica Esposito, Aaron Breslow, Jacob Sawyer, Elizabeth Geiger, Negar Morshedian, et al. 2017. "A Content Analysis of Scholarship on Consensual Nonmonogamies: Methodological Roadmaps, Current Themes, and Directions for Future Research." *Couple and Family Psychology: Research and Practice* 6 (1): 32–47. https://doi.org/10.1037/cfp0000074.

Bridges, Tristan. 2014. "A Very 'Gay' Straight? Hybrid Masculinities, Sexual Aesthetics, and the Changing Relationship between Masculinity and Homophobia." *Gender & Society* 28 (1): 58–82. https://doi.org/10.1177/0891243213503901.

Bridges, Tristan, and C. J. Pascoe. 2014. "Hybrid Masculinities: New Directions in the Sociology of Men and Masculinities." *Sociology Compass* 8 (3): 246–58. https://doi.org/10.1111/soc4.12134.

———. 2016. "Masculinities and Post-Homophobias." In *Exploring Masculinities: Identity, Inequality, Continuity, and Change*, 412–23. Oxford: Oxford University Press.

Brown, Anna. 2018. "Most Americans Say Higher Ed Is Heading in Wrong Direction, but Partisans Disagree on Why." Pew Research Center, July 26. https://www.pewresearch.org.

Brown, Gavin. 2008. "Urban (Homo)Sexualities: Ordinary Cities and Ordinary Sexualities." *Geography Compass* 2 (4): 1215–31. https://doi.org/10.1111/j.1749-8198.2008.00127.x.

Brown, Taylor N. T., Adam P. Romero, and Gary J. Gates. 2016. "Food Insecurity and SNAP Participation in the LGBT Community." Los Angeles: Williams Institute on Sexual Orientation and Gender Identity Law and Public Policy. https://williamsinstitute.law.ucla.edu.

Brown-Saracino, Japonica. 2015. "How Places Shape Identity: The Origins of Distinctive LBQ Identities in Four Small U.S. Cities." *American Journal of Sociology* 121 (1): 1–63. https://doi.org/10.1086/682066.

———. 2018. *How Places Make Us: Novel LBQ Identities in Four Small Cities*. Chicago: University of Chicago Press.

———. 2019. "Aligning Our Maps: A Call to Reconcile Distinct Visions of Literatures on Sexualities, Space, and Place." *City & Community* 18 (1): 37–43. https://doi.org/10.1111/cico.12378.

Budig, Michelle J., and Melissa J. Hodges. 2010. "Differences in Disadvantage: Variation in the Motherhood Penalty across White Women's Earnings Distribution." *American Sociological Review* 75 (5): 705–28. https://doi.org/10.1177/0003122410381593.

Budnick, J. 2016. "'Straight Girls Kissing'?: Understanding Same-Gender Sexuality beyond the Elite College Campus." *Gender & Society* 30 (5): 745–68. https://doi.org/10.1177/0891243216657511.

Bump, Philip. 2014. "There Really Are Two Americas: An Urban One and a Rural One." *Washington Post*, October 21.

Burke, Kelsy. 2016. *Christians under Covers: Evangelicals and Sexual Pleasure on the Internet*. Oakland: University of California Press.

Bye, Linda Marie. 2009. "'How to Be a Rural Man': Young Men's Performances and Negotiations of Rural Masculinities." *Journal of Rural Studies* 25 (3): 278–88. https://doi.org/10.1016/j.jrurstud.2009.03.002.

Cain, Demetria N., Chloe Mirzayi, H. Jonathon Rendina, Ana Ventuneac, Christian Grov, and Jeffrey T. Parsons. 2017. "Mediating Effects of Social Support and Internalized Homonegativity on the Association between Population Density and Mental Health among Gay and Bisexual Men." *LGBT Health* 4 (5): 352–59. https://doi.org/10.1089/lgbt.2017.0002.

Campbell, Hugh, and Michael Mayerfeld Bell. 2000. "The Question of Rural Masculinities." *Rural Sociology* 65 (4): 532–46. https://doi.org/10.1111/j.1549-0831.2000.tb00042.x.

Canaday, Margot. 2009. *The Straight State: Sexuality and Citizenship in Twentieth-Century America*. Princeton, NJ: Princeton University Press.

Cantú, Lionel. 2009. *The Sexuality of Migration: Border Crossings and Mexican Immigrant Men*, edited by Nancy Naples and Salvador Vidal-Ortiz. New York: NYU Press.

Caplan, Zoe. 2017. "The Problem with Square Pegs: Sexual Orientation Concordance as a Predictor of Depressive Symptoms." *Society and Mental Health* 7 (2): 105–20. https://doi.org/10.1177/2156869317701266.

Capó, Julio. 2017. *Welcome to Fairyland: Queer Miami before 1940*. Chapel Hill: University of North Carolina Press.

CareerBuilder. 2017. "Two in Five LGBT Workers Feel Bullied at Work, According to Recent CareerBuilder Survey." CareerBuilder. http://press.careerbuilder.com.

Carey, Nick. 2016. "In Rural-Urban Divide, U.S. Voters Are Worlds Apart." *Reuters*, November 11. https://www.reuters.com.

Carnevale, Anthony P., Nicole Smith, and Artem Gulish. 2018. "Women Can't Win: Despite Making Educational Gains and Pursuing High-Wage Majors, Women Still Earn Less Than Men." Washington, DC: Georgetown University, Center on Education and the Workforce. https://cew.georgetown.edu.

Carrillo, Héctor. 2017. *Pathways of Desire: The Sexual Migration of Mexican Gay Men.* Chicago: University of Chicago Press.

Carrillo, Héctor, and Jorge Fontdevila. 2014. "Border Crossings and Shifting Sexualities among Mexican Gay Immigrant Men: Beyond Monolithic Conceptions." *Sexualities* 17 (8): 919–38. https://doi.org/10.1177/1363460714552248.

Carrillo, Héctor, and Amanda Hoffman. 2016. "From MSM to Heteroflexibilities: Non-Exclusive Straight Male Identities and Their Implications for HIV Prevention and Health Promotion." *Global Public Health* 11 (7–8): 923–36. https://doi.org/10.1080/17441692.2015.1134272.

———. 2018. "'Straight with a Pinch of Bi': The Construction of Heterosexuality as an Elastic Category among Adult U.S. Men." *Sexualities* 21 (1–2): 90–108. https://doi.org/10.1177/1363460716678561.

Cassino, Dan. 2018. "Emasculation, Conservatism, and the 2016 Election." *Contexts* 17 (1): 48–53. https://doi.org/10.1177/1536504218766551.

Centers for Disease Control and Prevention. 2019. "HIV in the United States and Dependent Areas." Atlanta, GA. https://www.cdc.gov.

Cerna, Jonathan de la, and Karl Jade Cosido. 2020. "His Other Man: Straight Men's Romantic Relationships with Homosexual Partners." *Asia Pacific Journal of Academic Research in Social Sciences* 5 (1): 21–34.

Cha, Ariana Eunjung. 2019. "Proposed HHS Rule Would Strip Obama-Era Protections for LGBTQ Individuals." *Washington Post*, November 1. https://www.washingtonpost.com.

Chang, Mariko. 2015. "Women and Wealth: Insights for Grantmakers." New York: Asset Funders Network. https://assetfunders.org.

Charlton, Brittany M., Heather L. Corliss, Donna Spiegelman, Kerry Williams, and S. Bryn Austin. 2016. "Changes in Reported Sexual Orientation Following U.S. States' Recognition of Same-Sex Couples." *American Journal of Public Health* 106 (12): 2202–4. https://doi.org/10.2105/AJPH.2016.303449.

Chauncey, George. 1994. *Gay New York: Gender, Urban Culture, and the Making of the Gay Male World, 1890–1940.* New York: Basic Books.

Cheng, Simon, and Brian Powell. 2015. "Measurement, Methods, and Divergent Patterns: Reassessing the Effects of Same-Sex Parents." *Social Science Research* 52 (July): 615–26. https://doi.org/10.1016/j.ssresearch.2015.04.005.

Cho, Sumi, Kimberlé Williams Crenshaw, and Leslie McCall. 2013. "Toward a Field of Intersectionality Studies: Theory, Applications, and Praxis." *Signs* 38 (4): 785–810. https://doi.org/10.1086/669608.

Choo, Hae Yeon, and Myra Marx Ferree. 2010. "Practicing Intersectionality in Sociological Research: A Critical Analysis of Inclusions, Interactions, and Institutions in the Study of Inequalities." *Sociological Theory* 28 (2): 129–49. https://doi.org/10.1111/j.1467-9558.2010.01370.x.

Coffman, Katherine, Lucas Coffman, and Keith Marzelli Ericson. 2017. "The Size of the LGBT Population and the Magnitude of Antigay Sentiment Are Substantially Underestimated." *Management Science* 63 (10): 3168–86. https://doi.org/10.1287/mnsc.2016.2503.

Cohen, Alma, and Crystal Yang. 2018. "Judicial Politics and Sentencing Decisions." Working Paper 24615. National Bureau of Economic Research. https://doi.org/10.3386/w24615.

Cohen, Cathy J., Matthew Fowler, Vladimir E. Medenica, and Jon C. Rogowski. 2018. "Millennial Attitudes on LGBT Issues: Race, Identity, and Experience." University of Chicago. http://genforwardsurvey.com.

Cohen, Philip. 2018. "The Widening Political Divide over Science." December. University of Maryland. https://osf.io/preprints/socarxiv/u95aw.

Collins, Patricia Hill. 2015. "Intersectionality's Definitional Dilemmas." *Annual Review of Sociology* 41: 1–20. https://doi.org/10.1146/annurev-soc-073014-112142.

Compton, D'Lane, and Tristan Bridges. 2019. "2018 GSS Update on the U.S. LGB Population." Wordpress. *Inequality by (Interior) Design* (blog). April 12. https://inequalitybyinteriordesign.wordpress.com/2019/04/12/2018-gss-update-on-the-u-s-lgb-population/.

Connell, R. W., and James W. Messerschmidt. 2005. "Hegemonic Masculinity: Rethinking the Concept." *Gender & Society* 19 (6): 829–59. https://doi.org/10.1177/0891243205278639.

Connell, Raewyn. 1987. *Gender and Power: Society, the Person, and Sexual Politics.* Stanford, CA: Stanford University Press.

———. 2005. *Masculinities.* 2nd ed. Berkeley: University of California Press.

Conron, Kerith J., Shoshana K. Goldberg, and Carolyn T. Halpern. 2018. "Sexual Orientation and Sex Differences in Socioeconomic Status: A Population-Based Investigation in the National Longitudinal Study of Adolescent to Adult Health." *Journal of Epidemiology and Community Health* 72 (11): 1016–26. https://doi.org/10.1136/jech-2017-209860.

Courtenay, Will. 2006. "Rural Men's Health: Situating Risk in the Negotiation of Masculinity." In *Country Boys: Masculinity and Rural Life*, edited by Hugh Campbell, Michael Bell, and Margaret Finney, 139–58. University Park: Pennsylvania State University Press.

Cox, Daniel, Rachel Lienesch, and Robert P. Jones. 2017a. "Beyond Economics: Fears of Cultural Displacement Pushed the White Working Class to Trump." Washington, DC: Public Religion Research Institute. https://www.prri.org.

———. 2017b. "Who Sees Discrimination? Attitudes about Sexual Orientation, Gender Identity, Race, and Immigration Status: Findings from PRRI's American Values

Atlas." Washington, DC: Public Religion Research Institute. https://www.prri.org/research.

Cox, Daniel, Juhem Navarro-Rivera, and Robert P. Jones. 2016. "Race, Religion, and Political Affiliation of Americans' Core Social Networks." Washington, DC: Public Religion Research Institute. https://www.prri.org.

Crenshaw, Kimberle. 1991. "Mapping the Margins: Intersectionality, Identity Politics, and Violence against Women of Color." *Stanford Law Review* 43 (6): 1241–99. https://doi.org/10.2307/1229039.

Dameron, William. 2019. *The Lie: A Memoir of Two Marriages, Catfishing, and Coming Out*. Seattle, WA: Little A.

Davis, Georgiann. 2015. *Contesting Intersex: The Dubious Diagnosis*. New York: NYU Press.

Dean, James Joseph. 2014. *Straights: Heterosexuality in Post-Closeted Culture*. New York: NYU Press.

D'Emilio, John. 1997. "Capitalism and Gay Identity." In *Culture, Society, and Sexuality*, edited by Richard Parker and Peter Aggleton, 239–49. New York: Routledge.

Dentzman, Katherine, Ryanne Pilgeram, Paul Lewin, and Kelsey Conley. 2020. "Queer Farmers in the 2017 U.S. Census of Agriculture." *Society & Natural Resources*. https://doi.org/10.1080/08941920.2020.1806421.

Desmond, Matthew. 2006. "Becoming a Firefighter." *Ethnography* 7 (4): 387–421. https://doi.org/10.1177/1466138106073142.

Deterding, Nicole M., and Mary C. Waters. 2018. "Flexible Coding of In-Depth Interviews: A Twenty-first-Century Approach." *Sociological Methods & Research*, October. https://doi.org/10.1177/0049124118799377.

Diamond, Lisa. 2003. "What Does Sexual Orientation Orient? A Biobehavioral Model Distinguishing Romantic Love and Sexual Desire." *Psychological Review* 110 (1): 173–92. https://doi.org/10.1037/0033-295X.110.1.173.

———. 2009. *Sexual Fluidity: Understanding Women's Love and Desire*. Cambridge, MA: Harvard University Press.

Diaz, Andrea. 2018. "Officials Release Video from Gender Reveal Party That Ignited a 47,000-Acre Wildfire." *CNN*, November 28. https://www.cnn.com.

Diefendorf, Sarah. 2015. "After the Wedding Night: Sexual Abstinence and Masculinities over the Life Course." *Gender & Society* 29 (5): 647–69.

Diefendorf, Sarah, and Tristan Bridges. 2020. "On the Enduring Relationship between Masculinity and Homophobia." *Sexualities*. https://doi.org/10.1177/1363460719876843.

Doan, Long, Annalise Loehr, and Lisa R. Miller. 2014. "Formal Rights and Informal Privileges for Same-Sex Couples: Evidence from a National Survey Experiment." *American Sociological Review* 79 (6): 1172–95. https://doi.org/10.1177/0003122414555886.

Dodge, Brian, Debby Herbenick, M. Reuel Friedman, Vanessa Schick, Tsung-Chieh (Jane) Fu, Wendy Bostwick, Elizabeth Bartelt, et al. 2016. "Attitudes toward Bisexual

Men and Women among a Nationally Representative Probability Sample of Adults in the United States." *PLoS ONE* 11 (10): e0164430.

Downing, Janelle M., and Ellena Rosenthal. 2020. "Prevalence of Social Determinants of Health among Sexual Minority Women and Men in 2017." *American Journal of Preventive Medicine* 59 (1): 118–22. https://doi.org/10.1016/j.amepre.2020.01.007.

Duckworth, Kiera D., and Mary Nell Trautner. 2019. "Gender Goals: Defining Masculinity and Navigating Peer Pressure to Engage in Sexual Activity." *Gender & Society* 33 (5): 795–817. https://doi.org/10.1177/0891243219863031.

Duffin, Thomas P. 2016. "The Lowdown on the Down Low: Why Some Bisexually Active Men Choose to Self-Identify as Straight." *Journal of Bisexuality* 16 (4): 484–506. https://doi.org/10.1080/15299716.2016.1252301.

Dyar, Christina, and Brian A. Feinstein. 2018. "Binegativity: Attitudes toward and Stereotypes about Bisexual Individuals." In *Bisexuality: Theories, Research, and Recommendations for the Invisible Sexuality*, edited by D. Joye Swan and Shani Habibi, 95–111. Cham, Switzerland: Springer International. https://doi.org/10.1007/978-3-319-71535-3_6.

Dyar, Christina, Tenille C. Taggart, Craig Rodriguez-Seijas, Ronald G. Thompson, Jennifer C. Elliott, Deborah S. Hasin, and Nicholas R. Eaton. 2019. "Physical Health Disparities across Dimensions of Sexual Orientation, Race/Ethnicity, and Sex: Evidence for Increased Risk among Bisexual Adults." *Archives of Sexual Behavior* 48 (1): 225–42. https://doi.org/10.1007/s10508-018-1169-8.

Economist. 2016. "A Country Divided by Counties: America's Presidential Election over Time and Space." *Economist*, November 11. http://www.economist.com.

Egan, Patrick J. 2012. "Group Cohesion without Group Mobilization: The Case of Lesbians, Gays, and Bisexuals." *British Journal of Political Science* 42 (3): 597–616. https://doi.org/10.1017/S0007123411000500.

———. 2019. "Identity as Dependent Variable: How Americans Shift Their Identities to Align with Their Politics." *American Journal of Political Science*. https://doi.org/10.1111/ajps.12496.

Eliot, Lise. 2009. *Pink Brain, Blue Brain: How Small Differences Grow into Troublesome Gaps—and What We Can Do about It*. Boston: Houghton Mifflin Harcourt.

Emerson, Robert M., Rachel I. Fretz, and Linda L. Shaw. 1995. *Writing Ethnographic Fieldnotes*. Chicago: University of Chicago Press.

England, Paula. 2016. "Sometimes the Social Becomes Personal: Gender, Class, and Sexualities." *American Sociological Review* 81 (1): 4–28. https://doi.org/10.1177/0003122415621900.

England, Paula, Jonathan Bearak, Michelle J. Budig, and Melissa J. Hodges. 2016. "Do Highly Paid, Highly Skilled Women Experience the Largest Motherhood Penalty?" *American Sociological Review* 81 (6): 1161–89. https://doi.org/10.1177/0003122416673598.

England, Paula, Emma Mishel, and Mónica Caudillo. 2016. "Increases in Sex with Same-Sex Partners and Bisexual Identity across Cohorts of Women (but Not Men)." *Sociological Science* 3: 951–70. https://doi.org/10.15195/v3.a42.

Faderman, Lillian. 1991. *Odd Girls and Twilight Lovers: A History of Lesbian Life in Twentieth-Century America*. New York: Columbia University Press.

Falomir-Pichastor, Juan Manuel, and Gabriel Mugny. 2009. "'I'm Not Gay . . . I'm a Real Man!': Heterosexual Men's Gender Self-Esteem and Sexual Prejudice." *Personality and Social Psychology Bulletin* 35 (9): 1233–43. https://doi.org/10.1177/0146167209338072.

Farmer, Grant W., John R. Blosnich, Jennifer M. Jabson, and Derrick D. Matthews. 2016. "Gay Acres: Sexual Orientation Differences in Health Indicators among Rural and Nonrural Individuals." *Journal of Rural Health* 32 (3): 321–31. https://doi.org/10.1111/jrh.12161.

Fausto-Sterling, A. 2000. "The Five Sexes, Revisited." *Sciences* 40 (4): 18–23.

Feinstein, Brian A., Christina Dyar, Dennis H. Li, Sarah W. Whitton, Michael E. Newcomb, and Brian Mustanski. 2018. "The Longitudinal Associations between Outness and Health Outcomes among Gay/Lesbian versus Bisexual Emerging Adults." *Archives of Sexual Behavior* 48 (4): 1111–26. https://doi.org/10.1007/s10508-018-1221-8.

Fellows, Will. 1998. *Farm Boys: Lives of Gay Men from the Rural Midwest*. 2nd ed. Madison: University of Wisconsin Press.

Fetner, Tina. 2008. *How the Religious Right Shaped Lesbian and Gay Activism*. Minneapolis: University of Minnesota Press.

Fidas, Deena, and Liz Cooper. 2018. "A Workplace Divided: Understanding the Climate for LGBTQ Workers Nationwide." Washington, DC: Human Rights Campaign Foundation. https://assets2.hrc.org.

Fine, Cordelia. 2010. *Delusions of Gender: How Our Minds, Society, and Neurosexism Create Difference*. 1st ed. New York: Norton.

Fleckenstein, James R., and Derrell W. Cox. 2015. "The Association of an Open Relationship Orientation with Health and Happiness in a Sample of Older U.S. Adults." *Sexual and Relationship Therapy* 30 (1): 94–116. https://doi.org/10.1080/14681994.2014.976997.

Flood, Michael. 2008. "Men, Sex, and Homosociality: How Bonds between Men Shape Their Sexual Relations with Women." *Men and Masculinities* 10 (3): 339–59. https://doi.org/10.1177/1097184X06287761.

Flores, Andrew R., and Andrew Park. 2018. "Examining the Relationship between Social Acceptance of LGBT People and Legal Inclusion of Sexual Minorities." Los Angeles: Williams Institute on Sexual Orientation and Gender Identity Law and Public Policy. https://williamsinstitute.law.ucla.edu.

Florida, Richard. 2016. "How America's Metro Areas Voted," *Citylab*, November 29. https://www.citylab.com.

Fontdevila, Jorge. 2019. "Productive Pleasures across Binary Regimes: Phenomenologies of Bisexual Desires among Latino Men." *Sexualities* 23 (4): 645–65. https://doi.org/10.1177/1363460719839915.

Ford, Chandra L., Kathryn D. Whetten, Susan A. Hall, Jay S. Kaufman, and Angela D. Thrasher. 2007. "Black Sexuality, Social Construction, and Research Targeting 'The Down Low' ('The DL')." *Annals of Epidemiology* 17 (3): 209–16. https://doi.org/10.1016/j.annepidem.2006.09.006.

Forstie, Clare. 2020. "Theory Making from the Middle: Researching LGBTQ Communities in Small Cities." *City & Community* 19 (1): 153–68. https://doi.org/10.1111/cico.12446.

Foucault, Michel. 1988. *The History of Sexuality*. 1st Vintage Books ed. New York: Vintage Books.

Frederick, David A., H. Kate St. John, Justin R. Garcia, and Elisabeth A. Lloyd. 2018. "Differences in Orgasm Frequency among Gay, Lesbian, Bisexual, and Heterosexual Men and Women in a U.S. National Sample." *Archives of Sexual Behavior* 47 (1): 273–88. https://doi.org/10.1007/s10508-017-0939-z.

Freud, Sigmund. 1975. *Three Essays on the Theory of Sexuality*. New York: Basic Books.

Gahman, Levi. 2015. "Gun Rites: Hegemonic Masculinity and Neoliberal Ideology in Rural Kansas." *Gender, Place & Culture* 22 (9): 1203–19. https://doi.org/10.1080/0966369X.2014.970137.

Galinsky, Adena M., Martha K. McClintock, and Linda J. Waite. 2014. "Sexuality and Physical Contact in National Social Life, Health, and Aging Project Wave 2." *Journals of Gerontology: Series B* 69 (November): S83–98. https://doi.org/10.1093/geronb/gbu072.

Gamio, Lazaro. 2016. "Urban and Rural America Are Becoming Increasingly Polarized." *Washington Post*, November 17. https://www.washingtonpost.com.

Gansen, Heidi M. 2017. "Reproducing (and Disrupting) Heteronormativity: Gendered Sexual Socialization in Preschool Classrooms." *Sociology of Education* 90 (3): 255–72. https://doi.org/10.1177/0038040717720981.

Gates, Gary J. 2014. "LGBT Demographics: Comparisons among Population-Based Surveys." University of California, Los Angeles: Williams Institute on Sexual Orientation and Gender Identity Law and Public Policy. https://williamsinstitute.law.ucla.edu.

———. 2017. "In U.S., More Adults Identifying as LGBT." *Pew*, January 11. https://news.gallup.com.

Gattis, Maurice N., Paul Sacco, and Renee M. Cunningham-Williams. 2012. "Substance Use and Mental Health Disorders among Heterosexual-Identified Men and Women Who Have Same-Sex Partners or Same-Sex Attraction: Results from the National Epidemiological Survey on Alcohol and Related Conditions." *Archives of Sexual Behavior; New York* 41 (5): 1185–97. http://dx.doi.org/10.1007/s10508-012-9910-1.

Gerber, Lynne. 2011. *Seeking the Straight and Narrow: Weight Loss and Sexual Reorientation in Evangelical America*. Chicago: University of Chicago Press.

Ghaziani, Amin. 2014a. "Measuring Urban Sexual Cultures." *Theory and Society* 43 (3): 371–93. https://doi.org/10.1007/s11186-014-9225-4.

———. 2014b. *There Goes the Gayborhood?* Princeton, NJ: Princeton University Press.

———. 2019. "Cultural Archipelagos: New Directions in the Study of Sexuality and Space." *City & Community* 18 (1): 4–22. https://doi.org/10.1111/cico.12381.

Gieryn, Thomas F. 2000. "A Space for Place in Sociology." *Annual Review of Sociology* 26 (1): 463–96. https://doi.org/10.1146/annurev.soc.26.1.463.

Golombok, Susan, Sophie Zadeh, Susan Imrie, Venessa Smith, and Tabitha Freeman. 2016. "Single Mothers by Choice: Mother-Child Relationships and Children's

Psychological Adjustment." *Journal of Family Psychology* 30 (4): 409–18. https://doi.org/10.1037/fam0000188.

Gonzales, Gilbert, and Jesse M. Ehrenfeld. 2018. "The Association between State Policy Environments and Self-Rated Health Disparities for Sexual Minorities in the United States." *International Journal of Environmental Research and Public Health* 15 (6): 1136. https://doi.org/10.3390/ijerph15061136.

Gonzales, Gilbert, Julia Przedworski, and Carrie Henning-Smith. 2016. "Comparison of Health and Health Risk Factors between Lesbian, Gay, and Bisexual Adults and Heterosexual Adults in the United States: Results from the National Health Interview Survey." *JAMA Internal Medicine* 176 (9): 1344–51. https://doi.org/10.1001/jamainternmed.2016.3432.

González-López, Gloria. 2005. *Erotic Journeys: Mexican Immigrants and Their Sex Lives*. Berkeley: University of California Press.

Gottschalk, Lorene, and Janice Newton. 2009. "Rural Homophobia: Not Really Gay." *Gay & Lesbian Issues and Psychology Review* 5 (3): 153–59.

Gould, Elise, and Teresa Kroeger. 2017. "Women Can't Educate Their Way out of the Gender Wage Gap." Washington, DC: Economic Policy Institute. https://www.epi.org.

Gould, Skye, and Bob Bryan. 2018. "The Diverging Midterm Results Show There's a Growing Political Chasm in America: And Both Parties Look Like They're Digging In." *Business Insider*, November 12. https://www.businessinsider.com.

Gray, Mary L. 2009. *Out in the Country: Youth, Media, and Queer Visibility in Rural America*. New York: NYU Press.

Gray, Mary L., Colin R. Johnson, and Brian Joseph Gilley. 2016. *Queering the Countryside: New Frontiers in Rural Queer Studies*. New York: NYU Press.

Greenberg, Daniel, Maxine Najle, Oyindamola Bola, and Robert P. Jones. 2019. "Fifty Years after Stonewall: Widespread Support for LGBT Issues; Findings from American Values Atlas 2018." Washington, DC: Public Religion Research Institute. https://www.prri.org.

Greenberg, Daniel, Maxine Najle, Natalie Jackson, Oyindamola Bola, and Robert P. Jones. 2019. "Increasing Support for Religiously Based Service Refusals." Washington, DC: Public Religion Research Institute. https://www.prri.org.

Greenhouse, Linda. 2019. "Civil Rights Turned Topsy-Turvy." *New York Times*, August 29. https://www.nytimes.com.

Grzanka, Patrick. 2016. "Queer Survey Research and the Ontological Dimensions of Heterosexism." *Women's Studies Quarterly* 44 (3/4): 131–49. https://doi.org/10.1353/wsq.2016.0039.

Grzanka, Patrick R., ed. 2014. *Intersectionality: A Foundations and Frontiers Reader*. New York: Routledge.

Hagerman, Margaret Ann. 2016. "Reproducing and Reworking Colorblind Racial Ideology." *Sociology of Race and Ethnicity* 2 (1): 58–71. https://doi.org/10.1177/2332649215594817.

Hakim, Danny, and Michael Wines. 2018. "'They Don't Really Want Us to Vote': How Republicans Made It Harder." *New York Times*, November 3. https://www.nytimes.com.

Halberstam, Judith. 2005. *In a Queer Time and Place: Transgender Bodies, Subcultural Lives*. New York: NYU Press.

———. 2011. *The Queer Art of Failure*. Durham, NC: Duke University Press.

Hamilton, Laura, and Elizabeth A. Armstrong. 2009. "Gendered Sexuality in Young Adulthood: Double Binds and Flawed Options." *Gender & Society* 23 (5): 589–616. https://doi.org/10.1177/0891243209345829.

Hammack, Phillip L., David M. Frost, and Sam D. Hughes. 2018. "Queer Intimacies: A New Paradigm for the Study of Relationship Diversity." *Journal of Sex Research* 56 (4–5): 556–92. https://doi.org/10.1080/00224499.2018.1531281.

Han, Chong-suk. 2015. "No Brokeback for Black Men: Pathologizing Black Male (Homo)Sexuality through Down Low Discourse." *Social Identities* 21 (3): 228–43. https://doi.org/10.1080/13504630.2015.1041019.

Hart, Chloe Grace, Aliya Saperstein, Devon Magliozzi, and Laurel Westbrook. 2019. "Gender and Health: Beyond Binary Categorical Measurement." *Journal of Health and Social Behavior* 60 (1): 101–18. https://doi.org/10.1177/0022146519825749.

Hatzenbuehler, Mark L., Katherine M. Keyes, and Deborah S. Hasin. 2009. "State-Level Policies and Psychiatric Morbidity in Lesbian, Gay, and Bisexual Populations." *American Journal of Public Health* 99 (12): 2275–81. https://doi.org/10.2105/AJPH.2008.153510.

Hatzenbuehler, Mark L., Katie A. McLaughlin, Katherine M. Keyes, and Deborah S. Hasin. 2010. "The Impact of Institutional Discrimination on Psychiatric Disorders in Lesbian, Gay, and Bisexual Populations: A Prospective Study." *American Journal of Public Health* 100 (3): 452–59. https://doi.org/10.2105/AJPH.2009.168815.

Hatzenbuehler, Mark L., Conall O'Cleirigh, Chris Grasso, Kenneth Mayer, Steven Safren, and Judith Bradford. 2012. "Effect of Same-Sex Marriage Laws on Health Care Use and Expenditures in Sexual Minority Men: A Quasi-Natural Experiment." *American Journal of Public Health* 102 (2): 285–91. https://doi.org/10.2105/AJPH.2011.300382.

Havekes, Esther, Michael Bader, and Maria Krysan. 2016. "Realizing Racial and Ethnic Neighborhood Preferences? Exploring the Mismatches between What People Want, Where They Search, and Where They Live." *Population Research and Policy Review* 35: 101–26. https://doi.org/10.1007/s11113-015-9369-6.

Hayfield, Nikki. 2020. *Bisexual and Pansexual Identities: Exploring and Challenging Invisibility and Invalidation*. New York: Routledge.

Heath, Melanie. 2009. "State of Our Unions: Marriage Promotion and the Contested Power of Heterosexuality." *Gender & Society* 23 (1): 27–48. https://doi.org/10.1177/0891243208326807.

———. 2019. "Espousing Patriarchy: Conciliatory Masculinity and Homosocial Femininity in Religiously Conservative Families." *Gender & Society* 33 (6): 888–910. https://doi.org/10.1177/0891243219857986.

Hennen, Peter. 2008. *Faeries, Bears, and Leathermen: Men in Community Queering the Masculine*. Chicago: University of Chicago Press.

Henning-Smith, Carrie, and Gilbert Gonzales. 2018. "Differences by Sexual Orientation in Perceptions of Neighborhood Cohesion: Implications for Health." *Journal of Community Health* 43 (3): 578–85. https://doi.org/10.1007/s10900-017-0455-z.

Hensley, Christopher, Richard Tewksbury, and Jeremy Wright. 2001. "Exploring the Dynamics of Masturbation and Consensual Same-Sex Activity within a Male Maximum Security Prison." *Journal of Men's Studies* 10 (1): 59–71. https://doi.org/10.3149/jms.1001.59.

Herbenick, Debby, Vanessa Schick, Stephanie A. Sanders, Michael Reece, and J. Dennis Fortenberry. 2015. "Pain Experienced during Vaginal and Anal Intercourse with Other-Sex Partners: Findings from a Nationally Representative Probability Study in the United States." *Journal of Sexual Medicine* 12 (4): 1040–51. https://doi.org/10.1111/jsm.12841.

Herdt, Gilbert H. 1987. *The Sambia: Ritual and Gender in New Guinea.* New York: Holt, Rinehart, and Winston.

Herek, Gregory M. 2002. "Heterosexuals' Attitudes toward Bisexual Men and Women in the United States." *Journal of Sex Research* 39 (4): 264–74. https://doi.org/10.1080/00224490209552150.

Herring, Scott. 2010. *Another Country: Queer Anti-Urbanism.* New York: NYU Press.

Hochschild, Arlie Russell. 2016. *Strangers in Their Own Land: Anger and Mourning on the American Right.* New York: New Press.

Hooghe, Marc, and Ruth Dassonneville. 2018. "Explaining the Trump Vote: The Effect of Racist Resentment and Anti-Immigrant Sentiments." *PS: Political Science & Politics* 51 (3): 528–34. https://doi.org/10.1017/S1049096518000367.

Horowitz, Adam, and Charles J. Gomez. 2018. "Identity Override: How Sexual Orientation Reduces the Rigidity of Racial Boundaries." *Sociological Science* 5 (November): 669–93. https://doi.org/10.15195/v5.a28.

Horowitz, Juliana Menasce, Nikki Graf, and Gretchen Livingston. 2019. "Marriage and Cohabitation in the U.S." Washington, DC: Pew Research Center. https://www.pewsocialtrends.org.

Horwitz, Sar. 2016. "Getting a Photo ID So You Can Vote Is Easy: Unless You're Poor, Black, Latino, or Elderly." *Washington Post*, May 23. https://www.washingtonpost.com.

Howard, John. 1999. *Men like That: A Southern Queer History.* Chicago: University of Chicago Press.

Hudson, Jeffrey H. 2013. "Comprehensive Literature Review Pertaining to Married Men Who Have Sex with Men (MMSM)." *Journal of Bisexuality* 13 (4): 417–601. https://doi.org/10.1080/15299716.2013.842356.

Humphreys, Laud. 1970. *Tearoom Trade: Impersonal Sex in Public Places.* Chicago: Aldine.

Hunter, Marcus Anthony. 2010. "All the Gays Are White and All the Blacks Are Straight: Black Gay Men, Identity, and Community." *Sexuality Research and Social Policy* 7 (2): 81–92. https://doi.org/10.1007/s13178-010-0011-4.

Igielnik, Ruth. 2017. "Rural and Urban Gun Owners Have Different Experiences, Views on Gun Policy." Pew Research Center. https://www.pewresearch.org.

Ingraham, Chrys. 1994. "The Heterosexual Imaginary: Feminist Sociology and Theories of Gender." *Sociological Theory* 12 (2): 203. https://doi.org/10.2307/201865.

———. 2008. *White Weddings: Romancing Heterosexuality in Popular Culture*. 2nd ed. Hoboken, NJ: Taylor & Francis.

Jackson, Stevi. 1999. *Heterosexuality in Question*. London: Sage.

———. 2006. "Interchanges: Gender, Sexuality, and Heterosexuality: The Complexity (and Limits) of Heteronormativity." *Feminist Theory* 7 (1): 105–21. https://doi.org/10.1177/1464700106061462.

Jakubek, Joseph, and Spencer D. Wood. 2018. "Emancipatory Empiricism: The Rural Sociology of W. E. B. Du Bois." *Sociology of Race and Ethnicity* 4 (1): 14–34. https://doi.org/10.1177/2332649217701750.

Jerke, Bud W. 2011. "Queer Ruralism." *Harvard Journal of Law & Gender* 34 (1): 259–312.

Johnson, Colin R. 2013. *Just Queer Folks: Gender and Sexuality in Rural America*. Philadelphia: Temple University Press.

Jones, Maggie. 2018. "What Teenagers Are Learning from Online Porn." *New York Times*, February 7. https://www.nytimes.com.

Kail, Ben Lennox, Katie L. Acosta, and Eric R. Wright. 2015. "State-Level Marriage Equality and the Health of Same-Sex Couples." *American Journal of Public Health* 105 (6): 1101–5. https://doi.org/10.2105/AJPH.2015.302589.

Katz, Jonathan. 1995. *The Invention of Heterosexuality*. New York: Dutton.

———. 2001. *Love Stories: Sex between Men before Homosexuality*. Chicago: University of Chicago Press.

Kazyak, Emily. 2012. "Midwest or Lesbian? Gender, Rurality, and Sexuality." *Gender & Society* 26 (6): 825–48. https://doi.org/10.1177/0891243212458361.

Kersey, Alyssa J., Kelsey D. Csumitta, and Jessica F. Cantlon. 2019. "Gender Similarities in the Brain during Mathematics Development." *Science of Learning* 4 (1): 1–7. https://doi.org/10.1038/s41539-019-0057-x.

Killewald, Alexandra. 2013. "A Reconsideration of the Fatherhood Premium: Marriage, Coresidence, Biology, and Fathers' Wages." *American Sociological Review* 78 (1): 96–116. https://doi.org/10.1177/0003122412469204.

Kimmel, Michael S. 1996. *Manhood in America: A Cultural History*. Oxford: Oxford University Press.

Kinsey, Alfred C., Wardell Baxter Pomeroy, and Clyde E. Martin. 1948. *Sexual Behavior in the Human Male*. Philadelphia: W.B. Saunders.

Kitzinger, Celia, and Sue Wilkinson. 1995. "Transitions from Heterosexuality to Lesbianism: The Discursive Production of Lesbian Identities." *Developmental Psychology* 31 (1): 95–104. https://doi.org/10.1037/0012-1649.31.1.95.

Knowles, Eric, and Sarah DiMuccio. 2018. "How Donald Trump Appeals to Men Secretly Insecure about Their Manhood." *Washington Post*, November 29. https://www.washingtonpost.com.

Kosciw, Joseph G., Emily A. Greytak, Adrian D. Zongrone, Caitlin M. Clark, and Nhan L. Truong. 2018. "The 2017 National School Climate Survey: The Experiences of

Lesbian, Gay, Bisexual, Transgender, and Queer Youth in Our Nation's Schools." New York: GLSEN. https://www.glsen.org.

Krueger, Evan A., and Dawn M. Upchurch. 2019. "Are Sociodemographic, Lifestyle, and Psychosocial Characteristics Associated with Sexual Orientation Group Differences in Mental Health Disparities? Results from a National Population-Based Study." *Social Psychiatry and Psychiatric Epidemiology* 54 (6): 755–70. https://doi.org/10.1007/s00127-018-1649-0.

Krysan, Maria, and Kyle Crowder. 2017. *Cycle of Segregation: Social Processes and Residential Stratification*. New York: Russell Sage Foundation.

Kuperberg, Arielle, and Alicia M. Walker. 2018. "Heterosexual College Students Who Hookup with Same-Sex Partners." *Archives of Sexual Behavior* 47 (5): 1387–1403. https://doi.org/10.1007/s10508-018-1194-7.

Kunzel, Regina G. 2008. *Criminal Intimacy: Prison and the Uneven History of Modern American Sexuality*. Chicago: University of Chicago Press.

Labrecque, Lindsay T., and Mark A. Whisman. 2017. "Attitudes toward and Prevalence of Extramarital Sex and Descriptions of Extramarital Partners in the 21st Century." *Journal of Family Psychology* 31 (7): 952–57. https://doi.org/10.1037/fam0000280.

Lamont, Ellen. 2015. "The Limited Construction of an Egalitarian Masculinity: College-Educated Men's Dating and Relationship Narratives." *Men and Masculinities* 18 (3): 271–92. https://doi.org/10.1177/1097184X14557495.

Langer, Gary. 2017. "Unwanted Sexual Advances Not Just a Hollywood, Weinstein Story, Poll Finds." *ABC News*, October 17. https://abcnews.go.com.

Lapowsky, Issie. 2018. "A Dead-Simple Algorithm Reveals the True Toll of Voter ID Laws." *Wired*, January 4. https://www.wired.com.

Lavy, Victor, and Edith Sand. 2015. "On the Origins of Gender Human Capital Gaps: Short- and Long-Term Consequences of Teachers' Stereotypical Biases." Cambridge, MA: National Bureau of Economic Research. https://www.nber.org/papers/w20909.pdf.

Leap, Braden. 2017. "Survival Narratives: Constructing an Intersectional Masculinity through Stories of the Rural/Urban Divide." *Journal of Rural Studies* 55: 12–21.

Lee, Hailey. 2017. "One-Fifth of American Adults Have Experienced Sexual Harassment at Work, CNBC Survey Says." *CNBC*, December 19. https://www.cnbc.com.

Leonhardt, David, and Kevin Quealy. 2015. "How Your Hometown Affects Your Chances of Marriage." *New York Times*, May 15. https://www.nytimes.com.

Leslie, Isaac Sohn. 2017. "Queer Farmers: Sexuality and the Transition to Sustainable Agriculture." *Rural Sociology* 82 (4): 747–71. https://doi.org/10.1111/ruso.12153.

Levanon, Asaf, Paula England, and Paul Allison. 2009. "Occupational Feminization and Pay: Assessing Causal Dynamics Using 1950–2000 U.S. Census Data." *Social Forces* 88 (2): 865–91. https://doi.org/10.1353/sof.0.0264.

Levin, R. J. 2018. "Prostate-Induced Orgasms: A Concise Review Illustrated with a Highly Relevant Case Study." *Clinical Anatomy* 31 (1): 81–85. https://doi.org/10.1002/ca.23006.

Levine, Ethan Czuy, Debby Herbenick, Omar Martinez, Tsung-Chieh Fu, and Brian Dodge. 2018. "Open Relationships, Nonconsensual Nonmonogamy, and Monogamy among U.S. Adults: Findings from the 2012 National Survey of Sexual Health and Behavior." *Archives of Sexual Behavior* 47 (5): 1439–50. https://doi.org/10.1007/s10508-018-1178-7.

Lew, Kelley Newlin, Caroline Dorsen, and Thomas Long. 2018. "Prevalence of Obesity, Prediabetes, and Diabetes in Sexual Minority Men: Results from the 2014 Behavioral Risk Factor Surveillance System." *Diabetes Educator* 44 (1): 83–93. https://doi.org/10.1177/0145721717749943.

Lichter, Daniel, and David Brown. 2011. "Rural America in an Urban Society: Changing Spatial and Social Boundaries." *Annual Review of Sociology* 37: 565–92. https://doi.org.

Lick, David J., Laura E. Durso, and Kerri L. Johnson. 2013. "Minority Stress and Physical Health among Sexual Minorities." *Perspectives on Psychological Science* 8 (5): 521–48. https://doi.org/10.1177/1745691613497965.

Lin, Ken-Hou, and Jennifer Lundquist. 2013. "Mate Selection in Cyberspace: The Intersection of Race, Gender, and Education." *American Journal of Sociology* 119 (1): 183–215. https://doi.org/10.1086/673129.

Lindau, Stacy Tessler, L. Philip Schumm, Edward O. Laumann, Wendy Levinson, Colm A. O'Muircheartaigh, and Linda J. Waite. 2007. "A Study of Sexuality and Health among Older Adults in the United States." *New England Journal of Medicine* 357 (8): 762–74. https://doi.org/10.1056/NEJMoa067423.

Little, Jo. 2015. "The Development of Feminist Perspectives in Rural Gender Studies." In *Feminisms and Ruralities*, edited by Pini Barbara, Berit Brandth, and Jo Little, 107–18. Lanham, MD: Lexington Books.

Livingston, Gretchen. 2018. "Family Life Is Changing in Different Ways across Urban, Suburban, and Rural Communities in the U.S." Pew Research Center, June 19. https://www.pewresearch.org.

Livingston, Gretchen, and Anna Brown. 2017. "Intermarriage in the U.S. 50 Years after *Loving v. Virginia*." Pew Research Center, May 18. http://assets.pewresearch.org.

Lochlainn, Mary Ni, and Rose Anne Kenny. 2013. "Sexual Activity and Aging." *Journal of the American Medical Directors Association* 14 (8): 565–72. https://doi.org/10.1016/j.jamda.2013.01.022.

Loe, Meika. 2001. "Fixing Broken Masculinity: Viagra as a Technology for the Production of Gender and Sexuality." *Sexuality and Culture* 5 (3): 97–125. https://doi.org/10.1007/s12119-001-1032-1.

Löfström, Jan. 1997. "The Birth of the Queen/the Modern Homosexual: Historical Explanations Revisited." *Sociological Review* 45 (1): 24–41. https://doi.org/10.1111/1467-954X.00052.

Loofbourow, Lili. 2018. "The Female Price of Male Pleasure." *Week*, January 25. https://theweek.com.

Lourie, Michael A., and Belinda L. Needham. 2017. "Sexual Orientation Discordance and Young Adult Mental Health." *Journal of Youth and Adolescence* 46 (5): 943–54. https://doi.org/10.1007/s10964-016-0553-8.

Lundquist, J. H., and K.-H. Lin. 2015. "Is Love (Color) Blind? The Economy of Race among Gay and Straight Daters." *Social Forces* 93 (4): 1423–49. https://doi.org/10.1093/sf/sov008.

Lynch, David J. 2019. "Small Towns Are Dying Everywhere but Here." *Washington Post*, April 5. https://www.washingtonpost.com.

Lyons, Anthony, Warwick Hosking, and Tomas Rozbroj. 2015. "Rural-Urban Differences in Mental Health, Resilience, Stigma, and Social Support among Young Australian Gay Men." *Journal of Rural Health* 31 (1): 89–97. https://doi.org/10.1111/jrh.12089.

MacLellan, Lila. 2017. "The Biggest Myth about Our Brains Is That They Are 'Male' or 'Female.'" *Quartz*, August 27. https://qz.com.

Magliozzi, Devon, Aliya Saperstein, and L. Westbrook. 2016. "Scaling Up: Representing Gender Diversity in Survey Research." *Socius: Sociological Research for a Dynamic World* 2: 1–11. https://doi.org/10.1177/2378023116664352.

Malani, Peter, Sarah Clark, Erica Solway, Dianne Singer, and Matthias Kirch. 2018. "National Poll on Healthy Aging Sexual Health Report." Ann Arbor: University of Michigan.

Mallory, Christy, Taylor N. T. Brown, and Keith J. Conron. 2018. "Conversion Therapy and LGBT Youth." Los Angeles: Williams Institute on Sexual Orientation and Gender Identity Law and Public Policy.

Manning, Wendy D., Marshal Neal Fettro, and Esther Lamidi. 2014. "Child Well-Being in Same-Sex Parent Families: Review of Research Prepared for American Sociological Association Amicus Brief." *Population Research and Policy Review* 33 (4): 485–502. https://doi.org/10.1007/s11113-014-9329-6.

Marcin, Tim. 2018. "Sexual Assault Should Not Disqualify Kavanaugh If Proven, Majority of Republicans Believe: Poll." *Newsweek*, September 27. https://www.newsweek.com.

Martin, Emily. 1991. "The Egg and the Sperm: How Science Has Constructed a Romance Based on Stereotypical Male-Female Roles." *Signs* 16 (3): 485–501. https://doi.org/10.1086/494680.

Martin, Karin A. 2009. "Normalizing Heterosexuality: Mothers' Assumptions, Talk, and Strategies with Young Children." *American Sociological Review* 74 (2): 190–207. https://doi.org/10.1177/000312240907400202.

Martin, Karin A., and Emily Kazyak. 2009. "Hetero-Romantic Love and Heterosexiness in Children's G-Rated Films." *Gender & Society* 23 (3): 315–36. https://doi.org/10.1177/0891243209335635.

Martin, Robert D. 2018. "The Macho Sperm Myth." *Aeon*, August 23. https://aeon.co.

Martinez, Jaime, and Sybil G. Hosek. 2005. "An Exploration of the Down-Low Identity: Nongay-Identified Young African-American Men Who Have Sex with Men." *Journal of the National Medical Association* 97 (8): 1101–12.

Marwha, Dhruv, Meha Halari, and Lise Eliot. 2017. "Meta-Analysis Reveals a Lack of Sexual Dimorphism in Human Amygdala Volume." *NeuroImage* 147 (February): 282–94. https://doi.org/10.1016/j.neuroimage.2016.12.021.

Mason, Everdeen, Aaron Williams, and Kennedy Elliott. 2017. "The Dramatic Rise in State Efforts to Limit LGBT Rights." *Washington Post*, June 29. https://www.washingtonpost.com.

Mattson, Greggor. 2020. "Small-City Gay Bars, Big-City Urbanism." *City & Community* 19 (1): 76–97. https://doi.org/10.1111/cico.12443.

Maxwell, Angie, and Todd Shields. 2018. "The Impact of 'Modern Sexism' on the 2016 Presidential Election." Fayetteville, AR: Diane D. Blair Center of Southern Politics & Society. https://blaircenter.uark.edu/the-impact-of-modern-sexism/.

McCall, Leslie. 2005. "The Complexity of Intersectionality." *Signs* 30 (3): 1771–1800. https://doi.org/10.1086/426800.

McCarthy, Justin. 2020. "U.S. Support for Same-Sex Marriage Matches Record High." *Gallup*, June 1. https://news.gallup.com.

Mencken, F. Carson, and Paul Froese. 2019. "Gun Culture in Action." *Social Problems* 66 (1): 3–27. https://doi.org/10.1093/socpro/spx040.

Messerschmidt, James W. 2015. *Masculinities in the Making: From the Local to the Global*. Lanham, MD: Rowman & Littlefield.

Messner, Michael A. 1992. *Power at Play: Sports and the Problem of Masculinity*. Boston: Beacon.

Meyer, Ilan H. 2013. "Prejudice, Social Stress, and Mental Health in Lesbian, Gay, and Bisexual Populations: Conceptual Issues and Research Evidence." *Psychology of Sexual Orientation and Gender Diversity* 1 (S): 3–26. https://doi.org/10.1037/2329-0382.1.S.3.

Metzl, Jonathan M. 2019. *Dying of Whiteness: How the Politics of Racial Resentment Is Killing America's Heartland*. New York: Basic Books.

Milbank, Dana. 2016. "Yes, Half of Trump Supporters Are Racist." *Washington Post*, September 12. https://www.washingtonpost.com.

Miller, Maureen, Malin Serner, and Meghan Wagner. 2005. "Sexual Diversity among Black Men Who Have Sex with Men in an Inner-City Community." *Journal of Urban Health* 82: i26–i34. https://doi.org/10.1093/jurban/jti021.

Miller, Sarah A. 2016. "'How You Bully a Girl': Sexual Drama and the Negotiation of Gendered Sexuality in High School." *Gender & Society* 30 (5): 721–44. https://doi.org/10.1177/0891243216664723.

Minkowitz, Donna. 2017. "How the Alt-Right Is Using Sex and Camp to Attract Gay Men to Fascism." *Slate*, June 5.

Mishel, Emma. 2019. "Intersections between Sexual Identity, Sexual Attraction, and Sexual Behavior among a Nationally Representative Sample of American Men and Women." *Journal of Official Statistics* 35 (4): 859–84. https://doi.org/10.2478/jos-2019-0036.

Mitchell, Kristina M. W., and Jonathan Martin. 2018. "Gender Bias in Student Evaluations." *PS: Political Science & Politics* 51 (3): 648–52. https://doi.org/10.1017/S104909651800001X.

Mittleman, Joel. 2018. "Sexual Orientation and School Discipline: New Evidence from a Population-Based Sample." *Educational Researcher* 47 (3): 181–90. https://doi.org/10.3102/0013189X17753123.

———. 2019. "Sexual Minority Bullying and Mental Health from Early Childhood through Adolescence." *Journal of Adolescent Health* 64 (2): 172–78. https://doi.org/10.1016/j.jadohealth.2018.08.020.

Mize, Trenton D. 2016. "Sexual Orientation in the Labor Market." *American Sociological Review* 81 (6): 1132–60. https://doi.org/10.1177/0003122416674025.

Mize, Trenton D., and Bianca Manago. 2018. "Precarious Sexuality: How Men and Women Are Differentially Categorized for Similar Sexual Behavior." *American Sociological Review* 83 (2): 305–30. https://doi.org/10.1177/0003122418759544.

Mock, Brentin. 2016. "More Research Shows Voter ID Laws Hurt Minorities." *Citylab*, February 5. https://www.citylab.com.

Mohr, John W., and Amin Ghaziani. 2014. "Problems and Prospects of Measurement in the Study of Culture." *Theory and Society* 43 (3): 225–46. https://doi.org/10.1007/s11186-014-9227-2.

Monro, Surya, Sally Hines, and Antony Osborne. 2017. "Is Bisexuality Invisible? A Review of Sexualities Scholarship, 1970–2015." *Sociological Review* 65 (4): 663–81. https://doi.org/10.1177/0038026117695488.

Morris, Edward W. 2008. "'Rednecks,' 'Rutters,' and `Rithmetic: Social Class, Masculinity, and Schooling in a Rural Context." *Gender & Society* 22 (6): 728–51. https://doi.org/10.1177/0891243208325163.

Moss-Racusin, Corinne A., John F. Dovidio, Victoria L. Brescoll, Mark J. Graham, and Jo Handelsman. 2012. "Science Faculty's Subtle Gender Biases Favor Male Students." *Proceedings of the National Academy of Sciences* 109 (41): 16474–79. https://doi.org/10.1073/pnas.1211286109.

Motta, Matt. 2017. "Republicans Are Increasingly Antagonistic toward Experts: Here's Why That Matters." *Washington Post*, August 11. https://www.washingtonpost.com.

Movement Advancement Project. 2019. "Where We Call Home: LGBT People in Rural America." Boulder, CO. http://www.lgbtmap.org.

Munsch, Christin L., and Kjerstin Gruys. 2018. "What Threatens, Defines: Tracing the Symbolic Boundaries of Contemporary Masculinity." *Sex Roles* 79 (7): 375–92. https://doi.org/10.1007/s11199-017-0878-0.

Mustanski, Brian, Michelle Birkett, George J. Greene, Margaret Rosario, Wendy Bostwick, and Bethany G. Everett. 2014. "The Association between Sexual Orientation Identity and Behavior across Race/Ethnicity, Sex, and Age in a Probability Sample of High School Students." *American Journal of Public Health; Washington* 104 (2): 237–44.

Mustanski, Brian, Ethan Morgan, Richard D'Aquila, Michelle Birkett, Patrick Janulis, and Michael E. Newcomb. 2019. "Individual and Network Factors Associated with Racial Disparities in HIV among Young Men Who Have Sex with Men: Results from the RADAR Cohort Study." *JAIDS: Journal of Acquired Immune Deficiency Syndromes* 80 (1): 24. https://doi.org/10.1097/QAI.0000000000001886.

Mutz, Diana C. 2018. "Status Threat, Not Economic Hardship, Explains the 2016 Presidential Vote." *Proceedings of the National Academy of Sciences* 115 (19): E4330–39. https://doi.org/10.1073/pnas.1718155115.

Myers, Kristen, and Laura Raymond. 2010. "Elementary School Girls and Hetero-normativity: The Girl Project." *Gender and Society* 24 (2): 167–88. https://doi.org/10.1177/0891243209358579.

Nagoshi, Craig T., J. Raven Cloud, Louis M. Lindley, Julie L. Nagoshi, and Lucas J. Lothamer. 2019. "A Test of the Three-Component Model of Gender-Based Prejudices: Homophobia and Transphobia Are Affected by Raters' and Targets' Assigned Sex at Birth." *Sex Roles* 80 (3): 137–46. https://doi.org/10.1007/s11199-018-0919-3.

Newkirk, Vann R., II. 2018. "Voter Suppression Is Warping Democracy." *Atlantic*, July 17. https://www.theatlantic.com.

Newport, Frank. 2018. "In U.S., Estimate of LGBT Population Rises to 4.5%." *Gallup*, May 22. https://news.gallup.com.

Norton, Rictor. 2006. *Mother Clap's Molly House: The Gay Subculture in England, 1700–1830*. Hornchurch, UK: Chalford Press.

Ocampo, Anthony. 2012. "Making Masculinity: Negotiations of Gender Presentation among Latino Gay Men." *Latino Studies* 10 (4): 448–72. https://doi.org/10.1057/lst.2012.37.

O'Connor, Emma C., Thomas E. Ford, and Noely C. Banos. 2017. "Restoring Threatened Masculinity: The Appeal of Sexist and Anti-Gay Humor." *Sex Roles* 77 (9–10): 567–80. https://doi.org/10.1007/s11199-017-0761-z.

Office of Management and Budget. 2010. "2010 Standards for Delineating Metropolitan and Micropolitan Statistical Areas: Notice." *Federal Register* 75 (123): 37245–52.

Ofosu, Eugene K., Michelle K. Chambers, Jacqueline M. Chen, and Eric Hehman. 2019. "Same-Sex Marriage Legalization Associated with Reduced Implicit and Explicit Antigay Bias." *Proceedings of the National Academy of Sciences* 116 (18): 8846–51. https://doi.org/10.1073/pnas.1806000116.

Omi, Michael, and Howard Winant. 2015. *Racial Formation in the United States*. New York: Routledge/Taylor & Francis Group.

Orne, Jason. 2017. *Boystown: Sex & Community in Chicago*. Chicago: University of Chicago Press.

Oselin, Sharon S., and Kristen Barber. 2019. "Borrowing Privilege: Status Maneuvering among Marginalized Men." *Gender & Society* 33 (2): 201–23. https://doi.org/10.1177/0891243218823354.

Oswald, Ramona Faith, and Vanja Lazarevic. 2011. "'You Live Where?!': Lesbian Mothers' Attachment to Nonmetropolitan Communities." *Family Relations* 60 (4): 373–86. https://doi.org/10.1111/j.1741-3729.2011.00663.x.

Parker, Kim. 2015. "Among LGBT Americans, Bisexuals Stand Out When It Comes to Identity, Acceptance." Pew Research Center, February 20. https://www.pewresearch.org.

Parker, Kim, Juliana Menasce Horowitz, Anna Brown, Richard Fry, D'Vera Cohn, and Ruth Igielnik. 2018. "How Urban, Suburban, and Rural Residents Interact with Their Neighbors." Pew Research Center. https://www.pewsocialtrends.org.

Paschen-Wolff, Margaret M., Elizabeth Kelvin, Brooke E. Wells, Aimee N. C. Campbell, Nicholas A. Grosskopf, and Christian Grov. 2019. "Changing Trends in Substance Use and Sexual Risk Disparities among Sexual Minority Women as a

Function of Sexual Identity, Behavior, and Attraction: Findings from the National Survey of Family Growth, 2002–2015." *Archives of Sexual Behavior* 48 (4): 1137–58. https://doi.org/10.1007/s10508-018-1333-1.

Pascoe, C. J. 2011. *Dude, You're a Fag: Masculinity and Sexuality in High School.* New ed. Berkeley: University of California Press.

Pascoe, C. J., and Tristan Bridges, eds. 2015. *Exploring Masculinities: Identity, Inequality, Continuity, and Change.* Oxford: Oxford University Press.

Pascoe, C. J., and Tony Silva. 2019. "Sexuality in School." In *Education & Society*, edited by Thurston Domina, Benjamin Gibbs, Lisa Nunn, and Andrew Penner, 81–95. Berkeley: University of California Press.

Patil, Vrushali. 2018. "The Heterosexual Matrix as Imperial Effect." *Sociological Theory* 36 (1): 1–26. https://doi.org/10.1177/0735275118759382.

Pear, Robert, and Jeremy W. Peters. 2018. "Trump Gives Health Workers New Religious Liberty Protections." *New York Times*, January 18. https://www.nytimes.com.

Perry, Samuel L. 2019. "The Bible as a Product of Cultural Power: The Case of Gender Ideology in the English Standard Version." *Sociology of Religion* 81 (1): 68–92. https://doi.org/10.1093/socrel/srz022.

Peters, Jeremy W. 2017. "Fighting Gay Rights and Abortion with the First Amendment." *New York Times*, November 22. https://www.nytimes.com.

Pew Research Center. 2017. "Sharp Partisan Divisions in Views of National Institutions," July 10. https://www.people-press.org.

———. 2018. "Wide Gender Gap, Growing Educational Divide in Voters' Party Identification," March 20. https://www.people-press.org.

Phillips, Layli. 2005. "Deconstructing 'Down Low' Discourse: The Politics of Sexuality, Gender, Race, AIDS, and Anxiety." *Journal of African American Studies* 9 (2): 3–15. https://doi.org/10.1007/s12111-005-1018-4.

Pierce, Jason E. 2016. *Making the White Man's West: Whiteness and the Creation of the American West.* Boulder: University Press of Colorado.

Pini, Barbara, Berit Brandth, and Jo Little. 2015. *Feminisms and Ruralities.* Lanham, MD: Lexington Books.

Poon, Colleen S., and Elizabeth M. Saewyc. 2009. "Out Yonder: Sexual Minority Adolescents in Rural Communities in British Columbia." *American Journal of Public Health* 99 (1): 118–24.

Price-Feeney, Myeshia, Michele L. Ybarra, and Kimberly J. Mitchell. 2019. "Health Indicators of Lesbian, Gay, Bisexual, and Other Sexual Minority (LGB+) Youth Living in Rural Communities." *Journal of Pediatrics* 205 (February): 236–43. https://doi.org/10.1016/j.jpeds.2018.09.059.

Priebe, Gisela, and Carl Göran Svedin. 2013. "Operationalization of Three Dimensions of Sexual Orientation in a National Survey of Late Adolescents." *Journal of Sex Research* 50 (8): 727–38. https://doi.org/10.1080/00224499.2012.713147.

Prince, Barbara F., Kara Joyner, and Wendy D. Manning. 2019. "Sexual Minorities, Social Context, and Union Formation." *Population Research and Policy Review* 39 (1): 23–45. https://doi.org/10.1007/s11113-019-09528-z.

Raifman, Julia, Ellen Moscoe, S. Bryn Austin, Mark L. Hatzenbuehler, and Sandro Galea. 2018. "Association of State Laws Permitting Denial of Services to Same-Sex Couples with Mental Distress in Sexual Minority Adults: A Difference-in-Difference-in-Differences Analysis." *JAMA Psychiatry* 75 (7): 671–77. https://doi.org/10.1001/jamapsychiatry.2018.0757.

Raifman, Julia, Ellen Moscoe, S. Bryn Austin, and Margaret McConnell. 2017. "Difference-in-Differences Analysis of the Association between State Same-Sex Marriage Policies and Adolescent Suicide Attempts." *JAMA Pediatrics* 171 (4): 350–56. https://doi.org/10.1001/jamapediatrics.2016.4529.

Ramakrishna, Anil, Victor R. Martínez, Nikolaos Malandrakis, Karan Singla, and Shrikanth Narayanan. 2017. "Linguistic Analysis of Differences in Portrayal of Movie Characters." Los Angeles: University of Southern California. https://sail.usc.edu.

Reardon, Sean F., Erin M. Fahle, Demetra Kalogrides, Anne Podolsky, and Rosalía C. Zárate. 2019. "Gender Achievement Gaps in U.S. School Districts." *American Educational Research Journal* 56 (6): 2474–2508. https://doi.org/10.3102/0002831219843824.

Reback, Cathy J., and Sherry Larkins. 2010. "Maintaining a Heterosexual Identity: Sexual Meanings among a Sample of Heterosexually Identified Men Who Have Sex with Men." *Archives of Sexual Behavior* 39 (3): 766–73. https://doi.org/10.1007/s10508-008-9437-7.

Reiner, Andrew. 2017. "The Power of Touch, Especially for Men." *New York Times*, December 5. https://www.nytimes.com.

Relman, Eliza. 2020. "The 25 Women Who Have Accused Trump of Sexual Misconduct." *Business Insider*, May 1. https://www.businessinsider.com.

Reynolds, Chelsea. 2015. "'I Am Super Straight and I Prefer You Be Too': A Textual Analysis of Craigslist Posts Made by 'Straight' Men Seeking Homosexual Sexual Encounters Online." *Journal of Communication Inquiry* 39 (3): 213–31. https://doi.org/10.1177/0196859915575736.

Rich, Adrienne. 1980. "Compulsory Heterosexuality and Lesbian Experience." *Signs: Journal of Women in Culture and Society* 5 (4): 631–60. https://doi.org/10.1086/493756.

Rippon, Gina. 2019. *The Gendered Brain: The New Neuroscience That Shatters the Myth of the Female Brain*. New York: Random House.

Robert Wood Johnson Foundation. 2017. "Discrimination in America: Experiences and Views of LGBTQ Americans." National Public Radio, Robert Wood Johnson Foundation, Harvard T. H. Chan School of Public Health. https://www.rwjf.org.

———. 2018. "Life in Rural America." National Public Radio, Robert Wood Johnson Foundation, Harvard T. H. Chan School of Public Health. https://cdn1.sph.harvard.edu.

Robertson, Ronald E., Felix W. Tran, Lauren N. Lewark, and Robert Epstein. 2018. "Estimates of Non-Heterosexual Prevalence: The Roles of Anonymity and Privacy in Survey Methodology." *Archives of Sexual Behavior* 47 (4): 1069–84. https://doi.org/10.1007/s10508-017-1044-z.

Robinson, Brandon Andrew, and David A. Moskowitz. 2013. "The Eroticism of Internet Cruising as a Self-Contained Behaviour: A Multivariate Analysis of Men Seeking Men Demographics and Getting Off Online." *Culture, Health & Sexuality* 15 (5): 555–69. https://doi.org/10.1080/13691058.2013.774050.

Robinson, Brandon, and Salvador Vidal-Ortiz. 2013. "Displacing the Dominant 'Down Low' Discourse: Deviance, Same-Sex Desire, and Craigslist.org." *Deviant Behavior* 34 (3): 224–41. https://doi.org/10.1080/01639625.2012.726174.

Robinson, Christine M., and Sue E. Spivey. 2007. "The Politics of Masculinity and the Ex-Gay Movement." *Gender & Society* 21 (5): 650–75. https://doi.org/10.1177/0891243207306384.

Roediger, David. 2005. *Working toward Whiteness: How America's Immigrants Became White*. New York: Basic Books.

Roscigno, Vincent J. 2019. "Discrimination, Sexual Harassment, and the Impact of Workplace Power." *Socius* 5 (January). https://doi.org/10.1177/2378023119853894.

Rosenberg, Gabriel. 2016. "A Classroom in the Barnyard: Reproducing Heterosexuality in Interwar American 4-H." In *Queering the Countryside: New Frontiers in Rural Queer Studies*, edited by Mary Gray, Colin Johnson, and Brian Gilley, 88–108. New York: NYU Press.

Rosenberger, Joshua G., Vanessa Schick, Phillip Schnarrs, David S. Novak, and Michael Reece. 2014. "Sexual Behaviors, Sexual Health Practices, and Community Engagement among Gay and Bisexually Identified Men Living in Rural Areas of the United States." *Journal of Homosexuality* 61 (8): 1192–1207. https://doi.org/10.1080/0091836 9.2014.872525.

Ross, Lori E., Travis Salway, Lesley A. Tarasoff, Jenna M. MacKay, Blake W. Hawkins, and Charles P. Fehr. 2018. "Prevalence of Depression and Anxiety among Bisexual People Compared to Gay, Lesbian, and Heterosexual Individuals: A Systematic Review and Meta-Analysis." *Journal of Sex Research* 55 (4–5): 435–56. https://doi.org /10.1080/00224499.2017.1387755.

Rothstein, Richard. 2017. *The Color of Law: A Forgotten History of How Our Government Segregated America*. New York: Liveright.

Rotundo, E. Anthony. 1989. "Romantic Friendship: Male Intimacy and Middle-Class Youth in the Northern United States, 1800–1900." *Journal of Social History* 23 (1): 1–25. https://doi.org/10.1353/jsh/23.1.1.

———. 1993. *American Manhood: Transformations in Masculinity from the Revolution to the Modern Era*. New York: Basic Books.

Roughgarden, Joan. 2004. *Evolution's Rainbow: Diversity, Gender, and Sexuality in Nature and People*. 2nd ed. Berkeley: University of California Press.

Rubel, Alicia N., and Anthony F. Bogaert. 2015. "Consensual Nonmonogamy: Psychological Well-Being and Relationship Quality Correlates." *Journal of Sex Research* 52 (9): 961–82. https://doi.org/10.1080/00224499.2014.942722.

Rupp, Leila J. 2012. "Sexual Fluidity 'before Sex.'" *Signs: Journal of Women in Culture and Society* 37 (4): 849–56. https://doi.org/10.1086/664470.

Rust, Paul. 1992. "The Politics of Sexual Identity: Sexual Attraction and Behavior among Lesbian and Bisexual Women." *Social Problems* 39 (4): 366–86. https://doi.org/10.2307/3097016.

Saleh, Lena Denise, and Don Operario. 2009. "Moving Beyond 'the Down Low': A Critical Analysis of Terminology Guiding HIV Prevention Efforts for African American Men Who Have Secretive Sex with Men." *Social Science & Medicine* 68 (2): 390–95. https://doi.org/10.1016/j.socscimed.2008.09.052.

Sallaz, Jeffrey, and Jane Zavisca. 2007. "Bourdieu in American Sociology, 1980–2004." *Annual Review of Sociology* 33: 21–41.

Sánchez, Francisco J., and Eric Vilain. 2012. "'Straight-Acting Gays': The Relationship between Masculine Consciousness, Anti-Effeminacy, and Negative Gay Identity." *Archives of Sexual Behavior* 41 (1): 111–19. https://doi.org/10.1007/s10508-012-9912-z.

Savin-Williams, Ritch C. 2017. *Mostly Straight: Sexual Fluidity among Men*. Cambridge, MA: Harvard University Press.

Savin-Williams, Ritch C., and Zhana Vrangalova. 2013. "Mostly Heterosexual as a Distinct Sexual Orientation Group: A Systematic Review of the Empirical Evidence." *Developmental Review* 33 (1): 58–88. https://doi.org/10.1016/j.dr.2013.01.001.

Schalet, Amy T. 2011. *Not under My Roof: Parents, Teens, and the Culture of Sex*. Chicago: University of Chicago Press.

Schilt, Kristen, and Laurel Westbrook. 2009. "Doing Gender, Doing Heteronormativity: 'Gender Normals,' Transgender People, and the Social Maintenance of Heterosexuality." *Gender & Society* 23 (4): 440–64. https://doi.org/10.1177/0891243209340034.

Schippers, Mimi. 2016. *Beyond Monogamy: Polyamory and the Future of Polyqueer Sexualities*. New York: NYU Press.

Schrimshaw, Eric W., Karolynn Siegel, and Martin J. Downing. 2010. "Sexual Risk Behaviors with Female and Male Partners Met in Different Sexual Venues among Non-Gay-Identified, Nondisclosing MSMW." *International Journal of Sexual Health* 22 (3): 167–79. https://doi.org/10.1080/19317611003748821.

Schrock, Douglas, and Michael Schwalbe. 2009. "Men, Masculinity, and Manhood Acts." *Annual Review of Sociology* 35: 277–95.

Seidman, Steven. 2002. *Beyond the Closet: The Transformation of Gay and Lesbian Life*. New York: Routledge.

———. 2009. "Critique of Compulsory Heterosexuality." *Sexuality Research & Social Policy* 6 (1): 18–28. https://doi.org/10.1525/srsp.2009.6.1.18.

Serwer, Adam. 2017. "The Nationalist's Delusion." *Atlantic*, November 20. https://www.theatlantic.com.

Seto, Michael C. 2017. "The Puzzle of Male Chronophilias." *Archives of Sexual Behavior* 46 (1): 3–22. https://doi.org/10.1007/s10508-016-0799-y.

Sherkat, Darren E., Melissa Powell-Williams, Gregory Maddox, and Kylan Mattias de Vries. 2011. "Religion, Politics, and Support for Same-Sex Marriage in the United States, 1988–2008." *Social Science Research* 40 (1): 167–80. https://doi.org/10.1016/j.ssresearch.2010.08.009.

Siegel, Karolynn, and Étienne Meunier. 2019. "Traditional Sex and Gender Stereotypes in the Relationships of Non-Disclosing Behaviorally Bisexual Men." *Archives of Sexual Behavior* 48 (1): 333–45. https://doi.org/10.1007/s10508-018-1226-3.

Silva, Tony. 2017. "Bud-Sex: Constructing Normative Masculinity among Rural Straight Men That Have Sex with Men." *Gender & Society* 31 (1): 51–73. https://doi.org/10.1177/0891243216679934.

———. 2018. "'Helpin' a Buddy Out': Perceptions of Identity and Behaviour among Rural Straight Men That Have Sex with Each Other." *Sexualities* 21 (1–2): 68–89. https://doi.org/10.1177/1363460716678564.

———. 2019. "Straight Identity and Same-Sex Desire: Conservatism, Homophobia, and Straight Culture." *Social Forces* 97 (3): 1067–94. https://doi.org/10.1093/sf/soy064.

Silva, Tony, and Clare R. Evans. 2020. "Sexual Identification in the United States at the Intersections of Gender, Race/Ethnicity, Immigration, and Education." *Sex Roles.*

Silva, Tony J., and Rachel Bridges Whaley. 2018. "Bud-Sex, Dude-Sex, and Heteroflexible Men: The Relationship between Straight Identification and Social Attitudes in a Nationally Representative Sample of Men with Same-Sex Attractions or Sexual Practices." *Sociological Perspectives* 61 (3): 426–43. https://doi.org/10.1177/0731121417745024.

Smith, Sharon G., Xinjian Zhang, Kathleen C. Basile, Melissa T. Merrick, Jing Wang, Marcie-jo Kresnow, and Jieru Chen. 2018. "The National Intimate Partner and Sexual Violence Survey: 2015 Data Brief—Updated Release." National Center for Injury Prevention and Control, Centers for Disease Control and Prevention. https://www.cdc.gov.

Smith-Rosenberg, Carroll. 1975. "The Female World of Love and Ritual: Relations between Women in Nineteenth-Century America." *Signs* 1 (1): 1–29. https://doi.org/10.1086/493203.

Snorton, C. Riley. 2014. *Nobody Is Supposed to Know: Black Sexuality on the Down Low.* Minneapolis: University of Minnesota Press.

Solebello, Nicholas, and Sinikka Elliott. 2011. "'We Want Them to Be as Heterosexual as Possible': Fathers Talk about Their Teen Children's Sexuality." *Gender & Society* 25 (3): 293–315. https://doi.org/10.1177/0891243211403926.

Stacey, Judith. 2004. "Cruising to Familyland: Gay Hypergamy and Rainbow Kinship." *Current Sociology* 52 (2): 181–97. https://doi.org/10.1177/0011392104041807.

Stein, Arlene. 2001. *The Stranger Next Door: The Story of a Small Community's Battle over Sex, Faith, and Civil Rights.* Boston: Beacon.

Stewart, Lauren. 2018. "Power and Pleasure: Heteronormativity and Homophobia in Heterosexual Sex." PhD dissertation, University of Oregon. http://search.proquest.com.

Stoet, Gijsbert, and David C. Geary. 2018. "The Gender-Equality Paradox in Science, Technology, Engineering, and Mathematics Education." *Psychological Science* 29 (4): 581–93. https://doi.org/10.1177/0956797617741719.

Stone, Amy L. 2018. "The Geography of Research on LGBTQ Life: Why Sociologists Should Study the South, Rural Queers, and Ordinary Cities." *Sociology Compass* 12 (11): 1–15. https://doi.org/10.1111/soc4.12638.

———. 2019. "Frame Variation in Child Protectionist Claims: Constructions of Gay Men and Transgender Women as Strangers." *Social Forces* 97 (3): 1155–76. https://doi.org/10.1093/sf/soy077.

Sun, Hua, and Lei Gao. 2019. "Lending Practices to Same-Sex Borrowers." *Proceedings of the National Academy of Sciences* 116 (19): 9293–9302. https://doi.org/10.1073/pnas.1903592116.

Swank, Eric, Breanne Fahs, and David M. Frost. 2013. "Region, Social Identities, and Disclosure Practices as Predictors of Heterosexist Discrimination against Sexual Minorities in the United States." *Sociological Inquiry* 83 (2): 238–58. https://doi.org/10.1111/soin.12004.

Taggart, Tenille C., Craig Rodriguez-Seijas, Christina Dyar, Jennifer C. Elliott, Ronald G. Thompson, Deborah S. Hasin, and Nicholas R. Eaton. 2019. "Sexual Orientation and Sex-Related Substance Use: The Unexplored Role of Bisexuality." *Behaviour Research and Therapy* 115 (April): 55–63. https://doi.org/10.1016/j.brat.2018.12.012.

Tan, Anh, Wenli Ma, Amit Vira, Dhruv Marwha, and Lise Eliot. 2016. "The Human Hippocampus Is Not Sexually Dimorphic: Meta-Analysis of Structural MRI Volumes." *NeuroImage* 124 (January): 350–66. https://doi.org/10.1016/j.neuroimage.2015.08.050.

Tortorici, Zeb. 2007. "'Heran Todos Putos': Sodomitical Subcultures and Disordered Desire in Early Colonial Mexico." *Ethnohistory* 54 (1): 35–67. https://doi.org/10.1215/00141801-2006-039.

Twenge, Jean M., Ryne A. Sherman, and Brooke E. Wells. 2016. "Changes in American Adults' Reported Same-Sex Sexual Experiences and Attitudes, 1973–2014." *Archives of Sexual Behavior* 45 (7): 1713–30. https://doi.org/10.1007/s10508-016-0769-4.

Tyler, Meagan, and Peter Fairbrother. 2013. "Bushfires Are 'Men's Business': The Importance of Gender and Rural Hegemonic Masculinity." *Journal of Rural Studies* 30 (April): 110–19. https://doi.org/10.1016/j.jrurstud.2013.01.002.

United States Census Bureau. 2016. "QuickFacts: United States." Washington, DC.

U.S. Department of Health and Human Services. 2018. "Public Use Data File Documentation: 2015–2017 National Survey of Family Growth, User's Guide." Hyattsville, MD: Centers for Disease Control and Prevention.

Valentino, Nicholas A., Carly Wayne, and Marzia Oceno. 2018. "Mobilizing Sexism: The Interaction of Emotion and Gender Attitudes in the 2016 U.S. Presidential Election." *Public Opinion Quarterly* 82 (S1): 213–35. https://doi.org/10.1093/poq/nfy003.

Vandermaas-Peeler, Alex, Daniel Cox, Molly Fisch-Friedman, and Robert P. Jones. 2017. "One Nation, Divided, under Trump: Findings from the 2017 American Values Survey." Public Religion Research Institute. https://www.prri.org.

Vermes, Jason. 2020. "For LGBTQ in Rural Communities, Pride Festivals Can Be Key Connection but Pandemic Is Raining on the Parade." Canadian Broadcasting Corporation, June 14. https://www.cbc.ca.

Vicinus, Martha. 1984. "Distance and Desire: English Boarding-School Friendships." *Signs* 9 (4): 600–622.

Waidzunas, Tom. 2015. *The Straight Line: How the Fringe Science of Ex-Gay Therapy Reoriented Sexuality.* Minneapolis: University of Minnesota Press.

Waite, Linda J., Edward O. Laumann, Aniruddha Das, and L. Philip Schumm. 2009. "Sexuality: Measures of Partnerships, Practices, Attitudes, and Problems in the National Social Life, Health, and Aging Study." *Journals of Gerontology: Series B* 64B (suppl. 1): i56–66. https://doi.org/10.1093/geronb/gbp038.

Walker, Alicia. 2014. "'Our Little Secret': How Publicly Heterosexual Women Make Meaning from Their 'Undercover' Same-Sex Sexual Experiences." *Journal of Bisexuality* 14 (2): 194–208. https://doi.org/10.1080/15299716.2014.902347.

———. 2017. *The Secret Life of the Cheating Wife: Power, Pragmatism, and Pleasure in Women's Infidelity.* Lanham, MD: Lexington Books.

Warbelow, Sarah, and Breanna Diaz. 2017. "2017 State Equality Index." Washington, DC: Human Rights Campaign Foundation. https://assets2.hrc.org.

Ward, Jane. 2008. "Dude-Sex: White Masculinities and 'Authentic' Heterosexuality among Dudes Who Have Sex with Dudes." *Sexualities* 11 (4): 414–34. https://doi.org/10.1177/1363460708091742.

———. 2015. *Not Gay: Sex between Straight White Men.* New York: NYU Press.

Way, Niobe. 2013. *Deep Secrets: Boys' Friendships and the Crisis of Connection.* Cambridge, MA: Harvard University Press.

Weaver, Kevin S., and Theresa K. Vescio. 2015. "The Justification of Social Inequality in Response to Masculinity Threats." *Sex Roles* 72 (11–12): 521–35. https://doi.org/10.1007/s11199-015-0484-y.

West, Candace, and Don H. Zimmerman. 1987. "Doing Gender." *Gender & Society* 1 (2): 125–51. https://doi.org/10.1177/0891243287001002002.

Westbrook, Laurel, and Kristen Schilt. 2014. "Doing Gender, Determining Gender: Transgender People, Gender Panics, and the Maintenance of the Sex/Gender/Sexuality System." *Gender and Society* 28 (1): 32–57. https://doi.org/10.1177/0891243213503203.

Whitehead, Andrew L. 2010. "Sacred Rites and Civil Rights: Religion's Effect on Attitudes toward Same-Sex Unions and the Perceived Cause of Homosexuality." *Social Science Quarterly* 91 (1): 63–79. https://doi.org/10.1111/j.1540-6237.2010.00681.x.

Wienke, Chris, and Gretchen J. Hill. 2013. "Does Place of Residence Matter? Rural-Urban Differences and the Wellbeing of Gay Men and Lesbians." *Journal of Homosexuality* 60 (9): 1256–79. https://doi.org/10.1080/00918369.2013.806166.

Wilcox, Melissa M. 2001. "Of Markets and Missions: The Early History of the Universal Fellowship of Metropolitan Community Churches." *Religion and American Culture* 11 (1): 83–108.

Wilkinson, Lindsey, and Jennifer Pearson. 2013. "High School Religious Context and Reports of Same-Sex Attraction and Sexual Identity in Young Adulthood." *Social Psychology Quarterly* 76 (2): 180–202.

Willer, Robb, Christabel L. Rogalin, Bridget Conlon, and Michael T. Wojnowicz. 2013. "Overdoing Gender: A Test of the Masculine Overcompensation Thesis." *American Journal of Sociology* 118 (4): 980–1022. https://doi.org/10.1086/668417.

Williams, Aaron, and Armand Emamdjomeh. 2018. "America Is More Diverse Than Ever—but Still Segregated." *Washington Post*, May 10. https://www.washingtonpost.com.

Wilson, Jim. 2017. "California's Far North Deplores 'Tyranny' of the Urban Majority." *New York Times*, July 2.

Wojan, Tim, and Timothy Parker. 2017. "Innovation in the Rural Nonfarm Economy: Its Effect on Job and Earnings Growth, 2010–2014." Washington, DC: United States Department of Agriculture.

Wolff, Margaret, Brooke Wells, Christina Ventura-Dipersia, Audrey Renson, and Christian Grov. 2017. "Measuring Sexual Orientation: A Review and Critique of U.S. Data Collection Efforts and Implications for Health Policy." *Journal of Sex Research* 54 (4–5): 507–31. https://doi.org/10.1080/00224499.2016.1255872.

Wolfinger, Nicholas H. 2017. "America's Generation Gap in Extramarital Sex." Charlottesville, VA: Institute for Family Studies. https://ifstudies.org.

Wolitski, Richard, Kenneth Jones, Jill Wasserman, and Jennifer Smith. 2006. "Self-Identification as 'Down Low' among Men Who Have Sex with Men (MSM) from 12 U.S. Cities." *AIDS and Behavior* 10 (5): 519–29. https://doi.org/10.1007/s10461-006-9095-5.

Woods, Michael. 2009. "Rural Geography: Blurring Boundaries and Making Connections." *Progress in Human Geography* 33 (6): 849–58. https://doi.org/10.1177/0309132508105001.

Worthen, Meredith G. F. 2020. "The Young and the Prejudiced? Millennial Men, 'Dude Bro' Disposition, and LGBTQ Negativity in a U.S. National Sample." *Sexuality Research and Social Policy*, May. https://doi.org/10.1007/s13178-020-00458-6.

Zeeland, Steven. 1995. *Sailors and Sexual Identity: Crossing the Line between "Straight" and "Gay" in the U.S. Navy*. New York: Haworth Press.

Zimring, Carl. 2015. *Clean and White: A History of Environmental Racism in the United States*. New York: NYU Press.

INDEX

Aaron (North Dakota interviewee): on family stability, 111–12; porn and, 46; romantic relationships and, 128; on sex-only relationships utility, 74; stereotypes and, 173–74; wife's sexual abstinence and, 46

Abelson, Miriam, 24–25, 123

Adam (Wisconsin interviewee): bud-sex and, 149; compatible goals and, 61; FWBs and, 79; on marriage, 107; on not cheating, 154–55; same-sex marriage and, 132; sexless marriage of, 154–55; sports and, 106

affection, same-sex, 70–71

age: aging process and, 35; attraction and, 50; coming-of-age, 119–20; David on, 56; ED and, 42; free time and, 205n249; generational factors and, 33–34; growing older, 41–49; interviews and, 33–35; masculinity and, 119–20; not ready to give up sex, 41–49; NSFG and, 34–35

anal stimulation, as kink, 40

attachment: emotional, 76, 150–51, 162; to men, 205n7; to women, 42

attraction: age and, 50; biological influences and, 183; causality of, 50; changing, 50–54; flexibility of, 38–39, 42, 50; identity focus and, 6; Internet access and, 53–54; kink and, 39–41; occasional, 39; proportion of, 51, 206n21; sexual identity versus, 37, 205n1; social context and, 5–8; strength of, 5–6; unintentional changes in, 38, 41–42

behavior, sexual: identity focus and, 6; social context and, 5–8

Billy (Oregon interviewee): bud-sex and, 148; FWBs and, 75; whiteness and, 175

biphobia, 3, 8, 20

bisexuality: generational factors and, 34; interviewees and, 126, 132, 139–40, 208n3; reasons to not identify with, 127; rural identity and, 30–31; sexual partner preference for, 166–70; stigma toward, 138–40; women and, 139

Bob (Missouri interviewee): bud-sex and, 144, 147–48; FWBs and, 78–79; love and, 89–90; masculinity and, 118–19, 121, 123, 162–63; mutual interests and, 164; on rural straight culture, 97–98; sexual partner preference of, 162–63, 164

bottoming: anal stimulation and, 40; bud-sex and, 146–49; defined, 193n7; ED and, 45; masculinity and, 45; preferences of subjects related to, 147; Tom and, 44

Brandon (Oregon interviewee): bud-sex and, 148–49; darker skin tone attraction of, 173; homosexual lifestyle and, 129

Brett (South Dakota interviewee): on not cheating, 155–56; on rural straight culture, 97

Brian (Colorado interviewee): discretion and, 168; on marriage, 107; nonfriend sexual relationships and, 74; on not cheating, 154; racial identification of, 170, 211n8; religion and, 115–16; sexless marriage of, 47, 154

tions of, 94; intersex conditions and, 16; learning masculinity and heterosexuality in, 98–100; literature and, 20; marriage/family formation and, 91; masculinity and, 94, 98–100, 117–23; minority cultures and, 14, 198n106; MSM embedded in, 3; opposite attitudes and, 55; orgasm gap in, 18; partnerships with women and, 107–13; religion and, 113–17; research on, 95; same-sex affection within, 70–71; school/sports and, 104–7; sex as irrelevant in, 93; sexual harassment and, 19; socialization within, 16–17, 199n121; social mechanisms and, 182; social processes and, 95; theoretical and practical implications related to, 182–84; as umbrella concept, 20–21; violence and, 96–97; wage gap and, 199n140; Ward and, 15; white, 94; white racial category and, 14, 198n104. *See also* heterosexuality

threesomes, 28–29
Todd (Ohio interviewee), 100; father and, 102; homosexual lifestyle and, 129; whiteness and, 172
Tom (Washington interviewee): casual sex and, 150–51; ED and, 43–44; masculinity and, 124; on nonpenetrative sex, 44; on sex with women versus men, 44; stereotypes and, 173
topping: Cain and, 2; defined, 193n7; pegging and, 45; preferences of subjects related to, 147
transgender, binary ideas impacting, 17. *See also* lesbian, gay, bisexual, transgender, and queer
Travis (South Dakota interviewee): budsex and, 148; on his wife, 111; masculinity and, 121, 124
Trevor (Oklahoma interviewee): compatible feelings and, 65; FWBs and, 77

Trump, Donald: rural areas and, 4; sexual harassment and, 19
Trump Administration, legal equality and, 7
trust: gender beliefs and, 55–56; Pat on, 61–62

United States Supreme Court: legal equality and, 7; same-sex marriage and, 6
urban areas: masculinity and, 25–26, 30, 204n218; metropolitan area definition and, 202n207; queerness outside, 21–24; rural areas contexts compared with, 28–31; sexual identity history and, 8–9; sociological research focus on, 5

Val (Pacific Northwest interviewee): on cuddling, 66; on his wife, 111; love and, 87–88; masculinity and, 122, 124; on not cheating, 153; on straight identification, 93
versatile: defined, 193n7; preferences of subjects related to, 147
Vince (Michigan interviewee): FWBs and, 75; sports and, 105–6

Walker, Alicia, 150
Ward, Jane, 15, 210n3
weddings: heterosexuality and, 15; same-sex, 132
whiteness: darker skin tones and, 173; intersectional analysis and, 32–33; interviewees and, 171–78; Jose and, 178; as normalcy marker, 172; rationales for, 176; rural areas and, 170–71; sexual partner preference for, 170–75; as socially constructed, 178, 211n14; stereotypes and, 173–74; travel and, 175
Will (Missouri interviewee): bisexuality and, 132; on childhood family, 100; religion and, 114; shift in attraction of, 53

ABOUT THE AUTHOR

Tony Silva is Assistant Professor in the Department of Sociology at the University of British Columbia. His areas of expertise include inequality, gender, sexuality, rural sociology, and qualitative and quantitative methods.

Printed in the USA
CPSIA information can be obtained
at www.ICGtesting.com
JSHW021915261124
74362JS00013B/94